PRAISE FOR JAVASCRIP

"*JavaScript Crash Course* is the perfect no-n̶c̶   ̶nt
to roll their sleeves up and pick up the bas̶   ̶ac-
tions that often complicate a mastery of web programming, ...
works, build tools, and server tech, using real projects to give aspiring web
engineers a solid foundation."

—JED SCHMIDT, FOUNDER OF BROOKLYNJS

"*JavaScript Crash Course* is a fun, practical, hands-on introduction that I wish I
had when I was learning JavaScript. Readers can learn from the very basics
all the way through making real games and applications that are relevant to
'real-world' development practices."

—CASSIDY WILLIAMS (@CASSIDOO), STARTUP
ADVISOR AND CTO AT CONTENDA

"*JavaScript Crash Course* offers practical, pragmatic, and project-based education
on how to think about and work with JavaScript. Nick Morgan has the experience to introduce you to the language with examples that build on each other,
and he quickly dives into creating real projects. As you delve deeper into the
book, you'll realize that your building blocks are the internet itself. You'll find
yourself using audio and sound generation techniques, painting with the Canvas
API, and pulling in third-party JavaScript libraries. By the time you complete the
crash course, you'll be ready to start your own projects. Nick is providing a won-
derful service with his hands-on teaching, both here and in *JavaScript for Kids*.
I hope you enjoy the book as much as I did."

—SCOTT HANSELMAN (@SHANSELMAN),
VP OF DEVELOPER COMMUNITY AT
MICROSOFT

"Nick has managed to condense the foundational concepts of JavaScript into
concise, approachable descriptions that are easily accessible to beginners.
Throw in some fun lessons in graphics and sound to create a game, and you've
got an excellent and engaging JavaScript book that's well worth your time."

—NICHOLAS C. ZAKAS (@SLICKNET), CREATOR
OF ESLINT AND VETERAN JAVASCRIPT BOOK
AUTHOR

JAVASCRIPT CRASH COURSE

A Hands-On, Project-Based Introduction to Programming

by Nick Morgan

no starch press®

San Francisco

Printed in the United States of America

First printing

28 27 26 25 24   1 2 3 4 5

ISBN-13: 978-1-7185-0226-0 (print)
ISBN-13: 978-1-7185-0227-7 (ebook)

 Published by No Starch Press®, Inc.
245 8th Street, San Francisco, CA 94103
phone: +1.415.863.9900
www.nostarch.com; info@nostarch.com

Publisher: William Pollock
Managing Editor: Jill Franklin
Production Manager: Sabrina Plomitallo-González
Production Editor: Miles Bond
Developmental Editor: Nathan Heidelberger
Cover Illustrator: Gina Redman
Interior Design: Octopod Studios
Technical Reviewer: Angus Croll
Copyeditor: Rachel Head
Proofreader: Scout Festa
Indexer: BIM Creatives, LLC

Library of Congress Control Number: 2023030044

For customer service inquiries, please contact info@nostarch.com. For information on distribution, bulk sales, corporate sales, or translations: sales@nostarch.com. For permission to translate this work: rights@nostarch.com. To report counterfeit copies or piracy: counterfeit@nostarch.com.

To Lyra and Hazel

About the Author

Nick Morgan is the author of *JavaScript for Kids* (No Starch Press, 2014). He's a software engineer at Airbnb, working on some of the core services that keep the site running. Prior to that, he worked at Twitter, starting on the web team and writing JavaScript to help build the main website before moving to the backend Tweets service, where he helped design the Edit Tweet feature. Nick grew up in the UK and has a degree in music and sound recording from the University of Surrey. He lives in Colorado with his wife, two daughters, three cats, and one dog.

About the Technical Reviewer

Originally from the UK, Angus Croll now lives in the San Francisco Bay Area, where he currently works on all things performance at Netflix. A devotee of both literary fiction and JavaScript, he's the author of *If Hemingway Wrote JavaScript* (No Starch Press, 2014), as well as the official Babel song. He also wrote and maintains the popular Just utility library.

BRIEF CONTENTS

Project 3: Visualizing Data

CONTENTS IN DETAIL

PROJECT 2: MAKING MUSIC

12
GENERATING SOUNDS

13
WRITING A SONG

PROJECT 3: VISUALIZING DATA

14
INTRODUCING THE D3 LIBRARY

ACKNOWLEDGMENTS

First of all, thank you to my wife, Philly, and our kids, Lyra and Hazel, for making this all worth it. I'm sorry so many of my evenings have been taken up with writing, and I promise I won't write another book for at least a year!

Thanks to Bill Pollock for trusting me to write a second JavaScript book, to my editor Nathan Heidelberger for your excellent work in shaping my text (and for putting up with my many delays!), and to everyone else at No Starch for your work in turning this book into reality.

Thank you to my friend and tech reviewer Angus Croll for everything. Angus referred me to Twitter and later referred me to Bill Pollock—I wouldn't be here writing this if it weren't for him.

Finally, thanks to my parents for giving me the curiosity and optimism that ultimately led me to write this book.

INTRODUCTION

I vividly remember the first time I "wrote" JavaScript. I'd been messing around with web design and copy-pasted some code from another website to add some weird effects whenever the mouse hovered over certain parts of the page. I had no idea what the code was doing, but through trial and error I managed to get something working.

JavaScript is a very forgiving language—sometimes to a fault—and that made it a very gentle introduction to programming for me and countless others. So many people have chosen JavaScript as a first programming language because of how easy it is to get started: it's right there waiting for you in your web browser!

Who Is This Book For?

The aim of this book is to get you writing real JavaScript code as quickly as possible, teaching all the essentials without getting bogged down in the intricacies of the language. I don't expect you to have any prior programming experience. If you're comfortable using a computer for everyday tasks like browsing the internet and editing documents, you have everything you need to get started.

JavaScript Crash Course is written for individuals of all ages who want to learn JavaScript independently through hands-on examples and projects. Maybe you want to transition into a career in computer programming, or you want to pursue coding as a hobby. Perhaps you've worked in other programming languages, and you need to get up to speed in JavaScript. If you're a teacher and are looking for an easy way to introduce your students to programming, *JavaScript Crash Course* is a great option for you, too.

Why JavaScript?

There are hundreds of programming languages to choose from, but there are a few things that make JavaScript special. Most important is its relationship with web browsers, such as Google Chrome, Safari, Microsoft Edge, and Firefox. Almost every web browser can run JavaScript, which means the code you write in JavaScript can be run on any computer with a web browser. There's no need to install any additional special software. Almost all smartphone web browsers can run JavaScript, too, so you may have a JavaScript-enabled browser in your pocket or bag right now.

Because of its relationship to web browsers, JavaScript is an extremely important part of web development. If a website includes dynamic, interactive features, it was probably created with JavaScript. For example, YouTube uses JavaScript to show you previews of videos when you hover over their thumbnails, Threads uses JavaScript to load more posts as you scroll down the page, and Amazon uses JavaScript to power its Look Inside feature.

Beyond its use in web browsers, JavaScript is also heavily used on the *backend* of websites, or the part of the website code that runs on a server, delivering content to users (as opposed to the *frontend* code that runs directly on the user's device). This is possible via a technology called Node.js. Many top websites have a Node.js backend, letting you use the same language for the frontend and backend of your website, and even share code between the two.

Finally, JavaScript has become a very popular scripting language for various applications, from Photoshop (where you can automate image processing) to Gmail (where you can add automations that organize your email). With some JavaScript knowledge, you can bend these applications to your will!

While the language is useful in all these areas, this book will focus solely on browser-based JavaScript. There are a few reasons for this. First, as I've already mentioned, one of the great advantages of running JavaScript in a browser is that you don't have to install anything special to get started. I didn't want to begin the book with a tedious chapter on installing Node.js on your computer—a chapter that could become outdated as soon as it was written. Second, while virtually all websites use JavaScript for the frontend, JavaScript is just one among many possible languages for writing backend code. The browser is by far the most universally applicable context for learning JavaScript.

I still highly recommend checking out Node.js and other uses for JavaScript after you finish this book and have some experience with the language. You should see the book as a jumping-off point: the beginning, rather than the end, of your JavaScript education. For more on next steps once you've worked through the book, see the afterword.

What Can You Expect to Learn?

This book will teach you browser-based JavaScript. Beyond learning the JavaScript language itself, you'll also learn skills that will help you in *any* programming language, such as how to think about problems and how to structure programs. You'll build a foundation of programming knowledge that will stick with you throughout your professional and personal coding endeavors.

Part I of this book lays out the basics of the language. I've been very intentional about the ordering of language concepts and features, making sure that every new concept builds on previous ones and never introducing anything that doesn't have a solid foundation. Here's what you'll find in this part of the book:

Chapter 1: Getting Started　Shows you how to write your first lines of JavaScript in both a web browser and a text editor.

Chapter 2: The Basics　Introduces basic ingredients of JavaScript programs, like expressions, statements, and variables, and explains how to use simple data types to represent numbers, text, and true/false values.

Chapter 3: Compound Data Types　Discusses arrays and objects, which let you combine multiple pieces of data into more meaningful collections.

Chapter 4: Conditionals and Loops　Teaches you to add logic to your programs with control structures that can make decisions and repeat segments of code.

Chapter 5: Functions　Shows you how to create reusable pieces of code with functions.

Chapter 6: Classes　Helps you add more structure to your code with classes and object-oriented programming principles.

Part II of the book discusses how to use JavaScript to work with web browsers. This section explores important techniques for creating interactive web applications:

Chapter 7: HTML, the DOM, and CSS　Explains how to write web pages in HyperText Markup Language (HTML) and modify their content with JavaScript using the Document Object Model (DOM). You'll also learn how to apply basic styling to web pages using Cascading Style Sheets (CSS).

Chapter 8: Event-Based Programming   Shows how to trigger Java-Script code in response to user behaviors such as mouse clicks and key presses.

Chapter 9: The Canvas Element   Teaches you to draw graphics and animations in the browser with JavaScript using the Canvas API.

Finally, Part III of the book lets you put the skills you gained in Parts I and II to use through a series of projects. There are no dependencies between the projects, so you can tackle them in any order, or only work on the projects you find most interesting. I would recommend completing all of them if possible, as they all introduce some valuable general-purpose programming concepts. Each project spans two chapters:

Project 1: Creating a Game   Guides you through making your own version of the classic Atari game *Pong*. This project will put to use your skills with the Canvas API and tie together all the basics you learned about data structures, conditionals, and functions. After you've developed the game in Chapter 10, Chapter 11 shows you how to restructure its code using classes and object-oriented design principles.

Project 2: Making Music   Explores how to make music using Java-Script. Chapter 12 explains how to use the Web Audio API and a library called Tone.js to generate sounds. Then Chapter 13 puts together what you've learned to create a song. Once you've completed this project, you'll not only be able to create your own music, but you'll also have gained some experience working with complex third-party libraries.

Project 3: Visualizing Data   Introduces you to the world of data visualization using the popular D3 library. Chapter 14 teaches the basics of D3 and Scalable Vector Graphics (SVG), an alternative to the Canvas API for drawing in the browser. Then, in Chapter 15, you'll build an application to dynamically visualize data loaded from across the internet. This project illustrates how to request data through a third-party API, an important programming skill.

Online Resources

This book features a number of hands-on exercises so you can practice what you've learned. I encourage you to try them all out yourself, but if you get stuck or you just want to check your answers, solutions are available online at *https://codepen.io/collection/ZMjYLO*. There you'll also find complete, downloadable code files for the book's projects.

For updates and other information about the book, see the No Starch Press website at *https://nostarch.com/javascript-crash-course*.

PART I

THE LANGUAGE

This first part of the book introduces the fundamentals of the JavaScript language. You'll learn about the basic building blocks of any JavaScript program, including many core concepts that are relevant to any programming language.

First we'll look at two ways to write and execute JavaScript code: in the console of a browser or in a text editor (Chapter 1). Then, you'll learn how to represent individual pieces of data with variables and constants, and how to manipulate that data through statements and expressions (Chapter 2). Next, you'll see how to group individual values into more meaningful structures using JavaScript's compound data types, arrays and objects (Chapter 3).

The later chapters of this first part show you how to add structure to your code. First, you'll incorporate logic into your programs with conditionals and loops, which together allow you to make decisions and control the flow of code execution (Chapter 4). Then, you'll learn techniques for reusing and organizing code with functions (Chapter 5) and classes (Chapter 6).

1

GETTING STARTED

In this chapter, you'll get started writing your first JavaScript code. First, you'll learn how to enter code directly into a web browser, without having to install any specialized software. This approach is ideal for quickly testing out simple sequences of code. Next, you'll see how to write JavaScript in a separate text editor program, which is more appropriate as your code becomes more complex. We'll use both of these techniques for writing and executing JavaScript code throughout the book, so this chapter will prepare you for everything that's to come.

Using the JavaScript Console

The quickest way to run JavaScript code is through the *JavaScript console*. This is an interface in most web browsers that lets you enter individual lines of code and immediately see the results. We'll use the console in Google Chrome, the most popular browser. If you don't have Chrome installed, you can download and install it from *https://www.google.com/chrome*.

Once you have Chrome installed, follow these steps to access the JavaScript console:

1. Open Chrome and enter **about:blank** in the address bar. This will take you to a blank web page.
2. In Windows or Linux, press CTRL-SHIFT-J, or press OPTION-COMMAND-J if you're using macOS.
3. You should now see the JavaScript console, including the > prompt symbol where you can enter code. Click inside the console to put your cursor next to the prompt.

The console should look something like Figure 1-1. It may appear alongside the blank web page, rather than beneath it, depending on your browser settings.

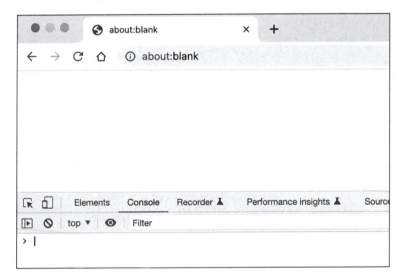

Figure 1-1: Google Chrome's JavaScript console

When you're learning a new programming language, it's customary to start by writing some code to display the message "Hello, world!" Let's try it out! Type the following into the console:

```
alert("Hello, world!");
```

In this book, when I ask you to enter code into the JavaScript console, I'll show the code in **bold**. If the code produces any output in the console, I'll show it directly below your input, not in bold.

When you're ready to run the code you've typed in, press ENTER. You should see a dialog appear in the browser containing the message "Hello, world!" as shown in Figure 1-2.

Figure 1-2: Hello, world!

You've just used JavaScript's alert function, which makes text pop up in a dialog. A *function* is a piece of code for performing a certain task—in this case, displaying a dialog. Functions can take *arguments*, which help specify how the task should be performed. The alert function takes one argument: a piece of text to display. Here, we've provided "Hello, world!" as the argument. You'll learn much more about functions in Chapter 5.

Click **OK** to dismiss the dialog and get back to the console. Then congratulate yourself on running your first JavaScript code.

Using a Text Editor

The JavaScript console is good for testing out a few lines of code, but it isn't so suitable for the larger projects we'll be working on later in the book. For those, it's more practical to use a *text editor*, a dedicated program for writing and editing code files. In this section, we'll create a similar "Hello, world!" program in a text editor.

For this book, I recommend using the Visual Studio Code text editor from Microsoft (VS Code for short). It's freely available for Windows, macOS, and Linux. Go to *https://code.visualstudio.com* and follow the instructions there to download and install the editor.

Once you've installed VS Code, create a new directory on your computer called *javascript_work* where you can save the code files you work on for this book. Then follow these steps to get ready to write your code:

1. Open VS Code.
2. Create a new file by selecting **File ▸ New File**.
3. You should be prompted to name the new file. Enter *hello.html*.
4. Next, you should be prompted to choose the new file's location. Select the *javascript_work* directory you just created and click **Create File**.
5. You should now be on a screen where you can edit your new file.

The *.html* extension in the filename indicates that this is an HTML file. HTML is a markup language used to describe the content of web pages. One way to run JavaScript code is to include it in an HTML file and then open the HTML file in a web browser. That's what we'll be doing here. Enter the contents of Listing 1-1 into your new file, exactly as written.

```
<html><body><script>
alert("Hello from hello.html!");
</script></body></html>
```

Listing 1-1: Writing JavaScript inside the file hello.html

As you type, you may notice that VS Code tries to predict what you're entering. This can be confusing at first, but once you get used to it, you'll likely find it helpful. Sometimes these predictions will be inserted automatically, while for others you'll have to press TAB to insert them.

The first and last lines of Listing 1-1 are HTML code, the bare minimum required to embed JavaScript into an HTML file. We'll explore HTML in detail in Chapter 7. For now, all you need to know is that it involves *tags* that identify different components of a web page. Most important for our purposes are the opening <script> tag at the end of the first line and the closing </script> tag at the beginning of the third line. When you load this file in a browser, everything between these tags (the second line in Listing 1-1) will be interpreted as JavaScript.

The JavaScript portion of the file is:

```
alert("Hello from hello.html!");
```

Here we're using the alert function, just as we did earlier in the console. This time we provide a different message, "Hello from hello.html!", to display in the dialog.

When you're finished entering the code, save the file. Now you're ready to open the file in Chrome and see the JavaScript code in action. Follow these steps:

1. Open a new tab in Chrome.
2. Press CTRL-O in Windows or Linux, or COMMAND-O in macOS, to bring up the Open File dialog.
3. Locate your *hello.html* file, select it, and click **Open**.

You should now see a dialog pop up containing the "Hello from hello.html!" message, as shown in Figure 1-3.

Figure 1-3: Hello from hello.html*!*

The browser recognized the code in the HTML file between the <script> and </script> tags as JavaScript and executed that code, causing the dialog to appear. If you don't see the dialog pop up, double-check the code in your *hello.html* file to make sure it matches Listing 1-1 exactly.

Summary

In this chapter, you learned two different ways to write and execute JavaScript code. First, you entered code into the JavaScript console in the Chrome web browser. You'll use this technique in the coming chapters to test out short snippets of code as you learn the basics of the language. Next, you embedded JavaScript in an HTML file using a text editor, then opened that file in Chrome to run the code. You'll use this technique in later chapters to develop more sophisticated projects.

2

THE BASICS

In this chapter, I'll introduce some of the basic ingredients that make up any JavaScript program. You'll learn about the fundamental units of JavaScript code that allow you to represent values and give instructions to the computer. You'll also learn how to assign a name to a value so you can refer to it later in your code.

This chapter also shows how JavaScript categorizes values into different data types based on the kind of information a value can represent. We'll focus on primitive data types that represent individual values, such as a single number or a single piece of text. You'll practice working with different primitive data types in the JavaScript console and explore some of the operations you can apply to them.

Expressions and Statements

The most basic building block in JavaScript is the *expression*, a fragment of code that represents a single value. The act of determining the value of an expression is known as *evaluation*. For example, 100 + 200 is an expression that evaluates to the number 300.

Another important JavaScript building block is the *statement*, which is a complete thought, like a sentence in English, instructing the computer to do something. Every JavaScript program consists of a series of statements. In Chapter 1, for example, we used the statement alert("Hello, world!"); to instruct the computer to display a dialog with the text *Hello, world!* in it. Whereas a sentence ends with a period, JavaScript statements end with a semicolon.

You can turn an expression into a statement simply by adding a semicolon to the end of it. For example, 100 + 200; is a statement instructing the computer to add two numbers together. Open up the JavaScript console and enter this statement. When you do this, it will evaluate the expression in the statement and print the result:

```
100 + 200;
300
```

The main expression in this statement, 100 + 200, is known as a *compound expression*, since it actually contains two smaller expressions, 100 and 200. These are examples of the simplest form of JavaScript expression, the *literal*, which is a direct representation of a fixed value in code. Specifically, 100 and 200 are *number literals*, since they directly correspond to the numeric values they represent, 100 and 200. By contrast, the compound expression 100 + 200 isn't a literal, since it doesn't directly correspond to its value of 300. The + in this compound expression doesn't represent a value at all. Rather, it's an *operator*, a symbol used to combine or manipulate expressions.

It's important to distinguish between values, which are the underlying pieces of data in a program, and expressions, which are the notations in code that tell JavaScript what the values should be. Both 300 and 100 + 200 have a value of 300, but they're two different expressions—one literal, one compound—that provide different ways of representing that value.

JavaScript expressions and statements complement each other. Expressions have values, but an expression by itself doesn't actually *do* anything. Conversely, statements do work by telling the computer to perform tasks, but statements themselves don't have values; they're just instructions. The power of programming comes from writing statements that use and manipulate the values of expressions to achieve the desired outcomes.

Numbers and Operators

JavaScript uses the *number* data type to store numeric values. You already started working with numbers in the previous section, where you also met the + operator, which adds two numbers together. JavaScript has operators for other common mathematical calculations, too, including subtraction (-), multiplication (*), and division (/). Try them out in the JavaScript console:

```
100 + 200;
300
10000 - 999;
9001
999 * 111;
110889
997002 / 999;
998
```

In cases like this, where the expression involves an operator (such as + or *), we often say the operator *returns* a value (rather than saying an expression is being *evaluated*). For instance, the * operator takes in the numbers 999 and 111 and returns their product, 110889.

Order of Operations

You can combine multiple numbers and operators in a single expression, in which case you need to think about the order in which the operations will be performed. Consider this example:

```
5 + 10 / 10 - 5;
1
```

When you have multiple operators like this, JavaScript uses the standard mathematical PEMDAS (parentheses, exponents, multiplication, division, addition, subtraction) rule to determine the order of calculations. The division operation in this expression takes place first, followed by the addition and subtraction, yielding a value of 1.

To force the addition and subtraction to happen first, use parentheses:

```
(5 + 10) / (10 - 5);
3
```

This time, the expression produces a different value, since the parentheses changed the order of operations.

Floating Point

So far we've limited ourselves to whole numbers, but JavaScript's number data type also accommodates fractional numbers, called *floating-point numbers* in programming terms. Here's an expression that produces a floating-point number:

```
10 / 4;
2.5
```

Floating-point numbers have limited precision, so the decimal component can't go on forever. Instead, they're truncated, as in the following example:

```
10 / 3;
3.3333333333333335
```

You may notice some weird quirks of floating-point math, where the answer isn't quite what you'd expect. For example, 0.1 + 0.2 doesn't work out to exactly 0.3. Instead, we get several extra decimal places:

```
0.1 + 0.2;
0.30000000000000004
```

This is due to the underlying mathematics of how computers represent numbers (search the web for "floating-point arithmetic" to learn more). In general, these quirks shouldn't affect you, but they could in certain circumstances. For example, if you're writing an application that works with monetary values, it could be a problem if $0.10 and $0.20 didn't sum to exactly $0.30. In this case, the usual solution is to convert your monetary values to cents (or the equivalent smallest denomination) before doing any math on them. For example, the number 0.10, representing an amount of dollars, would become 10, representing an amount of cents.

TRY IT YOURSELF

2-1. Use the JavaScript console to calculate the number of seconds in a day.

Bindings

In JavaScript, you can associate a name with a value so you can easily reference that value later in your code. This association is called a *binding*. Bindings are powerful tools because they provide a place to store the values your expressions generate. Without them, your programs would have no way of remembering the work they've already done.

One type of binding is a *variable*, which allows you to update the value associated with a particular name as needed. They're called variables because their values can change, or vary. Another type of binding is a *constant*, where you can't update the value associated with the name once it's been assigned. The value remains fixed, or constant.

Think of a variable or constant as a box with a label (the name) that holds a single item (the value). You put a value in the box, then look it up by name when you need it again. A variable allows you to put a new value in the box, while a constant will always contain the same value.

The name of a binding is also called its *identifier*, and creating an identifier is known as *declaration*: the binding's name is being declared. In JavaScript, a declaration is a special kind of statement that generates a new identifier. Let's look at how to declare and work with variables and constants.

Variables

JavaScript has two keywords for declaring variables: var and let. A *keyword* is a word built into the JavaScript language that's reserved for a particular purpose. Originally, the var keyword was the only option available, but let was later added to fix some of the shortcomings of var. Today, let is the preferred keyword for declaring variables, so that's what we'll use in this book, but don't be surprised if you encounter var while looking at older code.

Here's an example of using let to declare a variable:

```
let age;
undefined
```

This let declaration creates a new variable called age. A let declaration doesn't have a value, so the JavaScript console prints out the special value undefined.

Now that we've created a variable, let's write an expression to give it a value:

```
age = 35;
35
```

Giving a variable a value is called *assignment*, and you use the assignment operator (=) to do it. On the right side of the operator, you enter an expression (in this case, the number literal 35), and on the left, you enter the name of the variable that should be assigned the value of that expression (in this case, age).

An assignment using the = operator is a compound expression, just like expressions using + and other mathematical operators. The value of an assignment expression is the new value of the variable. In this case, we've set age to 35, so the console prints 35.

Assigning a value to a variable for the first time is called *initialization*. Programmers usually combine the declaration and initialization of a variable into a single line of code. For example, here we create a new variable called cats and assign it the value 2, all in the same statement:

```
let cats = 2;
undefined
```

Even though we're assigning the variable a value here, the prevailing rule is that the let declaration itself has no value, so the JavaScript console prints undefined.

To confirm the assignment worked, enter just the variable name into the console, followed by a semicolon:

```
cats;
2
```

Here, cats is an expression that evaluates to the current value of the cats variable, so the console prints that value.

Because cats is a variable, we're free to change its value using new assignment expressions. Here, for example, we update its value to 3:

```
cats = 3;
3
```

The nice thing about variables is that you can change their values whenever you need—for example, when you get another cat.

Constants

To declare a constant in JavaScript, we use the const keyword:

```
const PI = 3.141592653589793;
undefined
```

This creates a new constant called PI and assigns it the value 3.141592653589793, which is the approximate value of the number π.

Now we can use that constant to determine the circumference of a circle based on its diameter:

```
let diameter = 3;
undefined
let circumference = diameter * PI;
undefined
circumference;
9.42477796076938
```

Here we create a variable called diameter and assign it the value 3. Then we create another variable, circumference, and assign it a value of diameter * PI. Notice that we're using a compound expression consisting of a variable (diameter), a constant (PI), and a math operation (*) to set the value of a variable. A lot of programming boils down to creating constants and variables, and then manipulating them to create other constants and variables.

NOTE *Going forward, to keep the book's code listings from getting too cluttered, I'll stop showing the* undefined *that the console prints after a variable or constant is declared.*

Unlike with variables, you can't change the value of a constant once it's been created. For example, if you try to update the value of PI, JavaScript gives an error:

```
PI = 5.378;
Uncaught TypeError: Assignment to constant variable.
   at <anonymous>:1:4
```

Errors are how JavaScript tells you there's something wrong with your code. The important part of this error message is `Assignment to constant variable`. This indicates that we mistakenly tried to assign a new value to a constant.

Also unlike with variables, where you can separate the declaration from the initialization, you have to give a constant its value in its declaration. As a result, this won't work:

```
const TAU;
Uncaught SyntaxError: Missing initializer in const declaration
```

This error message tells us that the constant declaration is missing its initializer, meaning the constant should have been given a value.

Naming Conventions

You should give variables and constants descriptive names, so when you or somebody else is reading your code, it's clear what your variables and constants represent. For example, if you're writing code to control a car, you might want a variable that stores the speed of the car in miles per hour. The name `speedInMilesPerHour` is a bit too long, but given that MPH is a commonly understood abbreviation for miles per hour, a good variable name would be `speedInMPH`. A shorter name like `speed` might be okay, but only if it's obvious to everyone reading your code that speed is always in miles per hour. (Imagine if someone from Germany were reading your code and thought you were talking about kilometers per hour.) A bad name for this variable would be `s`, which tells the reader nothing.

JavaScript is case sensitive, which means it distinguishes between the variables `age`, `Age`, and `AGE`. Also, identifiers can't contain spaces. To work around that, a common convention for variable names is to use *camelCase*, where the first word in the name starts with a lowercase letter and each subsequent word starts with a capital letter, as in `speedInMilesPerHour`. (It's called camelCase because the capital letter in the middle looks like the hump of a camel.)

An alternative naming convention for variables is *snake_case*, where everything is lowercase and each word is separated by an underscore. (I guess this looks a bit like a snake if you squint.) In snake_case, we would write `speed_in_miles_per_hour` or `speed_in_MPH`.

Using snake_case can make variable names slightly clearer than camelCase, but it also makes them longer and harder to type quickly. JavaScript programmers tend to prefer camelCase, so that's what I'll use in this book.

Constants follow a separate naming convention from variables. There are two types of constants: *true constants*, which have values that will never change whenever you run the program (such as pi or the number of hours in a day), and values you've made constants because you don't want to accidentally change them in your code (such as the current user's name). For true constants, it's customary to use all-caps snake_case, like HOURS_IN_A_DAY. For constants you've created to avoid accidentally changing a value, use the same convention as for variables. In that case, the only difference is that the binding has been created using const rather than let.

CHOOSING BETWEEN LET AND CONST

It's not always obvious whether to use let or const when you're creating a binding. If you'll need to update the binding's value, use let to make it a variable. In other cases, it's up to you. Some programmers prefer to use let most of the time and reserve const only for true constants. Others use const wherever possible and switch to let only if they realize they need to update the value of a binding. The advantage of defaulting to let is that you don't need to stop and consider whether every binding could validly be changed. The advantage of defaulting to const is that you gain some safety from accidentally changing a value that shouldn't have been changed. Ultimately, the choice between the two approaches is a matter of style and personal preference.

Incrementing and Decrementing

When you're writing software, you'll often have to *increment* (increase) or *decrement* (decrease) the value of a variable by 1 or some other number. For example, you might use a variable to count the occurrences of a word in a document. Every time you see that word, you would increase the value of the variable by 1. Likewise, you might use a variable to keep track of how much money a player has in a game, increasing or decreasing it whenever the player earns or spends some.

One way to increment a variable is to initialize it, then change its value to itself plus 1:

```
let money = 100;
money = money + 1;
101
```

Here we declare a new variable called money and initialize it with the value 100. We then assign a new value to money by adding 1 to its existing value. It may seem paradoxical to see an expression like money = money + 1;, but this is actually quite a normal programming pattern. When JavaScript encounters an assignment expression like this, it first calculates the value of the expression on the right of the assignment operator, which in this case is money + 1. Because money is currently 100, money + 1 has a value of 101. JavaScript then updates the value of the variable on the left side of the assignment operator, which in this case is the same variable, money.

The key here is that JavaScript waits to change the value of the variable on the left of the operator until after it's calculated the value of the expression on the right of the operator. This is how the same variable can appear on both sides of the operator. In the end, money = money + 1 means "add 1 to money."

Because adding 1 to a variable is a very common task, JavaScript makes it easier with the increment operator (++). When you attach this operator to a variable, it increases the value of that variable by 1, without you having to write out a full assignment expression. Similarly, JavaScript's decrement operator (--) decreases the value of a variable by 1. Here, we use ++ and -- to change the value of a temperature variable:

```
let temperature = 70;
++temperature;
71
++temperature;
72
--temperature;
71
```

In this example, we've placed the increment and decrement operators *before* the variable we want to change. With the operators in this position, the output of the increment or decrement operation is the variable's updated value. For example, when temperature has a value of 70, ++temperature outputs a value of 71. This is called *prefix* incrementing and decrementing.

JavaScript also allows for *postfix* incrementing and decrementing, where the operator goes *after* the variable. In this case, the variable still increases or decreases by 1, but the value shown in the output is the variable's value *before* it was changed. Here's an example:

```
let books = 2;
books++;
❶ 2
books;
❷ 3
books--;
3
books;
2
```

We initialize the books variable with the value 2. Then books++ increments that value, but it returns the value of books from *before* it was incremented ❶. When we then ask for the value of books on its own, we can see that it has the new value ❷, confirming that the increment operation took place.

Whether you use prefix or postfix incrementing and decrementing, the effect on the variable is the same: its value increases or decreases by 1. The only difference is how the incrementing or decrementing expression itself evaluates. Luckily, most of the time when you use one of these operators, you won't actually need the value of the incrementing or decrementing expression itself—you'll just be modifying the value saved in the variable. Therefore, you can usually use the prefix and postfix versions interchangeably.

Addition and Subtraction Assignment

The increment operator increases a variable's value by 1, but sometimes you'll want to increase it by a different amount. For that, JavaScript has the addition assignment operator (+=). It increases the value of the variable on the left side of the operator by whatever value you place to the right of the operator, as shown here:

```
let price = 20;
price += 5;
25
```

Here we use += to increase the value of price by 5. Essentially, price += 5 is shorthand for price = price + 5. The += operator combines addition and assignment into one symbol.

Similarly, the subtraction assignment operator (-=) is a convenient way to subtract any value from a variable:

```
let cookies = 12;
cookies -= 5;
7
```

In this case, cookies -= 5 is shorthand for cookies = cookies - 5.

Multiplication and Division Assignment

The multiplication and division assignment operators, *= and /=, update a variable's value by multiplying or dividing it by the specified number. For example:

```
let tribbles = 6;
tribbles *= 2;
12
tribbles /= 3;
4
```

Similarly to the other shorthand assignment operators, these assignment operators translate to tribbles = tribbles * 2 and tribbles = tribbles / 3, respectively.

2-2. Use the *= operator to see the power of compound interest. If you have $100 and you gain 8 percent interest every year, how many years will it take to double your money? To find out, create a variable called savings and initialize it with the value 100. Then repeatedly use the *= operator to multiply this value by 1.08. (Tip: press the up arrow to reuse the previous input, instead of having to retype it over and over.)

Strings

JavaScript uses the *string* data type to represent text. It's called a string because the text is treated as a sequence, or string, of characters. For example, the string Hello! consists of six characters: H, e, l, l, o, and !.

A *string literal* is a direct representation of a string value. To create a string literal, simply surround some text with double quotation marks. Every character between the quotes is part of the string. For example, here we assign the string literal "Hello!" as the value of the variable greeting. Then we check the value of the variable:

```
let greeting = "Hello!";
greeting;
'Hello!'
```

You can also write string literals inside single quotation marks rather than double quotation marks. In fact, as shown in this example, when Chrome's JavaScript console outputs a string, it encloses the string in single quotes (even if you wrote it with double quotes). For consistency, I'll stick with double quotes when I'm writing strings throughout this book, although I'll also use single quotes to accurately reflect the output of the console.

Typically, strings mostly consist of letters, but as our "Hello!" example indicated, they can also include punctuation. Strings can contain spaces, too, as well as numerals, as in this example:

```
let price = "5 dollars";
price;
'5 dollars'
```

It's even possible to have a string that just contains numerals, such as "123", but it's important to distinguish this string from an actual number. The string literal "123" is a sequence of three characters, 1, 2, and 3, while the number literal 123 has a numerical value of 123.

JavaScript provides a lot of ways to manipulate strings. We'll look at some of these string operations next.

Joining Strings

When applied to strings rather than numbers, the + operator joins the strings together. This way, you can build up a longer message by combining various strings. Here's an example:

```
let first = "First string";
let second = "Second string";
let joined = first + second;
joined;
'First stringSecond string'
```

Here we assign two strings to the variables first and second. Then we use + to join the strings, storing the result in the variable joined. Notice that JavaScript doesn't add a space between the strings being joined—it just tacks the second string directly onto the end of the first. If you want a space in between, you have to add it explicitly by treating the space as its own string:

```
first + " " + second;
'First string Second string'
```

In this example, we join three string literals:

1. "First string"
2. " " (a string consisting of a single space)
3. "Second string"

As a result, we get a space between string and Second.

Finding the Length of a String

You'll often need to check the length of a string. For example, if you're making a reviews website, you might want to limit review length to something like 1,000 characters. To find out how many characters are in a string, add .length after the string to access its length property. (A *property* is a piece of information about something in your code; we'll discuss properties in more detail in Chapter 3.) Here we use .length to confirm that the string "abc" has three characters:

```
"abc".length;
3
```

In this case, we used .length on a string literal, but you can also use it on variables or constants that contain strings, as shown here:

```
let longString = "This is my very long string";
longString.length;
27
```

This code counts all the characters, including the spaces, in the string bound to the variable name longString.

Getting a Character from a String

To get a single character from a string, use that character's *index*. This is a number representing the character's position within the string. JavaScript always counts from zero, so index 0 refers to the first character in the string, index 1 to the second character, and so on. This is known as *zero-based indexing*.

Place the desired index in square brackets to access the character at that index, like so:

```
let alphabet = "ABCDEFG";
alphabet[0];
'A'
alphabet[1];
'B'
```

Here, alphabet[0] retrieves the first character of the string stored in the variable alphabet, and alphabet[1] retrieves the second character.

If you use an index beyond the length of the string, the expression evaluates to undefined:

```
alphabet[10];
undefined
```

The string in alphabet has only seven characters, at indices 0 through 6, so alphabet[10] is out of range.

Getting Multiple Characters from a String

To get a sequence of multiple characters (also called a *slice*) from a string, rather than just a single character, use the slice method. A *method* is a specific kind of function that's attached to a particular value or data type. (As we discussed in Chapter 1, a function is a named piece of code that carries out a task.) Methods are generally used to make a calculation about the thing they're attached to, or to update something about it. In this case, slice is one of many methods associated with the string data type that you can use to manipulate a given string.

The syntax for using, or *calling*, a method is to follow the value or variable you want to apply the method to with a period, then the name of the method, and then a set of parentheses. Inside the parentheses, you write any values that the method needs to do its job, separated by commas. As with other functions, these values are known as *arguments*. Methods can also produce a value, known as the method's *return value*.

The slice method takes two arguments, the start index (inclusive) and end index (exclusive) of the slice you want to extract, and returns the substring containing the specified range of characters. Here's an example:

```
let sentence = "My name is Nick.";
sentence.slice(3, 7);
'name'
```

Here, we store a string in the variable sentence and then call the slice method on that string by writing sentence.slice(3, 7). The first argument in the parentheses means we want the slice to start at index 3 of the string (the fourth character, the n in name). The second argument means we want the slice to go up to, but not include, index 7 of the string (the space after name). The net result is that the slice method returns the characters at indices 3, 4, 5, and 6, giving us the string "name".

NOTE   *We'll talk more about functions generally in Chapter 5, and about methods specifically in Chapter 6.*

Trimming Whitespace from a String

Whitespace refers to characters that wouldn't require any ink to print, such as spaces or tabs. The trim method removes any whitespace from the beginning or end of a string and returns a new string with that whitespace removed. This can be helpful, for example, if you're taking input from a user and they accidentally add a few spaces at the beginning and/or end, as shown here:

```
let inputText = " Here is my input    ";
inputText.trim();
'Here is my input'
inputText;
❶ ' Here is my input    '
```

The string stored in the variable inputText starts with a space before the word Here and ends with three extra spaces after the word input. When we call the trim method by writing inputText.trim(), we get a new string with those spaces removed. Notice, however, that the spaces *between* the words aren't affected; only the whitespace at the beginning and end of the string is trimmed. The trim method doesn't require any arguments, so we simply write an empty set of parentheses after the method name.

Because the trim method returns a new string, the original string stored in inputText is left unchanged. We can see this when we ask for the value of inputText at the end of the code listing: the output still has the spaces at the start and end of the string ❶.

Other Useful String Methods

JavaScript has many more string methods available besides slice and trim. I won't go into the details of all of them, but here are some useful ones:

str.**toLowerCase()**   Returns a new string with all the uppercase characters in *str* converted to lowercase.

str.**includes(***otherStr***)**   Returns true if *str* includes the string given as the *otherStr* argument.

str.**padStart(***num, char***)**   Returns a new string that has at least *num* characters, and adds the *char* character as many times as needed to the start of the string if it isn't already *num* in length.

str.**repeat(***count***)**   Returns a new string with *str* repeated *count* times.

TRY IT YOURSELF

2-3. Try out each of the methods listed in the "Other Useful String Methods" section. Make sure you test some *edge cases*, or situations where you call them with unusual input values. For example, what happens if you give the repeat method a count of 0? What about -1?

Escape Sequences

Sometimes you'll want to put special characters into your strings, like newline characters to create a line break in the middle of the string, or tab characters to create wider horizontal spacing. JavaScript lets you include these using *escape sequences*. An escape sequence is a series of characters, always starting with a backslash (\\), that gets converted to another character. For example, to insert a newline character into a string, use the \\n escape sequence:

```
"Hello\nWorld";
'Hello\nWorld'
```

For better or worse, when Chrome's JavaScript console evaluates a string with a special character and outputs the result, the special character remains in its escaped form. To see how the string appears with the escape sequence interpreted correctly, pass the string as an argument to the console.log method. This method prints data to the console, including any necessary formatting. For example:

```
console.log("Hello\nWorld");
Hello
World
```

The output of this method shows how the \\n escape sequence is interpreted as a line break between the two words in the string.

Table 2-1 lists some of the escape sequences you'll use most often.

Table 2-1: Common Escape Sequences

Escape sequence	Output
\'	Single quote
\"	Double quote
\\	Backslash
\n	Newline
\t	Tab

As the table indicates, if you want to include an actual backslash character in your string, you'll need to use \\. Similarly, if you want to include a double quote character in your double-quoted string, you'll need to use \". For example:

```
console.log("This string has \"double quotes\" and a \\ backslash character");
This string has "double quotes" and a \ backslash character
```

When you write a string inside double quotes, there's no need to use the \' escape sequence when you want a single quote, for example, as an apostrophe in a contraction. You can just write the single quote directly, as shown here:

```
console.log("You don't need to escape single quotes");
You don't need to escape single quotes
```

Similarly, when you write a string inside single quotes, there's no need to escape double quotes.

TRY IT YOURSELF

2-4. Create a string using all the escape sequences from Table 2-1.

Template Literals

A *template literal* is a special kind of string that can evaluate any expressions embedded within it. This gives you the flexibility to dynamically populate a string with the values of variables, the results of calculations, or other code, instead of having to type out every character of the string exactly or combine several variables into a string with the + operator.

Template literals are enclosed in backticks (`) instead of quotation marks. You incorporate code using *placeholder syntax*, which looks like this: ${}. The text inside the braces of the placeholder is treated as an expression and is evaluated before the final string is evaluated, as shown here:

```
let name = "Nick";
`Hello, ${name}!`;
'Hello, Nick!'
```

Here, the value of the name variable gets inserted into the string instead of the ${name} placeholder, resulting in the string "Hello Nick!" If we change the value of name, the same template literal will produce a different string:

```
name = "Dolly";
`Hello, ${name}!`;
'Hello, Dolly!'
```

You can place any expression in the placeholder braces, not just a simple variable. The expression will be evaluated, and the result will be inserted into the string. For example:

```
`There are ${60 * 60 * 24} seconds in a day`;
'There are 86400 seconds in a day'
```

In this case, JavaScript calculates the value of 60 * 60 * 24, converts it to a string, and incorporates it into the evaluated string.

Template literals have many applications, such as taking text input from a user and inserting it into a new string. They're especially useful when you need to make a string based on several variables. For example, say you're building a Mad Libs–type web application that takes in words of different parts of speech and combines them into sentences. The user has input the following three words, which you've stored in separate variables:

```
let noun = "moon";
let adverb = "strangely";
let adjective = "red";
```

Without template literals, you'd have to combine the variables into a string by repeatedly using the + operator:

```
"The " + noun + " was " + adverb + " " + adjective + ".";
'The moon was strangely red.'
```

This code is pretty tedious to write, especially as you want to include a space between each word and a period at the end of the sentence. It's much simpler to use a template literal:

```
`The ${noun} was ${adverb} ${adjective}.`;
'The moon was strangely red.'
```

In addition to making code easier to write, template literals also make it easier to read. It's much more apparent that this code is inserting a custom noun, adverb, and adjective into a sentence.

Undefined and Null

In JavaScript, the values undefined and null have a special meaning: they represent *nothing*. When JavaScript doesn't have a value for something, it returns undefined by default. For example, as you saw earlier in this chapter, if you create a variable without giving it a value, JavaScript automatically assigns that variable a value of undefined:

```
let nothing;
nothing;
undefined
```

You also get undefined when you execute a function that has no useful value to return in the console, such as the alert function we used in Chapter 1 to pop up a dialog in the browser:

```
alert("I have no value.");
undefined
```

Whereas JavaScript automatically uses undefined when something has no value, programmers generally use null to explicitly mark something as empty. For example, if you're writing some code that takes an address as user input, and the user doesn't supply their address, you can set the address variable to null instead:

```
let address = null;
address;
null
```

Functionally speaking, setting address to null isn't really any different from leaving the variable undefined, but it makes your intentions clearer. Someone else reading your code will see that you're deliberately marking address as an empty value, as opposed to it just not having been defined yet.

Booleans

The last primitive data type we'll consider is the *Boolean* type, which represents true/false values. There are only two Boolean literals: true and false. Here we create a Boolean variable using a literal and confirm its value:

```
let playing = true;
playing;
true
```

In this example, we're declaring a new variable called playing and initializing it with the Boolean literal true. You can imagine that this is some code in a game, and that the playing variable tells us if the game is currently active (true) or paused (false).

Booleans are an essential part of programming because they give us a way to talk about logic. If you want your program to behave differently for a particular condition, you need to be able to say whether or not that condition holds—that is, whether it's true or false. For example, if you're working on a video streaming website, you might need to know if the current user is under 18. If they are, you might hide certain content. You'd use a Boolean in this case to decide whether or not to hide the content.

Booleans have various operators associated with them. They fall into two groups: *logical operators*, which take Boolean values and return Boolean values, and *comparison operators*, which can take values of other types, such as numbers and strings, and return Boolean values.

Logical Operators

There are three Boolean logical operators: *and*, *or*, and *not*. The and operator (&&) takes two values, known as *operands*, and returns true only if both operands are true. This is useful for any case where you need two conditions to be true for something to happen. Let's continue the game example, and pretend we're writing the logic for a platform game. In this game, you can shoot fireballs, but only if you have a powerup *and* you're jumping. Here's how to express that in code:

```
let powerup = true;
let jumping = true;
powerup && jumping;
true
```

In this case, powerup is true and jumping is true, so powerup && jumping is also true. If you set either (or both) of those variables to false, however, powerup && jumping will also be false:

```
jumping = false;
powerup && jumping;
false
```

The or operator (||) returns true if *either* of its operands is true. This is useful if only one of several conditions needs to be true for something to happen. In our game, for example, let's say you die if a fireball hits you *or* if you touch a monster:

```
let hitByFireball = false;
let touchedMonster = true;
hitByFireball || touchedMonster;
true
```

Because one of the two operands is true, the expression hitByFireball ||
touchedMonster is true. The || operator will also return true if both operands
are true.

The not operator (!) takes only one operand and returns the inverse
of its value, so !true is false and !false is true. This is particularly useful if
you want something to happen when a condition is *not* true. In our game,
for example, we might have a variable called alive that tells us if the player
is currently alive. The game should end when the player is dead—that is,
when !alive is true (meaning alive itself is false):

```
let alive = false;
!alive;
true
```

Different logical operators are often combined to form more sophisticated logical expressions. For example, let's say you can jump in our game
only when you're not carrying a box and you're not swimming. In that case,
we'd use two Boolean variables to represent carrying a box and swimming,
use ! to invert each of those variables, and use && to check the two inverted
variables together, like so:

```
let carryingBox = true;
let swimming = false;
!carryingBox && !swimming;
false
```

You aren't swimming, but you *are* carrying a box, so the && operator returns
false, meaning you can't jump.

It can sometimes be hard to read more complex logical expressions, so
let's go through the steps JavaScript takes when evaluating the !carryingBox
&& !swimming expression. First, to simplify things, replace the variable names
with the Boolean values they're currently set to:

```
!true && !false
```

Next, replace the expressions !true and !false with their equivalent values, removing the ! operators:

```
false && true
```

Now we just have to remember that && returns true only if both its operands
are true. In this case, one of the operands is false, so we know that this
expression evaluates to false.

There's a useful trick for working with Boolean expressions like this.
The expression !a && !b can be rewritten as !(a || b). Think of this as
rewording the original description from "not carrying a box *and* not
swimming" to "not (carrying a box *or* swimming)." This trick is called
De Morgan's law (no relation!). It can also be used to convert !a || !b to
!(a && b).

Comparison Operators

JavaScript's comparison operators compare values and return a Boolean value based on the result of the comparison. For example, the === or "triple equals" operator checks if two values are equal. It returns true if they are, or false if they aren't. Here are some examples of the === operator in action:

```
5 === 5;
true
6 === 7;
false
2 + 2 === 4;
true
"hello" === "goodbye";
false
"hello" === "hel" + "lo";
true
false === false;
true
true === false;
false
```

Notice that === isn't just for comparing number literals; it can also work with numerical expressions like 2 + 2, string literals ("hello"), string expressions ("hel" + "lo"), and Booleans. It can compare values stored in variables as well:

```
let answer = 2 + 2;
answer === 5;
false
```

Here answer is set to 4, the value of 2 + 2, so the comparison with 5 is false.

The opposite of the === operator is !== (the first = is replaced by a !). This operator checks if two values are *not* equal. For example:

```
8 !== 8;
false
"apples" !== "oranges";
true
```

Using the !== operator is the same as using the === operator, then applying the ! operator to the result:

```
!(8 === 8);
false
!("apples" === "oranges");
true
```

JavaScript's other comparison operators check if one value is greater than or less than another. These include the standard mathematical operations of greater than (>), less than (<), greater than or equal to (>=), and less than or equal to (<=). Consider these examples:

```
1 > -1;
true
10 > 10;
false
10 >= 10;
true
-1 < 1;
true
10 < 10;
false
10 <= 10;
true
```

Notice in particular that comparing identical values with > or < returns false, but comparing them with >= or <= returns true.

These comparison operators can also be used with strings. One string is considered "greater than" another string if it would appear later in a dictionary. For example:

```
"cat" < "dog";
true
"abc" > "abbcdef";
true
```

The first comparison evaluates to true because the first letter of cat comes before the first letter of dog in the alphabet. In the second comparison, the first two characters of the strings are the same, but looking at the third character, c is later in the alphabet than b, so the first string is considered greater. It doesn't matter that the second string is longer; JavaScript compares the strings character by character and stops the comparison as soon as it's found a difference.

Type Coercion

Coercion is the act of automatically converting a value of one data type into a value of a different data type. JavaScript uses coercion in certain circumstances where values of different data types appear in the same expression. For example, if you use the + operator with a string on one side and a number on the other, JavaScript coerces the number to a string, then joins the two strings together:

```
"Current score: " + 10;
"Current score: 10"
```

Notice that 10 appears inside the quotes in the output, meaning it's become a string rather than a number. This kind of coercion makes it quite easy to incorporate numbers into strings for display to a user.

In some contexts, Boolean values are coerced into numbers, with false becoming 0 and true becoming 1. For example:

```
100 + true;
101
```

Here we've used the Boolean literal true with a number in a mathematical expression, so JavaScript coerces it to a 1, then adds 100 and 1 to produce 101.

Equality with Coercion

Earlier we used the triple equals operator (===) to check for equality. There's another operator, double equals (==), that applies coercion to its operands before checking for equality. For example, if you compare a number to a Boolean using ==, the Boolean will first be coerced into a number:

```
0 == false;
true
```

This comparison is true because the Boolean false is first coerced to a 0. If you make the same comparison using the triple equals operator, however, it will be false, since === doesn't permit type coercion:

```
0 === false;
false
```

It can be hard to guess what will be coerced to what when you use the == operator. Here are some other examples:

```
"1" == 1;
true
undefined == null;
true
undefined == false;
false
"" == 0;
true
"" == false;
true
```

When you compare a number with a string consisting of all numerals, such as "1", the string is coerced to the equivalent number, so "1" == 1 becomes 1 == 1, which evaluates to true. The == operator also returns true when undefined and null are compared to each other, but it returns false if undefined or null is compared to anything else. Meanwhile, an *empty string*—that is, a string that contains no characters, represented by a set of quotation marks with nothing in between ("")—is considered equivalent to the number 0 and the Boolean false.

The opposite of == is the != operator. It determines if two operands are *not equal*, after any appropriate type coercion. Some inequalities that are true using the strict !== operator become false with the coercive != operator. For example:

```
0 !== false;
true
0 != false;
false
```

Without coercion, 0 is not equal to false, so 0 !== false is true. With coercion, however, false becomes 0, so 0 != false is false.

It's important to be aware of the == and != operators, but because of the complicated rules governing type coercion, I'd recommend sticking to the strict === and !== operators as much as possible. You'll be less likely to encounter unexpected behavior in your code.

Truthiness

Truthiness is a special type of coercion that defines how non-Boolean values are treated as Booleans. This allows logical operators like && and ! to be used on any type of value. The way the operators work depends on whether JavaScript considers the value to be *truthy* (equivalent to true) or *falsy* (equivalent to false). The falsy values include undefined, null, the number 0, and an empty string (""). All nonzero numbers and nonempty strings are truthy.

The easiest way to check if a value is truthy or falsy is to apply two not operations to it using !!, meaning "not not," a double negative. This works because the ! operator always returns a Boolean, regardless of the data type of the value it's applied to. For example, say you want to verify that the number 0 is falsy. A single ! operation coerces the number to a Boolean, then inverts that Boolean, so !0 evaluates to true:

```
!0;
true
```

Adding a second ! reverses the Boolean again, giving the Boolean equivalent of the original value:

```
!!0;
false
```

This confirms that 0 is equivalent to false, or falsy.

You can use the same !! trick to check the other truthiness rules I mentioned earlier:

```
!!1;
true
!!"hi";
true
```

```
!!"";
false
!!undefined
false
!!null;
false
```

The output confirms that nonzero numbers and nonempty strings are truthy, while an empty string, undefined, and null are falsy.

When the && and || operators are applied to non-Booleans, they don't return a true or false value. Instead, they return one of the original operands. In the case of the && operator, if the first operand is truthy, the second operand is returned. If the first operand is falsy, the first operand is returned. Here are some examples:

```
15 && 17;
17
0 && 20;
0
undefined && null;
undefined
```

In the first case, 15 is truthy, so 17 is returned. In the other two cases, the first operand is falsy, so 0 and undefined are returned, respectively.

The || operator works the opposite way. If the first operand is falsy, it returns the second operand, and if the first operand is truthy, it returns the first operand, as shown here:

```
"" || "hello";
'hello'
"hello" || "goodbye";
'hello'
```

In the first case, the first operand is an empty string, which is falsy, so the second operand is returned. In the second case, the first operand is a nonempty string, which is truthy, so the first operand is returned.

Uses for Truthiness

You can leverage the behavior of && and || with truthy and falsy values in a number of ways. For example, the || operator can be used to give a variable a default value if one isn't provided. This could be helpful in a scenario where a user neglects to enter their name on a form:

```
let name;
name = name || "No name provided";
name;
'No name provided'
```

At the start of this example, `name` is created without being given a value, so it's `undefined`. Then we assign it a value using the Boolean expression `name || "No name provided"`. Since the first operand is falsy, the second operand is returned. As a result, `name` is given the default value `"No name provided"`. If, on the other hand, a name *had* been provided, `name` would be considered truthy, and so it would retain its value:

```
let name = "Nick";
name = name || "No name provided";
name;
'Nick'
```

Similarly, you can use `&&` or `||` to *short-circuit*, or skip, an expression. With `&&`, if the first operand is falsy, that's the operand that will be evaluated and returned, so JavaScript doesn't even bother evaluating the second operand. When the operands are just simple values, we don't really care if they're evaluated or not; all we care about is which value is returned. For example, in the expression `1 || 2 + 2`, it doesn't especially matter whether JavaScript calculates the result of `2 + 2`, because we know the first operand, `1`, is going to be returned. It *does* matter if an expression is evaluated when that expression has some kind of *side effect*, however, meaning that evaluating it does something other than just returning a value. For example, the alert function returns the value `undefined`, but more importantly has the side effect of displaying a dialog. But what if we want to only display a dialog in some circumstances?

For instance, say we want to use `alert` to display a player's score in a game, but only when the score isn't zero. We can make the `score` variable and the alert function the operands in an `&&` expression:

```
let score = 0;
score && alert(`Your score is ${score}!`);
0
```

Here `score` is `0`, so the first operand in the `&&` expression is falsy. The `&&` operator therefore returns this value and ignores the second operand, meaning alert is never called. We've short-circuited the function call.

Now consider what happens if `score` increases:

```
++score;
1
score && alert(`Your score is ${score}!`);
undefined
```

Here we use `++` to increment score, changing its value to `1`. This makes score truthy, so the second operand in the `&&` expression is evaluated, executing the alert function. The function returns `undefined`, but also has the (desired) side effect of displaying a dialog with the player's score (see Figure 2-1).

This page says

Your score is 1!

OK

Figure 2-1: The alert *function's side effect is displaying a message in a dialog.*

Essentially, we're using the && operator to decide whether or not to run some code (the alert function) based on a condition (whether or not score is 0). In Chapter 4, we'll look at control structures like if statements, which give a more explicit way of controlling whether and how our code is run.

Summary

This chapter introduced you to some of the fundamental building blocks of JavaScript programming. You learned that a statement is a complete thought in JavaScript, ending with a semicolon, that instructs the computer to do something, and that a statement can consist of one or more expressions (units of code that represent a value). You saw how to use bindings to give a value a name for later use, either as a variable, in which case the value can be updated later, or as a constant, in which case the value remains fixed.

You also learned about three primitive data types in JavaScript: numbers, strings, and Booleans. You applied math operations to numbers, including using shorthand like ++ and -- to increment or decrement them, and you practiced manipulating strings using various methods, including slicing and trimming whitespace. With Booleans, you learned how to use logical operators like and (&&), or (||), and not (!), and you saw how to generate Boolean values using comparison operators like === and !==. Finally, you learned how JavaScript sometimes coerces values from one data type to another, including how non-Booleans are treated as truthy or falsy, and you explored situations where this can come in handy, such as to short-circuit an expression.

3

COMPOUND DATA TYPES

In the previous chapter we discussed JavaScript's primitive data types, which represent a single piece of data, like a number or a string. Now we'll look at JavaScript's *compound data types*, arrays and objects, which combine multiple pieces of data into a single unit. Compound data types are an essential part of programming because they allow us to organize and work with collections of data of any size. You'll learn how to create and manipulate arrays and objects, and how to combine them into more complex data structures.

Arrays

A JavaScript *array* is a compound data type that holds an ordered list of values. The elements of an array can be of any data type. They don't all have to be the same type, although they typically are. For instance, an array might function as a to-do list by holding a series of strings describing tasks that need to be performed, or it might hold a collection of numbers representing temperature readings taken at regular intervals from a particular location.

Arrays are perfect for these sorts of structures because they collect the related values together in one place, and they have the flexibility to grow and shrink as values are added or removed. If you had a fixed number of to-do items—say, four—then you might use separate variables to hold them, but using an array enables you to hold an unbounded, changing number of items and keep them in a fixed order. Also, once you have your elements together in a single array, you can write code to efficiently operate on each item in the array in turn, as you'll see in Chapter 4.

Creation and Indexing

To create an array, list its elements separated by commas inside a pair of square brackets:

```
let primes = [2, 3, 5, 7, 11, 13, 17, 19];
primes;
▸ (8) [2, 3, 5, 7, 11, 13, 17, 19]
```

This array contains the first eight prime numbers and is stored in the `primes` variable. When you enter **primes;** the Chrome console should print the length of the array (8) followed by its elements.

Every element in an array has an index number associated with it. Like strings, arrays are zero-indexed, so the first element is found at index 0, the second at index 1, and so on. To access an individual element of an array, place its index number in square brackets after the name of the array. Here, for example, we access the first element of the `primes` array:

```
primes[0];
2
```

Because arrays are zero-indexed, the index of the last element of the array is one less than the array's length. So, the last element of our eight-element `primes` array is at index 7:

```
primes[7];
19
```

If you don't know how long an array is and you want to get its last element, you can first use dot notation to access its `length` property and look up the array's length, as we did with strings in Chapter 2:

```
primes.length;
8
primes[7];
19
```

Or, to do this in a single statement, you can simply subtract 1 from the length to get the element at the last index, like so:

```
primes[primes.length - 1];
19
```

If you use an index outside the range of the array, JavaScript returns undefined:

```
primes[10];
undefined
```

To replace an element in an array, assign the element a new value using indexing syntax:

```
primes[2] = 1;
primes;
▶ (8) [2, 3, 1, 7, 11, 13, 17, 19]
```

Here we add a 1 in the third position (index 2) of primes, replacing the value that was previously at that index. The console output confirms that 1 is the new third element in the array.

Arrays of Arrays

Arrays can contain other arrays. These *multidimensional arrays* are often used to represent two-dimensional grids of points, or tables. To illustrate this, let's make a simple tic-tac-toe game. We'll create an array (we'll call this the *outer* array) containing three elements, each of which is another array (we'll call these the *inner* arrays) representing one of the rows of the tic-tac-toe board. Each inner array will contain three empty strings to represent the squares within that row:

```
let ticTacToe = [
  ["", "", ""],
  ["", "", ""],
  ["", "", ""]
];
```

In order to make the code easier to read, I've put each inner array on a new line. Usually when you press ENTER (commonly to start a new line), the JavaScript console will run the line of code you just entered, but in this case, it's clever enough to realize that the first line isn't finished, because there's no closing square bracket to match the opening bracket. It will interpret everything up to the final closing bracket and semicolon as a single statement, even if you include additional brackets and carriage returns.

The Chrome console automatically applies indentation to the inner arrays, to indicate that they're nested inside the outer array. Chrome and VS Code by default use four spaces for each level of indentation, but this is a matter of personal preference. Throughout this book I'll be using two spaces for indentation, both because this is more common in modern JavaScript code and because it helps some of the bigger listings fit on the page.

I could have written this array on one line, as shown here, but this way it's harder to see its two-dimensionality:

```
let ticTacToeOneLine = [["", "", ""], ["", "", ""], ["", "", ""]];
```

Now let's see what happens when we ask the console for the value of the ticTacToe variable:

```
ticTacToe;
▶ (3) [Array(3), Array(3), Array(3)]
```

In this case, the length of the outer array is shown as (3), indicating that it's an array with three elements. Each element of the array is Array(3), which means each inner array is another three-element array.

To expand the view and see what's in those inner arrays, click the arrow on the left:

```
▼ (3) [Array(3), Array(3), Array(3)]
  ▶0: (3) ['', '', '']
  ▶1: (3) ['', '', '']
  ▶2: (3) ['', '', '']
  length: 3
  ▶[[Prototype]]: Array(0)
```

The first three lines show the values of the inner arrays at indexes 0, 1, and 2. After these, the outer array's length property is shown, with its value of 3. The final property, [[Prototype]], is where the array's built-in methods come from (more on this in Chapter 6).

We've created our tic-tac-toe board, but it's empty. Let's set an X in the top-right corner. The first inner array represents the top row; we access it with ticTacToe[0]. The top-right corner is the third element of that row, or index 2 of the inner array. Because ticTacToe[0] returns an array, we can just add [2] on the end to access the element we want: ticTacToe[0][2]. Knowing this, we can set this element to "X" as follows:

```
ticTacToe[0][2] = "X";
```

Now let's look at the value of ticTacToe again, clicking the arrow to expand the outer array:

```
ticTacToe;
▾ (3) [Array(3), Array(3), Array(3)]
  ▸0: (3) ['', '', 'X']
  ▸1: (3) ['', '', '']
  ▸2: (3) ['', '', '']
  length: 3
  ▸[[Prototype]]: Array(0)
```

The top-right corner of the tic-tac-toe board now contains an X.

Next, let's set an O in the bottom-left corner. The bottom row is index 2 of the outer array, and the leftmost square of that row is index 0 of the inner array, so we enter the following:

```
ticTacToe[2][0] = "O";
ticTacToe;
▾ (3) [Array(3), Array(3), Array(3)]
  ▸0: (3) ['', '', 'X']
  ▸1: (3) ['', '', '']
  ▸2: (3) ['O', '', '']
  length: 3
  ▸[[Prototype]]: Array(0)
```

Now there's an O in the bottom-left corner of the board.

To summarize, if you want to access an element in a nested array, use one set of square brackets to select the element in the outer array (which returns one of the inner arrays), then a second set to select the element in the inner array.

TRY IT YOURSELF

3-1. Play a game of tic-tac-toe against yourself, using the ticTacToe array. Remember, the first index number should be the row of the board, and the second index number should be the column.

Array Methods

JavaScript has several useful methods for working with arrays. We'll look at a few important ones in this section. Some of these methods modify the array in question, which is known as *mutation*. Example mutations include adding or deleting array elements, or changing the elements' order. Other methods create and return a new array while leaving the original array unchanged, which is useful if you still need the original array for other purposes.

It's important to be aware of whether or not the method you're using will mutate the array. For example, say you have an array containing the months of the year listed chronologically, but one part of your program needs them in alphabetical order. You'd want to be sure that alphabetizing the months doesn't inadvertently change the original, chronological array, or other parts of your program might start thinking April is the first month of the year. On the other hand, if you have an array representing a to-do list, you'd probably want the original array itself to be updated when a task is added or removed, rather than creating a new array.

Adding an Element to an Array

The push method mutates an array by adding a supplied element to the end of the array. The return value of the push method is the new length of the array. As an example, let's use push to build up an array of programming languages:

```
let languages = [];
languages.push("Python");
1
languages.push("Haskell");
2
languages.push("JavaScript");
3
languages.push("Rust");
4
languages;
▸ (4) ['Python', 'Haskell', 'JavaScript', 'Rust']
```

First we create a new array called languages and initialize it with [], an empty array. The first time we call the push method, we pass the value "Python". The method returns 1, which means there's now one element in the array. We do this three more times, and finally ask for the value of languages by entering languages;. This returns the four languages we added to the array, in the order we added them.

To add an element to the beginning of the array rather than the end, use the unshift method, like so:

```
languages.unshift("Erlang");
5
languages.unshift("C");
6
languages.unshift("Fortran");
7
languages;
▸ (7) ['Fortran', 'C', 'Erlang', 'Python', 'Haskell', 'JavaScript', 'Rust']
```

Here we've added three more languages to the front of the languages array. Because each element is added to the beginning of the array, they end up in the opposite order to how they were added. Like push, calling unshift returns the new length of the array.

Removing Elements from an Array

To mutate an array by removing its last element, use the pop method. Here we call the pop method on the languages array, deleting its last element:

```
languages.pop();
'Rust'
languages;
▶ (6) ['Fortran', 'C', 'Erlang', 'Python', 'Haskell', 'JavaScript']
```

The method returns the value of the element being removed, in this case "Rust". When we then check the array, it contains only six elements.

Because the pop method returns the array element being removed, it's particularly useful if you want to do something with that element as you're removing it. For example, here we delete another element from the languages array and use it in a message:

```
let bestLanguage = languages.pop();
let message = `My favorite language is ${bestLanguage}.`;
message;
'My favorite language is JavaScript.'
languages;
▶ (5) ['Fortran', 'C', 'Erlang', 'Python', 'Haskell']
```

This time when we call languages.pop() we store the method's return value in the bestLanguage variable, which we incorporate into a string using a template literal. When we print the resulting message, it includes the word *JavaScript*. This was the element removed from the array, which is now down to five languages.

To remove the *first* element from an array, rather than the last, use the shift method. Like pop, the shift method returns the removed element:

```
let worstLanguage = languages.shift();
message = `My least favorite language is ${worstLanguage}.`;
message;
'My least favorite language is Fortran.'
languages;
▶ (4) ['C', 'Erlang', 'Python', 'Haskell']
```

As with the previous example, we save the result of calling shift in a variable, this time called worstLanguage, and use it in a template literal. This variable contains the string "Fortran", and languages is left with four elements.

The four methods we've looked at so far, pop, unshift, push, and shift, are commonly used to implement more specialized data structures, like queues. A *queue* is a data structure that resembles a line of people, where new items are added to the end and items are removed and processed from the beginning. This is useful when you want to process data in the order it arrives. For example, imagine a Q and A app, where many users can ask questions. You could use an array to store the list of questions, with the push method adding each new question to the end of the array. When the answerer is ready to answer a question, they would use shift to get the first element in the array and remove it from the array. This ensures that only unanswered questions are in the array, and that they're answered in the order they were received.

TRY IT YOURSELF

3-2. Create a new empty array and save it in a variable called rainbow (see the section "Adding an Element to an Array" on page 42 to see how to create a new empty array). Your task is to add the colors of the rainbow ("Red", "Orange", "Yellow", "Green", "Blue", "Indigo", "Violet") to this array, but with a twist: you must start by adding "Green", and use push and unshift to add the rest. If you make a mistake, you can use pop or shift to remove the color you just added.

Combining Arrays

The concat method (short for *concatenate*) adds two arrays together. Here, for example, we start with two arrays, fish and mammals, and combine them into a new array, saving that into the animals variable:

```
let fish = ["Salmon", "Cod", "Trout"];
let mammals = ["Sheep", "Cat", "Tiger"];
let animals = fish.concat(mammals);
animals;
▶ (6) ['Salmon', 'Cod', 'Trout', 'Sheep', 'Cat', 'Tiger']
```

When you call concat on an array, a new array is created with all the elements from the first array (the array on which you called concat) followed by all the elements from the second array (the array passed as an argument to concat). The original arrays remain unchanged because, unlike the other methods we've looked at so far, concat isn't a mutating method. This is useful here, because we wouldn't want our fish array to suddenly contain the elements from mammals!

To combine three or more arrays, pass multiple arrays as arguments to concat, as in this example:

```
let originals = ["Hope", "Empire", "Jedi"];
let prequels = ["Phantom", "Clones", "Sith"];
let sequels = ["Awakens", "Last", "Rise"];
let starWars = prequels.concat(originals, sequels);
starWars;
▶ (9) ['Phantom', 'Clones', 'Sith', 'Hope', 'Empire', 'Jedi', 'Awakens', 'Last', 'Rise']
```

Here we create three separate arrays, originals, prequels, and sequels, representing the three sets of *Star Wars* movies. Then we use concat to combine them into a single nine-element starWars array. Notice that the elements in the combined array appear in the order in which the arrays were passed as arguments.

Finding the Index of an Element in an Array

To find out where a particular element is in an array, use the indexOf method. This method returns the index of the first occurrence of the specified element. If the element isn't found in the array, indexOf returns -1:

```
let sizes = ["Small", "Medium", "Large"];
sizes.indexOf("Medium");
1
sizes.indexOf("Huge");
-1
```

In this example, we want to check the position of "Medium" in the sizes array, and we get back the answer 1. Then, because "Huge" isn't in the array, we get the answer -1.

If the array contains multiple instances of the given value, indexOf returns the index of the first matching element only. For example, here's an array with the colors of the flag of Argentina:

```
let flagOfArgentina = ["Blue", "White", "Blue"];
flagOfArgentina.indexOf("Blue");
0
```

Even though "Blue" is found twice in the array, indexOf returns only the index of the first occurrence.

Turning an Array into a String

The join method converts an array into a single string, joining all the elements together, as shown here:

```
let beatles = ["John", "Paul", "George", "Ringo"];
beatles.join();
'John,Paul,George,Ringo'
```

Notice how the separate strings in the beatles array are combined into one string. By default, join places a comma between each element to form the returned string. To change this, you can give your own separator as an argument to join. For example, if you want nothing in between each element, pass an empty string as an argument:

```
beatles.join("");
'JohnPaulGeorgeRingo'
```

You can pass any valid string as a separator. In the next example, we pass a space, an ampersand, and a newline escape character to set each element on its own line. As you learned in Chapter 2, we have to use console.log for the newlines to display correctly in Chrome:

```
console.log(beatles.join("&\n"));
John&
Paul&
George&
Ringo
```

Keep in mind that the separator appears only *between* array elements, not after each one. This is why there isn't an extra ampersand and newline after Ringo.

If you use join on an array containing non-string values, those values will be converted to strings, as in this example:

```
[100, true, false, "hi"].join(" - ");
'100 - true - false - hi'
```

As with the previous joins, the result is one long string, joined together by the separator (in this case, " - "). The difference is that the non-string values (the number 100 and the Booleans true and false) had to be automatically converted to strings before the join. This example also shows how you can call array methods directly on array literals, rather than having to save the array into a variable first.

TRY IT YOURSELF

3-3. Use the join method to convert the array ["X", "X", "X"] into the string "XoXoX".

Other Useful Array Methods

Here are some other useful array methods you might want to try out:

*arr.*includes(*elem*) Returns true or false depending on whether a given *elem* is in the *arr* array.

*arr.*reverse() Reverses the order of elements in the array. This is a mutating method, so it modifies the original array.

*arr.*sort() Sorts the array elements, modifying the original array. If the elements are strings, they're sorted in alphabetical order. Otherwise, the sorting happens as if the elements were converted to strings.

*arr.*slice(*start, end*) Creates a new array by extracting elements from the original array starting at index *start*, up to but not including index *end*.

This method is equivalent to the slice method on strings, introduced in the previous chapter. If you call slice() without any arguments, the entire array is copied into a new array. This is useful if you need to use a mutating method like sort but you don't want to mutate the original array.

arr.splice(*index, count*)   Removes *count* elements from the array, starting at *index*.

Objects

Objects are another compound data type in JavaScript. They're similar to arrays in that they hold a collection of values, but they differ in that objects use strings called *keys* instead of numeric indices to access the values. Each key is associated with a specific value, forming a *key-value pair*.

Whereas arrays are commonly used to store ordered lists of elements of the same data type, objects are usually used to store multiple pieces of information about a single entity. These pieces of information often are not all of the same data type. For example, an object representing a person might hold information like the person's name (a string), their age (a number), whether or not they're married (a Boolean), and so on. Objects are better suited for this purpose than arrays because each piece of information is given a meaningful name—its key—rather than a generic index number. It's much clearer what the values 35 and true mean if they're stored in a person object under the keys "age" and "married" than it would be if they were stored in a person array under the indices 1 and 2.

Creating Objects

One way to create an object is with an *object literal*, which consists of a pair of braces ({ and }) enclosing a series of key-value pairs, separated by commas. Each key-value pair must have a colon between the key and the value. For example, here's an object literal called casablanca containing some information about that movie:

```
let casablanca = {
  "title": "Casablanca",
  "released": 1942,
  "director": "Michael Curtiz"
};
casablanca;
▶ {title: 'Casablanca', released: 1942, director: 'Michael Curtiz'}
```

Here we create a new object with three keys: "title", "released", and "director". Each key has a value associated with it. I've written each key-value pair on its own line to make the object literal easier to read, but this isn't strictly necessary. As you'll see in later examples, the key-value pairs can also all be written on the same line.

All object keys are strings, but if your key is a valid identifier, it's common practice to omit the quotes. A *valid identifier* is any series of characters that can be used as a JavaScript variable name. An identifier can consist of letters, numbers, and the characters _ and $, but it can't start with a number. It also can't contain other symbols, like *, (, or #, nor can it include whitespace characters like spaces and newlines. These other characters *are* allowed in object keys, but only if the key is enclosed in quotes. For example:

```
let obj = { key1: 1, key_2: 2, "key 3": 3, "key#4": 4 };
obj;
▸ {key1: 1, key_2: 2, key 3: 3, key#4: 4}
```

Here key1 and key_2 are valid identifiers, so they don't need quotes. However, key 3 contains a space and key#4 contains a hash mark, making them invalid identifiers. They must be enclosed in quotes to be used as object keys.

Accessing Object Values

To get the value associated with a key, call the name of the object with the string key in square brackets:

```
obj["key 3"];
3
casablanca["title"];
'Casablanca'
```

This is just like the syntax for accessing an element from an array, but instead of using the numeric index, you use the string key.

For keys that are valid identifiers, you can use dot notation instead of square brackets, with the key name coming after the dot:

```
obj.key_2;
2
```

This doesn't work for keys that aren't valid identifiers. For example, you can't write obj.key 3 because to JavaScript that looks like obj.key followed after the space by the number literal 3.

Notice that this dot notation looks like the syntax we used for accessing the length property of strings (in Chapter 2) and arrays (earlier in this chapter). That's because it's the same thing! A property is just another name for a key-value pair. Behind the scenes, JavaScript treats strings like objects, and arrays, too, are actually a special kind of object. When we write something like [1, 2, 3].length, we say we're accessing the array's length property, but we could also say we're getting the value associated with the array's length key. Likewise, when we write something like casablanca.title, we often say we're accessing the object's title property instead of the value associated with its title key.

Setting Object Values

To add a new key-value pair to an object, use the same bracket or dot notation used to look up a value. Here, for example, we set up an empty `dictionary` object, then add two definitions:

```
let dictionary = {};
dictionary.mouse = "A small rodent";
dictionary["computer mouse"] = "A pointing device for computers";
dictionary;
▶ {mouse: 'A small rodent', computer mouse: 'A pointing device for computers'}
```

We first create a new, empty object using a pair of empty braces. We then set two new keys, `"mouse"` and `"computer mouse"`, giving each a definition as a value. As before, we can use dot notation with the valid identifier `mouse`, but we need bracket notation for `"computer mouse"` because it contains a space.

Changing the value associated with a key that already exists follows the same syntax:

```
dictionary.mouse = "A furry rodent";
dictionary;
▶ {mouse: 'A furry rodent', computer mouse: 'A pointing device for computers'}
```

The output confirms that the definition for `mouse` has been updated.

Working with Objects

JavaScript has plenty of methods for working with objects; we'll examine a few of the most common ones here. Unlike with arrays, where the methods are called directly on the array you want to operate on, object methods are called as static methods by entering `Object.methodName()` and passing the object you want to operate on as an argument inside the parentheses. Here, `Object` is a *constructor*, a type of function used to create objects, and *static methods* are methods defined directly on the constructor instead of on a particular object. We'll discuss constructors in more detail in Chapter 6.

Getting an Object's Keys

To get an array of all the keys of an object, use the static method `Object.keys`. For example, here's how you could retrieve the names of my cats:

```
let cats = { "Kiki": "black and white", "Mei": "tabby", "Moona": "gray" };
Object.keys(cats);
▶ (3) ['Kiki', 'Mei', 'Moona']
```

The cats object has three key-value pairs, where each key represents a cat name and each value represents that cat's color. `Object.keys` returns just the keys, as an array of strings.

`Object.keys` can be helpful in cases like this where the only pieces of information you need from an object are the names of its keys. For example, you might have an object tracking how much money you owe your friends, where the keys are your friends' names and the values are the amounts owed. With `Object.keys` you can list just the names of the friends that you're tracking, giving you a general sense of whom you owe money to.

You might be wondering why keys is a static method—that is, why we need to call it with `Object.keys(cats)` rather than with `cats.keys()`. To understand why this is the case, consider this `piano` object:

```
let piano = {
  make: "Steinway",
  color: "black",
  keys: 88
};
```

The object has a property named `"keys"` that represents the number of keys on the piano. If methods like keys could be called directly on the `piano` object itself, the property name and method name would conflict, which isn't allowed. JavaScript has many more built-in object methods besides keys, and it would be tedious to have to remember all of their names to make sure they don't conflict with any of your objects' property names. To avoid this issue, the designers of the language made these object methods static. They're attached to the overall `Object` constructor instead of to individual objects like cat or `piano`, so there's no possibility of a naming conflict.

NOTE   *None of this is an issue with arrays. Method names must be valid identifiers, meaning they can't start with a number. Therefore, there's no way an array method could conflict with the array's numerical indices.*

Getting an Object's Keys and Values

To get an array of the keys *and* values of an object, use `Object.entries`. This static method returns an array of two-element arrays, where the first element of each inner array is a key and the second is its value. Here's how it works:

```
let chromosomes = {
  koala: 16,
  snail: 24,
  giraffe: 30,
  cat: 38
};
Object.entries(chromosomes);
▶ (4) [Array(2), Array(2), Array(2), Array(2)]
```

We create an object with four key-value pairs, showing how many chromosomes various animals have. `Object.entries(chromosomes)` returns an array containing four elements, each of which is a two-element array. To expand the outer array and view its full contents, click the arrow:

```
▼ (4) [Array(2), Array(2), Array(2), Array(2)]
  ▶0: (2) ['koala', 16]
  ▶1: (2) ['snail', 24]
  ▶2: (2) ['giraffe', 30]
  ▶3: (2) ['cat', 38]
  length: 4
  ▶[[Prototype]]: Array(0)
```

This shows that each inner array contains a key from the original object as its first element, and the associated value as its second element.

Converting an object into an array with `Object.entries` makes it easier to cycle through all of the object's key-value pairs and do something with each one in turn. We'll see how to do this with loops in Chapter 4.

Combining Objects

The `Object.assign` method lets you combine multiple objects into one. For example, say you have two objects, one giving the physical attributes of a book and the other describing its contents:

```
let physical = { pages: 208, binding: "Hardcover" };
let contents = { genre: "Fiction", subgenre: "Mystery" };
```

With `Object.assign`, you can consolidate these separate objects into one overall book object:

```
let book = {};
Object.assign(book, physical, contents);
book;
▶ {pages: 208, binding: 'Hardcover', genre: 'Fiction', subgenre: 'Mystery'}
```

The first argument to `Object.assign` is the *target*, the object that the keys from the other objects are assigned to. In this case, we use an empty object called book as the target. The remaining arguments are the *sources*, the objects whose key-value pairs are to be copied into the target. You can pass as many source objects after the initial target argument as you want—we're just doing two here. The method mutates and returns the target object with the key-value pairs copied from the source objects. The source objects themselves are untouched.

You don't have to create a new, empty object to use as the target for `Object.assign`, but if you don't, you'll end up modifying one of your source objects. For example, we could remove the first argument, book, from the previous call and still get an object with the same four key-value pairs:

```
Object.assign(physical, contents);
physical;
▶ {pages: 208, binding: 'Hardcover', genre: 'Fiction', subgenre: 'Mystery'}
```

The problem here is that physical is now the target object, so it gets mutated, gaining all the key-value pairs from contents. This usually isn't what you want, as the original, separate objects are often still important to other parts of your application. For this reason, it's common practice to use an empty object as the first argument to `Object.assign`.

Nesting Objects and Arrays

As with arrays, we can nest objects in other objects. We can also nest objects in arrays, and arrays in objects, to create more sophisticated data structures. For example, you might want to make an object representing a person that contained a `children` property containing an array of objects representing that person's children. We build these nested structures in two ways: by creating an object or array literal with nested object or array literals inside, or by creating the inner elements, saving them to variables, and then building up the composite structures using the variables. We'll examine both of these techniques here.

Nesting with Literals

First, let's build a nested structure using literals. We'll create an array of objects representing different book trilogies:

```
let trilogies = [
❶ {
    title: "His Dark Materials",
    author: "Philip Pullman",
    books: ["Northern Lights", "The Subtle Knife", "The Amber Spyglass"]
  },
❷ {
    title: "Broken Earth",
    author: "N. K. Jemisin",
    books: ["The Fifth Season", "The Obelisk Gate", "The Stone Sky"]
  }
];
```

The variable `trilogies` contains an array of two elements, ❶ and ❷, each of which is an object with information about a particular trilogy. Notice that each object has the same keys, since we want to store the same pieces of information about each trilogy. One of those keys, `books`, itself contains an array of strings representing the book titles within the trilogy. We thus have an array within an object within an array.

Accessing an element from one of these inner arrays requires a combination of array indexing and object dot notation:

```
trilogies[1].books[0];
'The Fifth Season'
```

Here, `trilogies[1]` means we want the second object in the outer array, `.books` means we want the value of that object's books key (which is an array), and [0] means we want the first element from that array. Putting it together, we get the first book from the second trilogy in the outer array.

Nesting with Variables

An alternative technique for making nested structures is to create objects containing the inner elements, assign those objects to variables, and then build the outer structure out of these variables. For example, say we want to create a data structure modeling the change in our pocket. We create four objects representing a penny, nickel, dime, and quarter, assigning each to its own variable:

```
let penny = { name: "Penny", value: 1, weight: 2.5 };
let nickel = { name: "Nickel", value: 5, weight: 5 };
let dime = { name: "Dime", value: 10, weight: 2.268 };
let quarter = { name: "Quarter", value: 25, weight: 5.67 };
```

Next, we use these variables to create an array representing the specific combination of coins in our pocket. For example:

```
let change = [quarter, quarter, dime, penny, penny, penny];
```

Notice that some of the coin objects appear in the array multiple times. This is one advantage of assigning the inner objects to variables before we create the outer array: an object can be repeated within the array without having to manually write out the object literal each time.

Accessing a value from one of the inner objects again requires a combination of array indexing and object dot notation:

```
change[0].value;
25
```

Here, change[0] gives us the first element of the change array (a quarter object) and .value gives us its value key.

An interesting consequence of building the array from object variables like this is that the repeated elements share a common identity. For example, change[3] and change[4] refer to the same penny object. If the US government decided to update the weight of a penny, we could update the weight property of the underlying penny object, and that update would be reflected in all the penny elements of the change array:

```
penny.weight = 2.49;
change[3].weight;
2.49
change[4].weight;
2.49
change[5].weight;
2.49
```

Here we change the weight property of penny from 2.5 to 2.49. Then we check the weight of each penny in the array, confirming that the update has carried over to each one.

TRY IT YOURSELF

3-4. Try changing the value property of quarter and check to see if that change is reflected in the change array. Now, change the weight of change[0]. Do you see that change reflected in quarter as well?

Exploring Nested Objects in the Console

The Chrome console makes it easy to explore nested objects, like we did earlier in this chapter with the nested ticTacToe array. To illustrate, we'll create a deeply nested object and try to look inside:

```
let nested = {
  name: "Outer",
  content: {
    name: "Middle",
    content: {
      name: "Inner",
      content: "Whoa..."
    }
  }
};
```

Our nested object contains three layers of objects, each with a name and content property. The value of content for the outer and middle layers is another object. Getting the value of the innermost object's content property requires a long chain of dot notation:

```
nested.content.content.content;
'Whoa...'
```

This is equivalent to asking for the content property of the content property of the content property of the outermost object.

Now try viewing the value of nested as a whole:

```
nested;
▶ {name: 'Outer', content: {...}}
```

The console just gives an abbreviated version with the value of the outer object's content property shown as {...} to imply that there's an object here but there isn't room to display it. Click the arrow to expand the view of the outer object. Now the next nested object (with name: "Middle") is shown in abbreviated form. Click the arrow to expand this object, too, and then one more time to expand the object with `name: "Inner"`. You should now see the entire content of the object in the console:

```
▼ {name: 'Outer', content: {...}}
  ▼ content:
    ▼ content:
        content: "Whoa..."
        name: "Inner"
      ▶ [[Prototype]]: Object
      name: "Middle"
    ▶ [[Prototype]]: Object
    name: "Outer"
  ▶ [[Prototype]]: Object
```

The `[[Prototype]]` properties refer to the `Object` constructor, which we've previously used to call object methods like `Object.keys` and `Object.assign`. We'll discuss prototypes in detail in Chapter 6.

Using the console like this to view complex objects is a very helpful debugging tool. You'll often be working with objects that come from different JavaScript libraries, or that contain data you fetch from a server, and you won't necessarily know the "shape" of the data—what properties the objects contain, how many levels of nesting they have, and the like. With the console, you can interactively explore the objects and see their contents.

Printing Nested Objects with JSON.stringify

Another way to view a nested object is to turn it into a JSON string. *JSON*, or *JavaScript Object Notation*, is a textual data format based on JavaScript object and array literals that's heavily used across the web and beyond to store and exchange information. The `JSON.stringify` method converts a JavaScript object into a JSON string. Let's pass it the `nested` object as an example:

```
JSON.stringify(nested);
'{"name":"Outer","content":{"name":"Middle","content":{"name":"Inner","content":"Whoa..."}}}'
```

The result is a string (it's enclosed in single quotes) containing a JSON representation of the `nested` object. Essentially, it's the equivalent of the original object literal we used to create `nested`. Just like JavaScript, JSON uses braces to enclose objects, colons to separate keys from values, and commas to separate different key-value pairs. All that's missing from this representation are the original line breaks and indentations we used to clarify the object literal's nested structure. To re-create those, we can pass `JSON.stringify` another argument representing the number of spaces to indent each new nested object:

```
nestedJSON = JSON.stringify(nested, null, 2);
console.log(nestedJSON);
```

```
{
  "name": "Outer",
  "content": {
    "name": "Middle",
    "content": {
      "name": "Inner",
      "content": "Whoa..."
    }
  }
}
```

The second argument to `JSON.stringify` lets you define a replacer function that can modify the output by replacing key-value pairs, but we don't have a need for that here, so we pass `null`. Passing `2` for the third argument modifies the behavior of `JSON.stringify` to add newlines after each property and after opening braces and brackets, and then two extra spaces of indentation for each additional level of nesting. If we viewed the result in the console directly, we'd see a bunch of \n escape characters for all the newlines. Instead, we store the result in a variable and pass it to `console.log`, giving us a well-formatted view of the object's nested hierarchy.

Calling `JSON.stringify` in this way is helpful for getting a quick visual representation of an object without having to repeatedly click the arrows in the console to expand each nested level. The method works on non-nested objects, too, but in that case the regular view of the object in the console is usually sufficient.

Summary

This chapter introduced you to JavaScript's compound data types, which allow you to combine multiple values into a single unit. By organizing data in this way, you can manipulate unbounded amounts of information more efficiently. You learned about arrays, which are ordered collections of values identified by numerical indices, usually all of the same data type, and about objects, which are collections of key-value pairs where each key is a string and the values are often of different data types. You've seen how arrays are useful for storing lists of similar values, such as a list of prime numbers or a list of programming languages. Meanwhile, objects are useful for collecting multiple pieces of information about a single entity, such as information about a particular book or movie.

4

CONDITIONALS AND LOOPS

Conditionals and *loops* are essential elements in programming. They add logic and structure to your programs by allowing your code to make decisions based on specific conditions. Together, conditionals and loops are known as *control structures* because they give you control over when and how often parts of your code should run. With conditionals, you can run a particular piece of code only if a certain condition is true. Meanwhile, loops enable you to repeatedly run a piece of code for as long as a condition remains true.

In this chapter you'll learn how to conditionally execute code with `if` statements and how to loop code with `while` and `for` statements. You'll also learn techniques for looping over the elements within a compound data type. This is especially useful if you need to perform an operation on every element of an array or object.

As we start to work with control structures, we'll begin writing more elaborate scripts that are less practical to enter directly into the console, where each statement executes as soon as you enter it. For this reason, we'll switch in this chapter to embedding JavaScript code in HTML files and then opening those files in the browser. This enables you to run an entire program at once, and lets you easily make changes and re-run the whole thing. To review how to do this, see "Using a Text Editor" in Chapter 1.

Making Decisions with Conditionals

Conditionals let you run a block of code when some condition you set is found to be true. For example, you might want to display a warning message only when your bank balance is below a certain threshold, or make the player in a game lose a life when they get hit by an enemy. You typically create these conditions using the comparison operators, like === and >, that we discussed in Chapter 2. You can also combine multiple conditions with logical operators like && and ||. The key is that the overall condition should evaluate to true or false.

There are two main kinds of conditional statement: if statements and if...else statements. We'll consider each type in turn.

if Statements

An if statement runs code if some condition is true, or skips that code if the condition is false. For example, let's create a program that logs a message to the console if a value is greater than a certain threshold. Open VS Code, create a new file called *if.html*, and enter the contents of Listing 4-1.

```
<html><body><script>
let speed = 30;
console.log(`Your current speed is ${speed} mph.`);
❶ if (speed > 25) {
    console.log("Slow down!");
}
</script></body></html>
```

Listing 4-1: An if statement

This code begins and ends with the same tags we used in Chapter 1 to embed JavaScript code in an HTML file. The JavaScript itself first initializes the speed variable to 30 and prints that value to the console using console.log. Then we use an if statement ❶ to check the value of speed and print another message if the value is greater than 25.

The if statement begins with the if keyword and has two main parts: the *condition*, which is written inside parentheses, and the code to run if the condition is true, called the *body*, which is written between a set of braces. Here, the condition is speed > 25 and the code to run if that's true is console.log("Slow down!"). Because we've set speed to be greater than 25, the condition is true, so the code in the body will run. Therefore, if you open *if.html* in your browser, you should see the following output in the JavaScript console:

```
Your current speed is 30 mph.
Slow down!
```

Our condition passed, so the Slow down! message was logged to the console. If the condition had been false, however, the code in the body of the if statement wouldn't have run. To see this for yourself, try updating *if.html* by initializing speed to 20 rather than 30. Then resave the file and reload the page. This time, you should just see the following output:

```
Your current speed is 20 mph.
```

Because speed > 25 now evaluates to false, the code inside the braces doesn't run. The code outside the if statement body does still run, however, so we still see the value of speed printed out thanks to the first console .log call.

if...else Statements

Often you'll want to run one piece of code when a condition is true, or another piece of code when that condition is false. For this, we use an if...else statement. To try it out, create a new file called *ifElse.html* and enter the contents of Listing 4-2.

```
<html><body><script>
let speed = 20;
console.log(`Your current speed is ${speed} mph.`);
if (speed > 25) {
❶ console.log("Slow down!");
} else {
❷ console.log("You're obeying the speed limit.");
}
</script></body></html>
```

Listing 4-2: An if...else *statement*

This code uses an if...else statement to check if speed is greater than 25. As in Listing 4-1, the conditional begins with the if keyword followed by the condition in parentheses. Unlike in Listing 4-1, however, the if...else statement has two bodies instead of just one, with the else keyword between them. The first body ❶ runs if the condition is true, and the second body ❷ runs if the condition is false. Each body is enclosed in its own set of braces. In this case, because speed is 20, the condition evaluates to false, so the second body runs. When you open the file in Chrome, you should see the following output:

```
Your current speed is 20 mph.
You're obeying the speed limit.
```

The message from the else body has been logged to the console. However, if you try setting speed to a higher value, like 30, the message from the if body will be logged instead.

TRY IT YOURSELF

4-1. Create a new file called *cointoss.html* with the usual HTML setup code, then add some JavaScript to simulate a coin toss. Generate a random number between 0 and 1 with Math.random(), and write an if...else statement that will log "heads" if the number is less than 0.5 or "tails" otherwise. Every time you reload this file, you'll get a new random heads or tails value.

More Complex Conditions

It's possible to use more complex Boolean expressions as conditions by incorporating logical operators. For example, say you only wanted to check a driver's speed during school hours. Assuming you have an hour variable that contains the current hour (using 24-hour time), you could do something like this:

```
if (speed > 25 && hour > 7 && hour < 16) {
```

The body of this if statement will run only if speed is greater than 25 and hour is greater than 7 but less than 16. In other words, a speed above 25 won't cause the body of the if statement to execute if it's outside school hours.

If your conditions get too complex, it can become hard to read your if statements. In that case, it's often best to write the Boolean expression separately and assign it to a new variable. Then you can use this variable as the condition for the if statement. For example, the previous conditional could be rewritten as:

```
let tooFastForSchool = speed > 25 && hour > 7 && hour < 16;
if (tooFastForSchool) {
```

Here we've assigned the same complex Boolean expression to the tooFastForSchool variable, then provided that variable to the if statement. Thanks to the meaningful variable name, the conditional now almost reads like a sentence: "If too fast for school, [do something]."

If it seems odd to lump the speed and hour tests into a single Boolean variable, a middle ground could be to put just the hour checks into a variable, like so:

```
let schoolHours = hour > 7 && hour < 16;
if (speed > 25 && schoolHours) {
```

Now the schoolHours variable holds true or false based on whether or not it's during school hours, and the if statement combines this variable with the speed test. In the end, the approach you choose comes down to the subjective question of how easy you find the code to read.

Chained if...else Statements

If you need your code to decide between three or more possible branches, you can chain together multiple if...else statements. For example, you can use this technique to log one of three possible messages depending on the value of the speed variable. Create a new file called *ifElseIf.html* with the code shown in Listing 4-3.

```
<html><body><script>
let speed = 20;
console.log(`Your current speed is ${speed} mph.`);
if (speed > 25) {
  console.log("Slow down!");
} else if (speed > 15) {
  console.log("You're driving at a good speed.");
} else {
  console.log("You're driving too slowly.");
}
</script></body></html>
```

Listing 4-3: A chained if...else statement with three bodies

This script is very similar to the if...else statement in Listing 4-2, except now there are three sections, each with its own body: if, else if, and else. Only one of the bodies—the first body whose condition is true—will run. Here's how it works:

1. First, we use if to check if speed is greater than 25. If it is, the first body runs, logging "Slow down!" to the console, and the remaining conditions are skipped.

2. Next, we use else if to add a second condition, testing if speed is greater than 15 and logging a different message if it is. If the code gets to this point, it'll be because speed > 25 was already found to be false, so essentially speed > 15 is testing if speed is between 15 and 25. We could make this explicit by writing else if (speed > 15 && speed <= 25), but since we already know speed can't be greater than 25, we don't need to specify the && speed <= 25 part.

3. Finally, we use else to log a third possible message if neither of the previous conditions was true.

In this case, we've set speed to 20, so only the else if branch should run, producing the following output:

```
Your current speed is 20 mph.
You're driving at a good speed.
```

Try experimenting with different values of speed to trigger the if and else branches instead.

You can chain as many else if clauses as you want between the initial if and the final else, as shown in Listing 4-4, to create any number of possible branches in your conditional structure.

```
if (speed > 25) {
  console.log("Slow down!");
} else if (speed > 20) {
  console.log("You're driving at a good speed.");
} else if (speed > 15) {
  console.log("You're driving a little bit too slowly.");
} else if (speed > 10) {
  console.log("You're driving too slowly.");
} else {
  console.log("You're driving far too slowly!");
}
```

Listing 4-4: A chained if...else statement with five bodies

This chained if...else statement has five possible bodies, depending on whether speed is greater than 25, 20, 15, 10, or none of these. As with the previous example, the order of conditions matters here. Making the comparisons in order from greatest to least allows us to define five ranges of possible values for speed, without having to explicitly define the upper bounds of the ranges. For example, we can write else if (speed > 15) rather than else if (speed > 15 && speed <= 20) for the third branch, since we've already confirmed by then that speed isn't greater than 20. Table 4-1 shows the full conditions for each branch in Listing 4-4.

Table 4-1: Full Conditions and Outputs for Listing 4-4

Condition	Output
speed > 25	Slow down!
speed > 20 && speed <= 25	You're driving at a good speed.
speed > 15 && speed <= 20	You're driving a little bit too slowly.
speed > 10 && speed <= 15	You're driving too slowly.
speed <= 10	You're driving far too slowly!

Note that we could reverse the order of the conditions and bodies and end up with the same effect. Reversed, the conditions would be speed <= 10, speed <= 15, speed <= 20, and speed <= 25. The speed > 25 case would be handled in the else block. The important thing to recognize is that the conditions are checked one by one, in sequence, so checking the second condition implies that the first condition was false. Also, notice that the opposite of > is <= (think which case would be hit if speed were exactly 10).

DO YOU NEED BRACES?

It's possible to write if and if...else statements without braces, as long as the body consists of a single statement. For example:

```
if (speed > 25)
  console.log("Slow down!");
else
  console.log("You're driving under the speed limit.");
```

Omitting the braces from the if and else bodies is valid here, since each body contains only one statement. We've still put each body on a separate line and indented it for clarity, but this, too, isn't strictly necessary. The bodies can go on the same lines as the if and else keywords, as shown here:

```
if (speed > 25) console.log("Slow down!");
else console.log("You're driving under the speed limit.");
```

These examples work fine, but if you have more than one line in the body, you need to include the braces to specify where the body of the conditional ends and the code after the conditional begins. It's also good coding style to indent the body. In this book, we'll always use braces and indentation, for consistency.

Repeating Code with Loops

Loops are another form of control structure in JavaScript that let you repeatedly run the same code as many times as necessary. For example, you could use a loop to print out each item on a shopping list. Without a loop, this wouldn't be possible because you don't necessarily know ahead of time how many items there are on the list. Loops are also useful when you want to keep running the same piece of code until some condition becomes true; for example, repeatedly asking a user to enter their date of birth until they provide a valid date.

You'll learn about four kinds of loops in this chapter: while loops, for loops, for...in loops, and for...of loops. Let's start with while loops.

while Loops

Similar to an if statement, a while loop depends on a conditional test. Just like an if statement, a while loop will skip executing its code altogether if the condition is initially found to be false. Unlike an if statement, however, a while loop will keep running the code in its body as long as the condition is true, rechecking the condition before each new repetition. In other words, it repeatedly runs a block of code *while* some condition is true. This is useful when you need to execute a piece of code multiple times, allowing your program to keep running as long as it's needed, instead of just running through once and stopping.

To see how a while loop works, create a new file called *while.html* and enter the contents of Listing 4-5.

```
<html><body><script>
let speed = 30;
❶ while (speed > 25) {
  console.log(`Your current speed is ${speed} mph.`);
  speed--;
}
❷ console.log(`Now your speed is ${speed} mph.`);
</script></body></html>
```

Listing 4-5: A while loop

This script sets speed to 30, then uses a while loop ❶ to bring that speed within the limit. We write the while loop using the while keyword, followed by a condition in parentheses and a body in braces, much like an if statement. Here, our condition checks if speed is greater than 25. Our body logs the value of speed to the console, then uses the decrement operator (--) to decrease speed by one. This gives us a new value of speed to test the next time through the loop. The while loop will keep repeating the body until the condition is false, producing the following output:

```
Your current speed is 30 mph.
Your current speed is 29 mph.
Your current speed is 28 mph.
Your current speed is 27 mph.
Your current speed is 26 mph.
Now your speed is 25 mph.
```

Let's think about what happens when this code runs. The first time we hit the while loop, speed is 30, so the condition (speed > 25) is true. This means the body of the while loop runs once, outputting Your current speed is 30 mph. and decrementing speed from 30 to 29. At the end of the loop body, we go back to the start and check the condition again. Since speed is now 29, the condition is still true, so we run the body again, printing Your current speed is 29 mph. and decrementing speed to 28. Then we go back to the start and check the condition yet again, and so on. Finally, the fifth time through the loop, speed decrements from 26 to 25. When we then check the condition for a sixth time, it evaluates to false (25 isn't greater than 25). This causes JavaScript to stop looping and jump to the first line of code following the while loop ❷, which outputs the final line of text.

for Loops

A for loop is another, more structured style of JavaScript loop. Like a while loop, a for loop keeps repeating as long as some condition is true. But unlike in a while loop, in a for loop the code for managing the repetitions appears at the start of the loop, separate from the loop body.

   Often, loops have a particular *looping variable* that keeps track of the state of the loop. A common pattern is to set the looping variable to a starting value, update it somehow, and check some condition based on the looping variable to decide whether the repetition should stop. For example, our while loop in Listing 4-5 follows this pattern, with speed serving as the looping variable. We set speed to 30 before entering the loop, decrement speed each time through the loop, and keep looping until speed is no longer greater than 25.

   A for loop is just a more convenient way to write this pattern. With for loops, we move the code to set up and update the looping variable into the first line of the loop, within the same set of parentheses where we write the loop condition. To illustrate, let's rewrite the previous example to use a for loop instead of a while loop. Save the contents of Listing 4-6 in *for.html*.

```
<html><body><script>
for (let speed = 30; speed > 25; speed--) {
  console.log(`Your current speed is ${speed} mph.`);
}
</script></body></html>
```

Listing 4-6: A for loop

We declare the for loop with the for keyword, followed by a set of parentheses containing three components, each with its own loop management task:

1. Initialize the looping variable (let speed = 30).
2. Set the looping condition (speed > 25).
3. Update the looping variable (speed--). The update will occur after each repetition of the loop.

These three components are separated by semicolons.

Inside the loop body, we have a single statement logging the value of speed to the console. Notice that we no longer have to decrement speed as part of the loop body, as we did in the while loop; this is covered by the third part of the loop management code in parentheses. Likewise, we no longer have to initialize speed before declaring the loop; that, too, is handled inside the parentheses.

Running this script will produce mostly the same output as the while loop from Listing 4-5:

```
Your current speed is 30 mph.
Your current speed is 29 mph.
Your current speed is 28 mph.
Your current speed is 27 mph.
Your current speed is 26 mph.
```

The only difference is that we can't log the final speed after the loop ends, as we did with the while loop. This is because the speed variable is declared as part of the code for the loop itself, rather than before the loop. As such, speed is confined to the *scope* of the loop, meaning code outside the loop doesn't have access to it. This is actually one of the advantages of for loops: the looping variable exists just for the loop and can't be accidentally used or changed in other parts of the code.

There's nothing you can do with a for loop that you can't do with a while loop, but most programmers find for loops easier to read than the equivalent while loops, because all the looping logic is gathered in one place.

WHAT IS SCOPE?

All bindings in JavaScript have *scope*, which is the area of code in which they're accessible. For example, if you declare a variable with `let` inside a `while` loop, that variable can't be used outside of the `while` loop. If, however, you declare the variable outside of the loop, it can be used inside the loop. The same goes for variables declared in the body of an `if` statement. Each nesting of control structure (or function definition, as you'll see in Chapter 5) adds a new layer of scope. Bindings defined in the outer layers can be accessed by the inner layers, but not vice versa. Consider this example:

```
let name = "Philadelphia";

if (name.length > 10) {
  let message = `Hi ${name}, you have a really long name!`;
}

console.log(message);
```

The body of this `if` statement can access `name` and incorporate it into a template literal to generate a message, since `name` was declared outside the `if` statement. However, trying to access `message` outside the conditional won't work, since `message` doesn't have scope beyond the `if` statement in which it's declared. If you run this code, it'll produce an `Uncaught ReferenceError` when it gets to the `console.log` call, saying that the variable `message` hasn't been defined. To successfully print the message, we'd need to move the `console.log` call to within the body of the `if` statement, where `message` has scope.

Similarly, variables defined in the initialization segment of a `for` loop have scope only within the loop. In this example, we can access and log the looping variable `i` within the body of the `for` loop:

```
for (let i = 0; i < 10; i++) {
  console.log(`This is repetition ${i}`);
}
console.log(i);
```

However, calling `console.log(i)` after the loop ends will trigger another `Uncaught ReferenceError`, since `i` is no longer in scope.

for...of Loops

A `for...of` loop cycles through the items in an array. Whereas a `while` loop or `for` loop keeps looping as long as some condition is true, a `for...of` loop goes over each item in an array, one at a time, and stops when it runs out of items. This is quite useful, as it's common to have to apply the same action to each member of an array. For example, if you had an array of numbers, you could create a bar chart by looping over those numbers and drawing a rectangle to the screen for each one, using the number to set the rectangle's height in pixels. Similarly, if you had an array of objects about movies, you could loop over the movies and print their titles.

Let's have a look at a for...of loop in action. Create a new file called *forOf.html* containing the contents of Listing 4-7.

```
<html><body><script>
let colors = ["Red", "Green", "Blue"];

for (let color of colors) {
  console.log(`${color} is a color.`);
}
</script></body></html>
```

Listing 4-7: Looping over an array with a for...of loop

This code logs a sentence for each color in the array colors, then stops. We first create the array, containing the strings "Red", "Green", and "Blue". We then use the statement for (let color of colors) to set the looping variable color to each element in colors, one at a time. The first time through the loop, color will be set to "Red". The second time, it will be set to "Green". Finally, the third time around, it will be set to "Blue". When the array runs out of items, the loop ends. This script should output the following:

```
Red is a color.
Green is a color.
Blue is a color.
```

It's also possible to use a regular for loop to loop over the items in an array, as in Listing 4-8.

```
for (let index = 0; index < colors.length; index++) {
  console.log(`${colors[index]} is a color.`);
}
```

Listing 4-8: Using a for loop instead of a for...of loop to loop over an array

Here, the looping variable index represents the index of each item in the array. Our loop setup code initializes index to 0 and increments it until it's no longer less than the length of the colors array (remember that the highest index in an array of length N will be $N-1$). Within the body of the loop, we access the current color using colors[index].

For a long time, this for loop style was the only way to loop over an array in JavaScript. It's worth being able to recognize it, as you may see it in a lot of older code. These days, the for...of style is more common. However, one benefit of the old for loop technique is that it gives you access to the array indices. This is helpful because it's sometimes important to know which element of the array you're currently working with. For example, you might want to do something different with even and odd elements, or you might just want to print out the indices along with the elements' values to make a numbered list. You can do that with a for...of loop, too, by using the entries method on the array. To see how it works, create a new *forOfEntries.html* file and enter the contents of Listing 4-9.

```
<html><body><script>
let colors = ["Red", "Green", "Blue"];
for (let [index, item] of colors.entries()) {
  console.log(`${index}: ${item} is a color.`);
}
</script></body></html>
```

Listing 4-9: Using a for...of loop with entries to access the indices in an array

In the previous chapter you saw how applying the `Object.entries` method to an object gives you an array of arrays, where each inner array contains one of the object's keys and its associated value. Here, calling entries on the colors array does a similar thing, giving the array `[[0, "Red"], [1, "Green"], [2, "Blue"]]`. The syntax `let [index, item]` is called *destructuring assignment*. It splits each two-element array from `colors.entries` (for example, `[0, "Red"]`) into two separate variables, `index` for the index number and `item` for the corresponding value. This way we can incorporate the indices into the logged messages, creating the following output:

```
0: Red is a color.
1: Green is a color.
2: Blue is a color.
```

Note that it's also possible to use destructuring assignment in regular assignment statements, outside `for...of` loops, to break up an array into separate variables. For example, you could turn an array of three numbers representing RGB color values into individual r, g, and b variables like this:

```
let rgbcolor = [125, 100, 0];
let [r, g, b] = rgbcolor;
```

Thanks to the destructuring assignment, r now has the value 125, g has the value 100, and b has the value 0. We won't be using this syntax much in this book, but it's good to be able to recognize it.

TRY IT YOURSELF

4-2. Much like looping over the elements in an array, it's also possible to use for...of to loop over the letters in a string. Write a for...of loop that will loop over your name, printing each letter on a separate line, like this:

```
N
i
c
k
```

(continued)

```
N 0
i 1
c 2
k 3
```

for...in Loops

A for...in loop cycles through the keys in an object. It works similarly to a for...of loop, picking out each key in turn and stopping when there are no more keys. The difference is that for...in loops apply to objects instead of arrays, looping over the keys, not the values. Save the contents of Listing 4-10 as *forIn.html* to try it out.

```
<html><body><script>
let me = {
  "first name": "Nick",
  "last name": "Morgan",
  "age": 39
};

for (let key in me) {
  console.log(`My ${key} is ${me[key]}.`);
}
</script></body></html>
```

Listing 4-10: Looping over the keys in an object with a for...in loop

Here we create a me object with three key-value pairs (feel free to fill in your own name and age). Then we use a for...in loop to loop over the keys. Similar to for...of loop syntax, writing for (let key in me) creates a looping variable key and sets it to each key from the me object, one at a time. The first time through the loop key is set to "first name", the second time through it's set to "last name", and so on. Within the loop body, we use the notation me[key] to access the value associated with the current key, incorporating it into a message, along with the key itself. The output should look something like this:

```
My first name is Nick.
My last name is Morgan.
My age is 39.
```

We could have achieved the same result using `Object.entries(me)` to get an array of pairs of keys and values, and a `for...of` loop to loop over those. As usual, the choice is mostly a personal one.

Summary

This chapter showed you how to add logic and structure to your code using conditionals and loops. These control structures let you determine when and how often your code should run. Conditionals like `if` and `if...else` statements run code based on whether or not a certain condition is true. Some loops, like `while` and `for`, repeat the same code multiple times until a certain condition is met. Other loops, like `for...of` and `for...in`, are for cycling through the elements of an array or object.

5

FUNCTIONS

As you learned in Chapter 1, a *function* is a self-contained block of code for performing a certain task. We've already used some of JavaScript's built-in functions, such as `alert` and `console.log`, but you can also create your own custom functions to perform the tasks particular to your application. Then you can *call* these functions to run the associated code. Packaging code into functions in this way makes your programming more effective, as you don't have to repeat the code every time you want to use it.

In this chapter, you'll learn different techniques for writing your own functions. You'll see how to provide input to functions and receive output from them. You'll also see how functions can be treated as ordinary values, just like a number or a string. In particular, we'll explore how functions can serve as input or output for other, higher-order functions.

Declaring and Calling Functions

Before you can use a custom function, you have to establish what the function is called and what it does. One way is to use a *function declaration*, a block of code that defines a function. To illustrate, we'll declare a simple function called sayHello that takes in someone's name and logs a custom greeting for that person to the console. Open the JavaScript console in Chrome and enter the following:

```
function sayHello(name) {
  console.log(`Hello, ${name}!`);
}
```

A function declaration has four parts. First, we use the function keyword to tell JavaScript we're creating a function. Next, we give the function a name—in this case, sayHello. After that, we provide a comma-separated list of the function's parameters, surrounded by parentheses. *Parameters* are pieces of information that the function needs to do its job. In this case, our function has one parameter, name, indicating that the function needs to be supplied with someone's name in order to create a greeting. (If a function has no parameters, we simply write an empty set of parentheses.) Finally, we write the function's body, surrounded by braces. This is the code that should be executed when the function is called. In our example, the body consists of a call to console.log to print out a greeting, with the value of the name parameter inserted via a template literal.

Now that we've declared our sayHello function, we can call it whenever we want to greet someone. Each time we call the function, we'll need to provide a value for the name parameter. That value is called an *argument*, and it's specified in parentheses when the function is called. By passing the function different arguments, we can create different custom greetings. For example:

```
sayHello("Nick");
Hello, Nick!
undefined
sayHello("Mei");
Hello, Mei!
undefined
```

The first time we call our sayHello function, we pass "Nick" as an argument in the parentheses after the function name. As a result, the message Hello, Nick! is logged to the console. The second time we call the function, we pass "Mei" as an argument, so the message Hello, Mei! is logged. In each case, the value of the argument is bound to the function's name parameter, and the function body runs with the name parameter set to that value.

Essentially, you can think of name as a variable within the function that takes on the value of the corresponding argument (such as "Nick" or "Mei") when the function is called.

The distinction between parameters and arguments is subtle but important. Parameters are generic names for a function's inputs, whereas arguments are the actual input values passed to the function when you call it. Each function has only one set of parameters, but every time you call the function it can have a new set of arguments. In this way, parameters make your functions highly customizable. The sayHello function, for example, has one parameter, name, but it can be called with a different argument each time. We've seen it called with sayHello("Nick") and sayHello("Mei"), but the possibilities are endless: sayHello("Kitty"), sayHello("Dolly"), sayHello("world"), and so on.

Notice that each call to sayHello outputs undefined as well as the custom greeting. This extra line of output is the function's return value. sayHello returns undefined because we didn't explicitly give it a return value; we'll look at how to do that next.

Return Values

A *return value* is a value that a function produces for use elsewhere in your code. In many cases, you'll want a function to take in some inputs using parameters, process those inputs in some way, and output the result. That output is the return value. For example, let's declare a function that takes in two numbers and returns their sum:

```
function add(x, y) {
  return x + y;
}
```

This add function has two parameters, x and y. The function body consists of the return keyword followed by the expression x + y. When the function is called, JavaScript will evaluate this expression, adding x and y together, and return the result, as shown here:

```
add(1, 2);
3
```

We call add with the arguments 1 and 2, which become the values for parameters x and y, respectively. (The arguments are matched with the parameters in the order in which they're given.) The function sums the two arguments and returns the resulting value, 3.

When we call a function in the Chrome console, its return value is automatically printed out—but it's important to distinguish between a function explicitly logging text to the console, as we saw sayHello do earlier, and a function returning a value, as add is doing here. When a function logs a value using console.log, the only place that value exists is in the log; we can't make further use of it later. By contrast, when a function returns a value, we can then use that value later in our code. The fact that the return value is also displayed in the console is largely irrelevant. It helps us see what the function is doing, but logging to the console isn't the add function's main purpose, unlike the sayHello function.

One way to make use of a function's return value is to call the function as part of an assignment expression, so the return value will be stored in a variable. Then we can work with that variable later in the code. For example:

```
let sum = add(500, 500);
undefined
`I walked ${sum} miles`;
'I walked 1000 miles'
```

Here we declare the variable sum and initialize it to the return value of the add function, which we call with the arguments 500 and 500. The console shows undefined even though add has a return value because, as discussed in Chapter 2, declaring a variable always prints undefined. We then use the function's return value by incorporating sum into a template literal to create the string "I walked 1000 miles".

Notice that it wouldn't be possible to do something similar with our sayHello function as it's currently written. For example, we can't use it to generate the greeting "Hello, Nick!" and then write some code to incorporate that greeting into a longer string. The sayHello function returns undefined, because we didn't use the return keyword to explicitly give it a return value. It merely logs the greeting to the console, and there's no way to access the greeting once it's been logged.

It's not necessary to store a function's return value in a variable to use it. A function call that returns a value can be used anywhere a value can be used, just as you can use variables and literal values interchangeably. For instance, the previous example could be rewritten like so:

```
`I walked ${add(500, 500)} miles`;
'I walked 1000 miles'
```

Here, instead of calling add separately and storing the result in a variable, we call the function from within the template literal. Its return value is inserted directly into the resulting string, producing the same message as before. It's often more readable to store the return value in a variable, but both approaches are equally valid.

TRY IT YOURSELF

5-1. Rewrite the sayHello function so it returns the `Hello, ${name}!` greeting instead of logging it. Then write some code to use the returned greeting. For example, apply the toUpperCase string method to convert the greeting to all caps.

Parameter Types

The data types of function parameters in JavaScript are not fixed. This is because JavaScript is a *dynamically typed* programming language, in which the types of variables and parameters can change while the program is running, as opposed to a *statically typed* language, in which the types of variables and parameters are determined before the program is run.

To illustrate, so far we've been using the add function to add numbers together, but there's nothing stopping us from using it to concatenate two strings:

```
add("Hello, ", "world!");
'Hello, world!'
```

Here we pass the function two strings as arguments, so the + operator in the function body is interpreted to mean string concatenation rather than numerical addition. The function therefore combines the strings and returns the result.

By extension, we could also pass arguments of other types, or even mix data types within the same function call:

```
add(true, false);
1
add(1, '1');
'11'
```

In these cases, JavaScript's rules around type coercion, discussed in Chapter 2, come into play. When we try to add two Booleans with add(true, false), JavaScript converts the Booleans to the numbers 1 and 0 before the addition, producing the number 1. When we try to add a number and a string with add(1, "1"), JavaScript converts both of the operands to strings and concatenates them, producing the string "11".

Dynamic typing brings a lot of flexibility to JavaScript, but if you aren't careful, it can also open the way for some confusing bugs. It's essential to have a good idea of the types you're using, to make sure you're not passing a string to a function that expects a number, for example.

Side Effects

A *side effect* is anything a function does that makes a difference outside of the function itself, apart from returning a value. Side effects can be intended or unintended, and include updating the value of a variable declared outside the function, modifying an array or object declared outside the function, or outputting a string to the console.

Some functions, like our add function, have no side effects and are called only for their return value. Other functions, like sayHello, have no return value and are called only for their side effects. It's also possible to write functions that return a value *and* have side effects. For example, we can redefine add to log some information to the console and update a variable, in addition to returning the sum of its arguments:

```
let addCalls = 0;

function add(x, y) {
  addCalls++;
  console.log(`x was ${x} and y was ${y}`);
  return x + y;
}
```

Here we declare the variable addCalls, which we'll use to keep track of how often the add function is called. Then we write our updated add function declaration. The function now increments addCalls and logs the values of its parameters to the console, before returning the sum of the parameters, as before.

Let's try calling the revised function:

```
let sum = add(Math.PI, Math.E);
x was 3.141592653589793 and y was 2.718281828459045
addCalls;
1
sum;
5.859874482048838
```

The function call has the side effect of logging the two values to the console before adding them together. It also has the side effect of updating the addCalls variable, changing its value from 0 to 1. Additionally, the function has the (non–side effect) result of returning the sum of its arguments, which we've stored in the sum variable.

If we made further calls to add, the variable addCalls would keep incrementing each time, giving us a running count of the number of times the function is called. You don't typically need to keep track of the number of times a function is called like this, although you could use such a mechanism to restrict how often a program is allowed to call some function that requires a lot of processing power (a technique known as *rate limiting*). You could achieve this by periodically resetting the counter—perhaps every minute—and skipping the function call if the counter goes over some threshold.

Passing a Function as an Argument

In JavaScript, functions are *first-class citizens*, which means they can be used like any other value, such as a number or a string. For example, you can store a function in a variable or pass a function as an argument to another function. The latter is especially common, as there are many functions that delegate work to other functions. When a function is passed as an argument, it's often referred to as a *callback* because the function it's passed to is said to "call it back" by executing it.

We'll illustrate this with JavaScript's built-in `setTimeout` function, which allows you to delay the calling of another function. It takes two arguments: a function to call, and a time in milliseconds (ms) to wait before calling that function. Here's how it works:

```
function sayHi() {
  console.log("Hi!");
}
setTimeout(sayHi, 2000);
1
Hi!
```

First we create a simple function with no arguments, `sayHi`, which just calls `console.log`. We then call `setTimeout`, passing the `sayHi` function and the number `2000` (indicating 2,000 ms, or 2 seconds) as arguments. Once you press ENTER, `setTimeout` should immediately return a *timeout ID*—in this case, 1—which is a unique identifier you could use to cancel the delayed function call if desired. Then, after two seconds, the `sayHi` function is called, and the string `"Hi!"` is logged to the console.

NOTE   *To cancel a function call delayed with `setTimeout`, call the `clearTimeout` function, passing the timeout ID as an argument.*

Notice that when we pass a function as an argument, we write its name without parentheses: in this case, `sayHi` rather than `sayHi()`. A function name without parentheses simply *refers* to the function, while a function name with parentheses actually *calls* the function. We can see this distinction in the JavaScript console:

```
❶ sayHi;
ƒ sayHi() {
    console.log("Hi!");
}

❷ sayHi();
Hi!
undefined
```

Executing just plain `sayHi;` without parentheses ❶ prints the function's definition but doesn't call it. However, executing `sayHi();` with parentheses ❷ calls the `sayHi` function, printing the string `"Hi!"` and returning `undefined`.

Other Function Syntaxes

So far in this chapter we've focused on creating functions using function declarations, but JavaScript also supports other ways to create functions. Function declarations follow a straightforward format and use a similar syntax to how functions are defined in many other languages, like C++

and Python. They're perfectly fine when you're writing functions that you intend to call directly, like the sayHello and add functions that we've discussed. However, once you start treating functions as values by passing them as arguments and the like, the other styles of creating functions become more useful. We'll turn to those now, starting with function expressions.

Function Expressions

A *function expression*, also known as a *function literal*, is a code literal whose value is a function, just as 123 is a literal whose value is the number 123. Whereas a function declaration creates a function and binds it to a name, a function expression is an expression that evaluates to (returns) a function, for you to do with what you will.

Syntactically, a function expression looks very similar to a function declaration, with two main differences. First, a function expression doesn't have to include a name, although you can include one if you want. Function expressions without names are also called *anonymous functions*. Second, a function expression can't be written at the start of a line of code, or Java-Script will think it's a function declaration; there has to be some code before the function keyword. This is why function expressions are often used in contexts where functions need to be treated as values.

For example, you can define a function expression and assign it as the value of a variable, all in one statement, as shown here:

```
let addExpression = function (x, y) {
  return x + y;
};
```

The function keyword appears on the right side of an assignment statement, rather than at the start of a line, so JavaScript treats this as a function expression. In this case, we're assigning the function expression to the addExpression variable. The function itself is anonymous, since we don't provide a name after the function keyword (you'll see an example where we do this in the "Named Function Expressions" box on the following page). It has two parameters, x and y, specified in parentheses, just like our original add function. The body returns the sum of the parameters and is enclosed in braces, much like the body of a function declaration, but notice that we need to put a semicolon after the closing brace to signify the end of the statement assigning the function to a variable.

Although the function itself is technically anonymous, it's now bound to the addExpression variable. We can therefore call the function by putting a pair of parentheses containing the necessary arguments after the variable name, just like calling any named function:

```
addExpression(1, 2);
3
```

Entering addExpression(1, 2) calls the function, returning the sum of the two arguments.

NAMED FUNCTION EXPRESSIONS

You can optionally include a name in a function expression after the function keyword. For instance:

```
let addExpressionNamed = function add(x, y) {
  return x + y;
};
```

Here we give the function expression a name, add, although notice that we're still assigning the function to a separately named variable, addExpressionNamed. In fact, the add name isn't in scope outside of the function body itself. This means that we can't call the function by name, for example, with add(1, 2). We have to call it using the variable name the function was assigned to: addExpressionNamed(1, 2).

Naming function expressions isn't as common as leaving them anonymous, but this syntax can be useful for debugging purposes, to help distinguish one function expression from another. You can see this if you use console.log to log the values of addExpression and addExpressionNamed. The former will just show the anonymous function expression, while the latter will include the add name in the output, which is useful if you don't know which function you're logging to the console.

In many respects, function expressions and function declarations are interchangeable, so choosing between the two approaches is often just a matter of style. For example, defining our function for adding two numbers as a function expression and assigning it to a variable is largely equivalent to defining it using a function declaration, as we did originally. When it comes to passing functions as arguments, however, function expressions offer certain advantages. Earlier, for example, we declared the sayHi function, then passed its name to setTimeout as an argument. A more common way to do this is to write an equivalent function expression directly in the setTimeout function's arguments list, without first assigning it to a variable:

```
setTimeout(function () {
  console.log("Hi!");
}, 2000);
2
Hi!
```

Previously we called setTimeout(sayHi, 2000), passing the name of a function as the first argument, but this time we're passing a function expression instead. The function expression defines an anonymous function for logging "Hi!" to the console (the equivalent of the sayHi function we declared earlier). Notice that the `function` keyword isn't the first thing in the line of code, a requirement for function expressions, and that the closing brace is followed by a comma, since the function expression is part of a list of arguments.

As before, calling `setTimeout` returns a timeout ID, this time 2. Then, when our anonymous function is called two seconds later, `Hi!` appears in the console. Using a function expression in this case is more concise, since we don't have to separately define the delayed function before passing it to `setTimeout`.

Arrow Functions

JavaScript has yet another syntax for defining functions, called *arrow function expressions*, or *arrow functions* for short. An arrow function is a more compact version of a function expression, and in most cases the choice between the two is purely stylistic. You can use an arrow function anywhere a normal function expression would work, and save yourself a bit of typing in the process. For example, here's how to make a function that adds two numbers using arrow function syntax:

```
let addArrow = (x, y) => {
  return x + y;
};
```

An arrow function doesn't use the `function` keyword. Instead, it begins with the arguments list—in this case, `(x, y)`—followed by an arrow (`=>`) and the function body. Here we're assigning the arrow function to the `addArrow` variable, which lets us call it just like other functions:

```
addArrow(2, 2);
4
```

We defined `addArrow` using *block body* syntax, where the body is placed between braces and each statement within the body is written on its own indented line. If the body consists of just a single statement, however, there's an even simpler syntax, called *concise body*:

```
let addArrowConcise = (x, y) => x + y;
```

Here the body is written on the same line as the rest of the statement, and it isn't surrounded by braces. Also, the `return` keyword is implied, meaning the expression in the body (in this case, x + y) is automatically understood to be the function's return value. This concise body syntax is great for writing simple functions, but if your function body involves multiple statements, you'll have to use the block body syntax (and include the `return` keyword if the function has an explicit return value).

If the arrow function has exactly one parameter, you can further simplify the syntax by omitting the parentheses around the parameter name:

```
let squared = x => x * x;
squared(3);
9
```

This arrow function takes in a number, x, and returns its square (x * x). Since x is the function's only parameter, we don't need to put it in parentheses. This works for both block body and concise body syntax.

Like function expressions, arrow functions provide an efficient way to define functions that are passed as arguments. To illustrate, we'll consider JavaScript's built-in setInterval function. Like setTimeout, it takes another function and a time in milliseconds as arguments, but unlike setTimeout, it repeatedly calls the provided function, waiting the specified amount of time between each call. Here, for example, we pass setInterval an arrow function that logs the string "Beep" to the console:

```
setInterval(() => {
  console.log("Beep");
}, 1000);
3
Beep
```

Our arrow function takes no arguments, so it begins with an empty set of parentheses for the parameter list. The closing brace at the end of the body is followed by a comma to separate the arrow function from the next argument to setInterval, which specifies a one-second pause (1,000 ms) between repetitions.

When we execute this code, it first returns an interval ID for canceling the repetition—in this case, 3. Then, after a one-second delay, the first "Beep" is logged. After that, a number should appear on the left of the console output and increment every second to show how many times console.log("Beep") has been called. Chrome uses this trick to keep the console from filling up with duplicate lines of output. When you're ready for the code to stop Beep-ing, refresh the browser page, or call the clearInterval function, passing the interval ID. In our example, that would be clearInterval(3).

TRY IT YOURSELF

5-2. You've now seen three different ways of creating functions: function declarations, function expressions, and arrow functions. Write each of the following in all three styles:

- A function that takes a number from 0 to 5 and returns the English word for that number. For example, 1 should return "one". Hint: use an array to define the mapping from numbers to strings.

(continued)

- A function with no parameters that prints how many times it's been called. Hint: define a variable outside of the function to keep track of the number of calls, like we did in the "Side Effects" section on page 77.
- A function that prints the current date and time. Hint: you can get the current date and time with new Date().

Rest Parameters

Sometimes you want your function to accept a variable number of arguments. For example, say you want to make a function that takes someone's name and their favorite colors, and prints them out in a sentence. You don't know ahead of time how many favorite colors the user will enter, so you want to make your function flexible enough to handle however many colors are passed in. In JavaScript, you can do this with a *rest parameter*, a special type of parameter that collects a variable number of arguments into an array.

Rest parameters work with any style of function definition. Here we use one to create an arrow function that lists the user's favorite colors:

```
let myColors = (name, ...favoriteColors) => {
  let colorString = favoriteColors.join(", ");
  console.log(`My name is ${name} and my favorite colors are ${colorString}.`);
};
myColors("Nick", "blue", "green", "orange");
My name is Nick and my favorite colors are blue, green, orange.
```

A rest parameter looks like an ordinary parameter preceded by three periods, and it always has to be the last parameter listed in the function definition. When the function is called, any regular parameters, listed first, are matched to the first provided arguments, in order. Then, the rest parameter bundles the remaining arguments into an array. In our example, name is a regular parameter, and favoriteColors is the rest parameter. When we call the function, the argument "Nick" is assigned to the name parameter. The remaining arguments, "blue", "green", and "orange", are gathered into a single array and assigned to the favoriteColors parameter. Because favoriteColors is an array, we can use the join method to convert it into a string, separating each color by a comma and a space. Then we incorporate the color string into a larger string using a template literal and use console .log to print it.

Since favoriteColors is a rest parameter, we can use the function with as few or as many colors as we want:

```
myColors("Boring", "gray");
My name is Boring and my favorite colors are gray.
myColors("Indecisive", "red", "orange", "yellow", "green", "blue", "indigo", "violet");
My name is Indecisive and my favorite colors are red, orange, yellow, green, blue, indigo, violet.
```

No matter how many arguments we provide, the function still works.

Here's another example of using a rest parameter, this time to sum all the numbers provided as arguments:

```
function sum(...numbers) {
  let total = 0;
  for (let number of numbers) {
    total += number;
  }
  return total;
}
sum(1, 2, 3, 4, 5);
15
sum(6, 7, 8, 9, 10, 11, 12, 13);
76
```

This time we've used a function declaration instead of an arrow function, and the function's only parameter is the rest parameter. Because there are no other parameters, all the arguments are collected into an array and assigned to the numbers rest parameter. Then we use a for...of loop to add the numbers together.

Higher-Order Functions

A *higher-order function* is a function that takes another function as an argument, or that outputs another function as its return value. You've already seen two higher-order functions in this chapter: setTimeout and setInterval, which both take a callback function to execute later as an argument. JavaScript has many other built-in higher-order functions as well. We'll consider some here, and discuss how to write your own higher-order functions.

Array Methods That Take Callbacks

There are a number of built-in methods for working with arrays that take a callback function. Remember, a method is a type of function that operates on an object, such as an array. In most cases, the callback passed to these higher-order array methods is called once for each item in the array. Let's take a look at a few examples.

Finding an Array Element

The find array method finds the first element in an array that matches some criterion. You specify the criterion with a callback function that returns a Boolean true/false value. For example, if we wanted to find the first item in our shopping list with more than six characters, we could do the following:

```
let shoppingList = ["Milk", "Sugar", "Bananas", "Ice Cream"];
shoppingList.find(item => item.length > 6);
'Bananas'
```

The callback function we pass to find is item => item.length > 6. This callback takes advantage of two useful syntactic features of arrow functions. First, because our function has only one parameter, item, we can leave off the parentheses around the parameter list. Second, because the function body involves only one statement, item.length > 6, we can use concise body syntax, leaving off the return keyword and the braces around the body. These features let us define the logic for finding the element as compactly as possible, making arrow functions ideal for writing simple callbacks.

The find method runs the callback for each element in the array in turn. The callback takes in the element and returns true or false based on whether the element has more than six characters. If the callback returns true for a given element, the find method returns that element and halts the search. In this case, the method returns "Bananas" rather than "Ice Cream" since "Bananas" comes earlier in the array.

If no item is found that meets the criterion, the find method returns undefined:

```
shoppingList.find(item => item[0] === "A");
undefined
```

This time we pass find a callback that checks if an element starts with the letter A. None of the shopping list items do, so the method returns undefined.

Filtering the Elements of an Array

The filter method returns a new array containing all the elements from the original array that satisfy some criterion. As with the find method, the criterion is specified using a callback. To illustrate, we'll update our original find example by changing the method name to filter. This will give us a list of *all* items with more than six characters, rather than just the first item that passes this test:

```
let shoppingList = ["Milk", "Sugar", "Bananas", "Ice Cream"];
shoppingList.filter(item => item.length > 6);
▶ (2) ['Bananas', 'Ice Cream']
```

This filters out the array elements whose character lengths are too short, while leaving both "Bananas" and "Ice Cream" in the resulting array.

Transforming Each Element of an Array

Sometimes you'll want to transform each element in an array and store the results in a new array. For instance, you might have an array of numbers that all need to be operated on in the same way. You could do this using a for...of loop, as we discussed in Chapter 4, but a more concise technique is to use the map array method. It applies the same callback to each element of an array and returns a new array containing the results. Here, for example, we use map to take in an array of numbers and produce an array of those numbers' cubes:

```
let numbers = [1, 2, 3, 4, 5, 6, 7, 8, 9, 10];
let cubes = numbers.map(x => x * x * x);
cubes;
▶ (10) [1, 8, 27, 64, 125, 216, 343, 512, 729, 1000]
```

Our callback function, x => x * x * x, takes an array element and cubes it. The map method applies this callback to each element in the numbers array, returning a new array of the first 10 perfect cubes while leaving the original array unchanged. Compare the concise syntax of passing map an arrow function with the equivalent code using a for...of loop:

```
let numbers = [1, 2, 3, 4, 5, 6, 7, 8, 9, 10];
let cubes = [];
for (let x of numbers) {
  cubes.push(x * x * x);
}
cubes;
▶ (10) [1, 8, 27, 64, 125, 216, 343, 512, 729, 1000]
```

The result is the same, but with map we're able to declare and populate the cubes array in a single line of code, instead of first declaring cubes as an empty array and then filling it up within the body of the for...of loop.

The map method is also useful if you have an array of similar objects and you want to extract the same piece of information from each one. For example, say you have an array of objects that represent items in a store, each with a name and a price property, and you want to get an array of just the prices. You can pass map a callback function accessing each object's price property, like so:

```
let stockList = [
  { name: "Cheese", price: 3 },
  { name: "Bread", price: 1 },
  { name: "Butter", price: 2 }
];
let prices = stockList.map(item => item.price);
prices;
▶ (3) [3, 1, 2]
```

Here, the callback function is item => item.price, which takes an item and returns the value of that item's price property. The map function applies the callback to each object in the original array in turn, and creates a new array with all the prices.

In general, it's preferable to use map rather than the equivalent loop whenever possible, both for the map method's conciseness and for the code's *self-documenting* nature (the method name map implies that you're making a new array that copies and modifies elements from another array, without the need for further comment). A loop would be more appropriate when your needs are more custom, for example, if the number of elements in the output array doesn't match the number in the original array.

Custom Functions That Take Callbacks

To create your own higher-order function that takes a callback as an argument, simply include a name for the callback in the function's list of parameters, just as you'd name any other parameter. Then, when you want to call the callback within the function body, add parentheses after the parameter name, just like calling any other function. Let's illustrate this by declaring a doubler function that takes in a callback and calls it twice:

```
function doubler(callback) {
  callback();
  callback();
}
doubler(() => console.log("Hi there!"));
Hi there!
Hi there!
```

When we define the doubler function, we give it a callback parameter. Then, in the function body, we write callback() twice to make two calls to the function passed to this parameter. When we call doubler, we pass it a function that logs "Hi there!" to the console, so this message gets logged twice. Notice that this callback function doesn't require any arguments, so we've written an empty set of parentheses before the arrow symbol.

As we've discussed, JavaScript has no conception of set data types for function parameters, so there's nothing stopping us from trying to pass a value that isn't a function as an argument to doubler. If we do, though, we'll get an error when JavaScript tries to call the non-function:

```
doubler("hello");
▶Uncaught TypeError: callback is not a function
    at doubler (<anonymous>:2:5)
    at <anonymous>:1:1
```

Here we pass doubler a string instead of a function, so we get a TypeError.

The callback we passed to doubler didn't require any arguments, but you can also set up a higher-order function so its callback takes arguments. Here, for example, we create a function that calls another function some number of times, passing the current number of times into the callback:

```
function callMultipleTimes(times, callback) {
  for (let i = 0; i < times; i++) {
    callback(i);
  }
}
```

We declare the callMultipleTimes function to have two parameters: a function to call (callback) and a number of times to call it (times). (Note that unlike setTimeout and setInterval, where the callback is the first parameter, our function here follows the more common JavaScript convention of having the callback be the last parameter.) The function body consists of a for loop in which we call `callback(i)`, passing the looping variable i as an argument to the callback.

Because the callback function is passed a single argument, we know that the callback function we pass to `callMultipleTimes` should have a single parameter. For example:

```
callMultipleTimes(3, time => console.log(`This was time: ${time}`));
This was time: 0
This was time: 1
This was time: 2
```

Here we pass an arrow function as a callback. It has a single time parameter. The function incorporates time into a message that gets logged to the console. Each time this callback is executed, time takes on the current value of looping variable i, inserting the numbers 0, 1, and 2 into the logged message, respectively.

Functions That Return Functions

So far we've focused on higher-order functions that take in functions as arguments, but a higher-order function can also output a function as its return value. For example, say you want to create various functions that add a suffix to the end of a string, such as adding "!!!" at the end to make the string seem more exciting, or "???" to make it seem more puzzling. Rather than manually defining a separate function for adding each possible suffix, or making a function with text and suffix parameters and having to supply the suffix every time you call it, you can define a higher-order function that takes in a suffix and returns a function that will append that suffix to a string:

```
function makeAppender(suffix) {
❶ return function (text) {
  ❷ return text + suffix;
  };
}
```

There are two return keywords here. The first ❶ is used by the higher-order makeAppender function to return an anonymous function. It's followed by the function keyword, indicating that we're defining a function to be returned. The second return keyword ❷ is inside the anonymous function itself. When *that* function is called, it returns the value of the anonymous function's text parameter concatenated with the makeAppender function's suffix parameter.

To be able to call the inner function, we first have to get access to it by calling the outer function:

```
let exciting = makeAppender("!!!");
exciting("Hello");
'Hello!!!'
```

Calling makeAppender("!!!") returns a new function, which we assign to the exciting variable. This variable now contains the function expression that was returned from makeAppender, which takes a string as an argument. When we call exciting("Hello"), we get the string "Hello!!!", the result of concatenating the "Hello" and "!!!" strings together.

The benefit of our higher-order makeAppender function is that we can use it to generate additional functions for appending other suffixes besides "!!!". For example:

```
let puzzling = makeAppender("???");
puzzling("Hello");
'Hello???'
let winking = makeAppender(" ;-)");
winking("Hello");
'Hello ;-)'
```

Here makeAppender returns two more functions, which we assign as values to the puzzling and winking variables. We had to define only a single higher-order function, but we now have three different suffix-appending functions to choose from, and we can reuse them as much as we like:

```
winking("Goodbye");
'Goodbye ;-)'
puzzling("Goodbye");
'Goodbye???'
exciting("Goodbye");
'Goodbye!!!'
```

Notice that each function we returned from makeAppender remembers the value of suffix that we passed in, which is how it can keep appending the same suffix. Each of these functions was defined within the scope of makeAppender, so even though the call to makeAppender has completed, the inner function it returned is able to hold onto other values from that same scope, including suffix.

We discussed scope in Chapter 4, noting, for example, how variables defined within a while or for loop can't be accessed outside of the loop. Similarly, variables defined inside a function have scope only within that function, so they typically disappear once the function call ends. Scope gets more interesting with nested functions, however, as in the example at hand. You might expect the scope of the outer makeAppender function to "disappear" after we call it, but the inner function retains access to the variables and arguments from that scope, as long as we keep a reference to the inner function (which we do through the variables exciting, puzzling, and winking). Functions that hold onto variables and parameters from their enclosing scopes are known as *closures* because they "close over" their environments. (Imagine that the inner function has a dome over it that preserves all the variables in its scope.)

TRY IT YOURSELF

5-3. Write a function called makeWrapper that takes a prefix and a suffix, and returns a new function that adds the prefix and suffix to a provided string. For example, you could enter let bracketWrapper = makeWrapper("[", "]"); and then call bracketWrapper("Bracket me!"); to get the string "[Bracket me!]". Likewise, you could enter let bracesWrapper = makeWrapper("{", "}"); and then call bracesWrapper("Brace Me!"); to get the string "{Brace me!}".

Summary

In this chapter, you learned how to make your code more readable and concise by creating and working with your own custom functions. You saw the three main styles of defining functions—function declarations, function expressions, and arrow functions—and experimented with block body and concise body syntax. You learned how to provide input to a function by passing values to its parameters as arguments, and you learned how to take advantage of a function's work, either through its return value, its side effects, or both. You also saw how functions can be assigned as values to variables, and how they can be passed to or returned from higher-order functions.

6

CLASSES

Classes are a powerful programming tool for generating multiple objects with shared characteristics and behaviors. They're a core part of *object-oriented programming*, a style of coding that revolves around creating objects that contain both data and functions for manipulating that data. In an object-oriented multiplayer game, for example, you might represent each player as an object of a Player class, and each enemy as an object of an Enemy class. The classes would establish what kind of data a player or enemy should have and would include functions to make the player or enemy do things, like move around or attack.

In this chapter, you'll learn how to create JavaScript classes, and how to use those classes to create individual objects. You'll also learn how to leverage *inheritance* to share behavior between different classes. Using classes and object-oriented programming in this way gives your code structure and can make it easier to read, write, and understand, especially if your program involves lots of entities with common behaviors.

Creating Classes and Instances

A *class* is like template for making standardized objects. In Chapter 3 we discussed how an object is a compound data type consisting of key-value pairs, and you saw how to create objects by manually writing out object literals. Classes automate that process, allowing you to instead create objects using a syntax similar to calling a function.

A class lays out two main things:

1. What properties each object of that class should have. (Remember that *property* is another term for a key-value pair in an object.)
2. What functions the object should have access to. (When they're defined and called as part of a class, functions are called *methods*.)

The Player class in a game, for example, might include properties such as the player's name, health level, position in the environment, and so on. It might have methods for moving, firing a weapon, picking up an item, and more. The class could be used to create multiple different players.

FUNCTIONS VS. METHODS

It's easy to confuse functions with methods, since they're both pieces of code that accomplish a task. The difference is that a method is always associated with an object, whereas a function stands alone. In Chapter 5, we practiced writing custom, standalone functions that weren't associated with particular objects. Meanwhile, we've already looked at some methods in Chapters 2 and 3—for example, the slice method associated with strings and the push method associated with arrays. For our purposes, you can think of strings and arrays as specialized types of objects.

Methods are defined on objects, but more importantly, they're *called* on objects using dot notation. The object on the left of the dot is sometimes called the *receiver*, because it receives the method call. For example, when you call myArray.push(2), the receiver is myArray. Internally, methods are able to access and modify their receiver using the this keyword, as you'll see later in this chapter. By contrast, functions aren't called using dot notation, so they don't have a receiver object.

Objects created from a class are known as *instances* of that class. Each player's character in the game would be an instance of the Player class, for example. Each instance fills in the generic template of the class with its own details. A specific Player instance would have its own name, health level, and position, distinct from those of other Player instances. All instances can use the class's methods, however.

To see how this works, we'll create a simple Player class for a hypothetical 2D game. For now, we'll just give the player a position, defined by a set of x- and y-coordinates, and a method for moving that changes those coordinates. Enter the following in the JavaScript console to declare the class:

```
class Player {
❶ constructor(startX, startY) {
    this.x = startX;
    this.y = startY;
  }

❷ move(dx, dy) {
    this.x += dx;
    this.y += dy;
  }
}
```

We start with the class keyword to indicate we're declaring a new class, followed by the class's name, Player. It's customary for class names to start with an uppercase letter. Next comes the class body, enclosed in braces, just like a function body. Inside the body we define two methods, constructor ❶ and move ❷. Declaring a class method is like declaring a function, but we don't use the function keyword.

If a class has a method called constructor, as our Player class does, that method will be called automatically anytime you create an instance of the class. The constructor performs any necessary setup for the object being created, including receiving any parameters that define the instance and laying out what properties the object should have. In this case, our Player class's constructor takes in two parameters, startX and startY, and assigns them to the new instance's x and y properties, which together keep track of the player's position in the 2D game. The this keyword refers to the current instance being created, so this.x = startX means "take the value of startX and assign it to the new Player object's x property." Notice that we're using the same dot notation we've used elsewhere to access the properties of an object; the only difference here is that this serves as a placeholder for the new object's name.

The move method updates the player's position by changing the x and y properties based on the provided dx and dy parameters. The *d* in dx and dy is short for the Greek letter *delta*, which often refers to the amount something changes, as in "change in the x value" and "change in the y value."

Now that we've declared the Player class, we can make instances of it. For example:

```
let player1 = new Player(0, 0);
```

We create a new instance of the Player class using the new keyword followed by the class name. After the class name, we write a set of parentheses, much as we would when calling a function. The parentheses contain any arguments that need to be passed to the class's constructor method.

When you create a new instance of a class with new, some magic happens. First, a new, empty object is created. Then a hidden link from this object to the class is created, which is how JavaScript is able to tell which class created the object and what methods the object should therefore have access to. Next, the class's constructor method is called automatically. Inside the constructor, the new object being created is available via the keyword this, allowing you to set properties on the object. Any arguments you provide in the parentheses after the class name are passed to the constructor method's parameters. After the constructor method has been called, the new object is returned.

In our example, when we enter let player1 = new Player(0, 0);, JavaScript creates a new object and gives it a hidden link to the Player class. It then calls the class's constructor method, passing the arguments 0 and 0 to the constructor's startX and startY parameters. The constructor takes these parameters and uses this.x and this.y to set the new object's x and y properties to 0. Finally, the new object is returned and assigned to the player1 variable.

We can now interact with the new object. Here, for example, we look up its position, tell it to move, then look up its position again to confirm the move method worked:

```
player1.x;
0
player1.y;
0
player1.move(3, 4);
player1.x;
3
player1.y;
4
```

We access the object's x and y properties using player1.x and player1.y, respectively. They both show the value 0, since that's what we passed to the constructor. Next, we call the move method, which we defined in the Player class. Because instances have a hidden link to the class that created them, they're able to call methods defined on that class. We use dot notation to call the method, just like calling the built-in methods associated with strings or arrays.

When you call a method on an object, the this keyword inside the method definition is set to the current object (the receiver). When we call player1.move(3, 4), for example, this inside the body of the move method is bound to the player1 object. That's how one method is able to be shared by multiple objects: this becomes whatever object is receiving the method call at any given time.

The move method updates the object's x and y properties by adding dx and dy to their current values. For example, when we call player1.move(3, 4) we're setting x to 0 + 3 and y to 0 + 4. When we again look up the object's x and y properties, we can see that this worked: player1.x has become 3 and player1.y has become 4. If we then made another call to move, for example, player1.move(2, 2), x would become 5 and y would become 6.

TRY IT YOURSELF

6-1. Create a new instance of Player called player2. Try calling move with different values on player1 and player2. You'll see that each object has its own x and y properties, but that both objects have access to the move method.

Inheritance

Inheritance is a mechanism in object-oriented programming for defining relationships between different classes. Just as a child inherits genes from its parents, a "child" class inherits properties and methods from a "parent" class, taking on the parent's properties and methods. This is useful when you have multiple classes that should share a general set of behaviors, in addition to each class having some unique behaviors of its own. You can define the general behaviors as part of a parent class, also called a *superclass*. Then you can define the child classes, also called *subclasses*, to inherit these behaviors and augment them with other, specialized behaviors. This saves you from having to repeat the general code when you define each subclass.

To illustrate, in our 2D game, human-controlled players and computer-controlled enemies probably have a lot in common. They both need x and y properties representing their position, for example, and they both need a move method to change their position. However, they also have some differences. Perhaps enemies have the ability to attack a player if the player comes too close, but not the other way around—the goal of the game is for players to avoid, not kill, the enemies.

We can use inheritance to realize this scheme with minimal code. We'll create a new class called Actor representing *any* participant in the game. It will hold the general code both players and enemies should have, such as the move method. We'll then define Player and Enemy as subclasses of Actor. They'll each inherit the general code from the Actor superclass, while also adding their own code particular to just players or enemies.

First, here's the definition of the Actor class. It's mostly a copy of our previous Player class, but with a new name. We're also adding another

method, called `distanceTo`, that calculates the distance between two partici-
pants in the game:

```
class Actor {
  constructor(startX, startY) {
    this.x = startX;
    this.y = startY;
  }

  move(dx, dy) {
    this.x += dx;
    this.y += dy;
  }

  distanceTo(otherActor) {
    let dx = otherActor.x - this.x;
    let dy = otherActor.y - this.y;
    return Math.hypot(dx, dy);
  }
}
```

The `distanceTo` method takes another `Actor` (or any object with an x- and
y-coordinate) as a parameter and returns the distance to that object. It's
quite common for objects to be passed to other objects' methods in this
way. The distance is determined by calculating the horizontal distance
(`otherActor.x - this.x`) and the vertical distance (`otherActor.y - this.y`), and
then using the built-in `Math.hypot` method to find the length of the hypot-
enuse of the triangle formed by the two distances. This is the standard
mathematical technique, based on the Pythagorean theorem, for finding
the distance between two points on a 2D plane.

Although it's technically possible to create an instance of the `Actor`
class, it's not really meant to be instantiated. Classes like `Actor` that are just
meant to be extended by subclasses are sometimes known as *abstract classes*,
because they represent an abstract concept, like a generic entity in a game.
Meanwhile, classes that are meant to be instantiated, such as the `Player` and
`Enemy` classes we'll define momentarily, are sometimes known as *concrete classes*,
because they represent something solid, such as actual players or enemies.

Next, we'll redefine the `Player` class to inherit from `Actor`. We'll add a
new property specific to players called `hp` (for *hit points*), representing the
player's health level—the `Enemy` class doesn't need this property, since only
players, not enemies, can be attacked:

```
class Player extends Actor {
  constructor(startX, startY) {
    super(startX, startY);
  ❶ this.hp = 100;
  }
}
```

This time we declare the class with the extends keyword to establish
`Player` as a subclass of `Actor`. We have to write only the class's constructor

method, since it inherits the move and distanceTo methods from Actor. The constructor takes startX and startY parameters, just as before.

The first thing we do in the constructor is call super(startX, startY). Inside a subclass's constructor method, the super keyword refers to the constructor from the superclass—in this case, the Actor class's constructor. As a result, when we create a new instance of Player, the Player constructor is called automatically, which in turn calls the Actor constructor (via super). We pass startX and startY to the Actor constructor, which uses these values to set the Player object's x and y properties. Then, back in the Player class's constructor, we set the new Player instance's hp property to 100 ❶. This way each new player will start with 100 hit points (full health).

Next, we'll create our Enemy class. It, too, will inherit from the Actor class, extending it with an attack method for attacking players (the Player class doesn't need this method, since only enemies can attack):

```
class Enemy extends Actor {
  attack(player) {
    if (this.distanceTo(player) < 4) {
      player.hp -= 10;
      return true;
    } else {
      return false;
    }
  }
}
```

We declare the Enemy class to extend Actor, just like the Player class. Unlike with Player, however, the Enemy class doesn't have any extra properties (such as hp) that need to be set in the constructor. As such, the class doesn't have its own constructor method. When a subclass doesn't define a constructor, its parent class's constructor is called automatically when a new instance of the subclass is created. Thus, new Enemy instances will still be given an initial position thanks to the Actor superclass's constructor method, but we don't need to show this explicitly in the Enemy class declaration.

Without a constructor, the Enemy class's only unique method is attack. It takes in a Player object as a parameter and checks the distance to that object, using the distanceTo method inherited from the Actor class. (Notice that we call the method using this.distanceTo, again using the this keyword to reference the current instance of the Enemy class.) If the distance is less than 4, the enemy can attack, reducing the player's hp value by 10. We return true to indicate that this was a successful attack. If the attack fails because the player is too far away, we return false instead.

Now that we have our Player and Enemy classes, we can see how they interact. Let's create an instance of each class, move them around, and have the enemy attack the player:

```
let player = new Player(1, 2);
let enemy = new Enemy(3, 4);
player.hp;
```

```
100
enemy.distanceTo(player);
2.8284271247461903
enemy.attack(player);
true
player.hp;
90
player.move(5, 5);
enemy.attack(player);
false
player.hp;
90
```

First we create an instance of each class, at the positions (1, 2) and (3, 4). The Player object starts out at full health, as player.hp demonstrates. The two objects are about 2.8 units apart, which we confirm by calling enemy.distanceTo(player). At this point, the enemy is close enough to successfully attack the player, so we call its attack method using enemy.attack(player). The method returns true, indicating a hit, and checking player.hp shows the attack has reduced the player's health to 90. Next, we move the player by 5 units in the x and y directions. The move puts the player out of range of the enemy, so the enemy's second attack is unsuccessful, returning false. A last check of player.hp shows the player's health remains at 90.

Notice in this code that we've called the distanceTo method on an Enemy object and the move method on a Player object. These were both methods defined on the Actor class, but they're available on the Enemy and Player classes as well, proving the subclasses successfully inherited from their superclass. We can also verify this using the instanceof keyword, which tests whether an object is an instance of a particular class. Here, for example, we try it out with the player object:

```
player instanceof Player;
true
player instanceof Actor;
true
player instanceof Enemy;
false
```

As you may expect, player is an instance of Player. What might be surprising is that player is also an instance of Actor. When a subclass like Player inherits from a superclass like Actor, instances of the subclass are also considered to be instances of the superclass. On the other hand, player is not an instance of Enemy, even though the Player and Enemy classes share a common superclass.

In this example, we've used a single level of inheritance: an Actor superclass with Player and Enemy subclasses. A more sophisticated game might use multiple levels of inheritance to create different subtypes of players and enemies. For example, there might be Witch, Elf, and Centaur classes, all subclasses of Player (which in turn is a subclass of Actor). These subclasses would share some common abilities, defined on the Player superclass (as

well as any methods defined on Actor), while also having their own specialized abilities defined on the individual subclasses. Likewise, Enemy might
have subclasses such as Troll, Demon, and Harpy.

Prototype-Based Inheritance

When JavaScript was first created, there were no classes, but it was still possible to share behaviors between objects using *prototype-based inheritance*.
This older system, which still works today alongside the class system, relies
on two mechanisms:

1. A *constructor* function that creates and returns new objects. In this context, a constructor is just a regular, standalone function (not a function
   defined within a class), but it's called using the new keyword.
2. A *prototype*, an example object that the constructor uses as a model for
   the objects it creates. The newly created objects inherit methods and
   properties from the prototype object.

JavaScript was one of the only mainstream languages to use prototype-
based inheritance rather than classes. Recognizing this, the committee
that develops the language eventually decided to add support for classes, in
order to make JavaScript more palatable to newcomers with a background in
other modern programming languages. When they added classes, however,
they built the new feature on top of the existing support for prototype-based
inheritance. In other words, JavaScript's class-based inheritance is essentially
an alternative syntax for prototype-based inheritance. (This is sometimes
known as *syntactic sugar*, because it makes the syntax more palatable.)

If you're comfortable using classes, it isn't essential that you learn about
prototype-based inheritance. However, since classes are a relatively new
JavaScript feature, it's still common to encounter prototype-based inheritance in older code, so it's worth being able to recognize how it works.

Exploring prototype-based inheritance also illuminates some of JavaScript's inner workings, including the significance of the mysterious [[Prototype]] property you've been seeing in the Chrome console. Even if you don't end up programming with prototype-based inheritance, understanding some of these underlying details can make it easier to use classes.

Using Constructors and Prototypes

As I mentioned, prototype-based inheritance involves a constructor function that creates instances of objects, and a prototype object that the instances inherit methods and properties from. This works because JavaScript creates links between the constructor, the prototype, and the new instance being created. Let's take a look at this in action. We'll create a new constructor function called Cat, and add a method called sayHello to its prototype. This will allow us to create Cat objects that have access to the sayHello method:

```
function Cat(name) {
  this.name = name;
}
Cat.prototype.sayHello = function () {
  console.log(`Miaow! My name is ${this.name}.`);
};
```

We first create a constructor function called Cat with a name parameter. Constructor functions, like class names, usually start with a capital letter. The constructor's body uses this.name = name to set the new object's name property to the value of the provided name parameter. As with classes, the this keyword in a constructor refers to the object being produced.

When the Cat constructor function is created, it's automatically given a property called prototype. It might sound weird that functions can have properties, but a JavaScript function is actually a kind of object; the Cat function can have a prototype property just like a person object can have name and age properties. This property is accessible as Cat.prototype, using the same dot notation we'd use to access a property of any other object.

The value of Cat.prototype is itself an object, the prototype that Cat instances should be modeled after. By adding methods to this prototype object, we can control what methods any Cat instances will inherit. In this case, we use Cat.prototype.sayHello to add a sayHello method to the prototype. The method logs a greeting that includes the value of this.name to the console. When sayHello is called as a method on a particular instance, this in the method definition refers to that instance—just as it would in a method defined on a class—so this.name refers to the value of the instance's name property.

NOTE *Notice that Cat.prototype.sayHello chains multiple dot notations together: Cat .prototype refers to the object stored in the Cat function's prototype property, and .sayHello refers to the sayHello property of that object. That property doesn't exist yet, so here we're adding it to the object and setting its value to a function expression.*

We've created a `Cat` constructor and added a method to its prototype. Now let's use the constructor to create a new instance that will inherit from the prototype:

```
let kiki = new Cat("Kiki");
kiki.sayHello();
Miaow! My name is Kiki.
undefined
```

Here we create a new object from the `Cat` constructor by calling it with the `new` keyword, passing `"Kiki"` as an argument for the constructor's `name` parameter. We store the resulting object in the `kiki` variable. Notice that if we'd declared `Cat` as a class rather than a constructor function, the syntax for creating an object would be exactly the same: `new Cat("Kiki")`. The only difference is whether we're thinking of `Cat` as the name of a function or the name of a class.

Next, we call the `sayHello` method on the new instance. Because `kiki` was created using the `Cat` constructor, it has a hidden link to `Cat.prototype`, which JavaScript uses to locate the `sayHello` definition. Since `sayHello` was called as a method on the `kiki` object, the `this` keyword in `sayHello` is set to `kiki`.

Although I'm calling the link between instance and prototype "hidden," the Chrome console lets you inspect it via the special `[[Prototype]]` property. Let's see what we can find out about `kiki`. Enter **kiki;** into the console and click the arrow at the side to inspect it:

```
kiki;
▼ Cat {name: 'Kiki'}
  name: "Kiki"
  ▶[[Prototype]]: Object
```

The first line of the output tells us that `kiki` was created with the `Cat` constructor. Next, we see that `kiki` has a `name` property with a value of `"Kiki"` (this was assigned when the constructor was called). We also see that `kiki` has a `[[Prototype]]` property whose value is an object. This is the "hidden" link I've been talking about to the prototype that this instance inherited from. It's the same object referenced by `Cat.prototype` (the `prototype` property of the `Cat` constructor function). Click the arrow to expand `[[Prototype]]` and see what's inside:

```
▼ Cat {name: 'Kiki'}
  name: "Kiki"
  ▼[[Prototype]]: Object
    ▶sayHello: ƒ ()
    ▶constructor: ƒ Cat(name)
  ❶ ▶[[Prototype]]: Object
```

We can see that the prototype object has three properties. The first, `sayHello`, has a value that's a function, as the ƒ () indicates. This is the sayHello method we added to the prototype. The second, constructor, refers to the Cat constructor function. This cements the link between the constructor function and the prototype the constructor uses to create new instances. Finally, the prototype itself has its own [[Prototype]] property ❶, which we'll explore shortly.

Comparing Constructors and Classes

In prototype-based inheritance, the chain of references from an instance to its prototype and a prototype to its constructor is how JavaScript knows where to find the methods and properties for that instance. It turns out classes use these same techniques. To demonstrate, let's create a Dog class that mirrors the functionality of our Cat constructor:

```
class Dog {
  constructor(name) {
    this.name = name;
  }

  sayHello() {
    console.log(`Woof! My name is ${this.name}.`);
  }
}
```

The constructor method here is equivalent to the Cat constructor function, and the sayHello method is equivalent to Cat.prototype.sayHello. Now let's make a Dog instance and compare it to the kiki instance by expanding the [[Prototype]] properties:

```
let felix = new Dog("Felix");
felix;
▼ Dog {name: 'Felix'}
   name: "Felix"
   ▼[[Prototype]]: Object
      ▶ constructor: class Dog
      ▶ sayHello: ƒ sayHello()
      ▶[[Prototype]]: Object
kiki;
▼ Cat {name: 'Kiki'}
   name: "Kiki"
   ▼[[Prototype]]: Object
      ▶ sayHello: ƒ ()
      ▶ constructor: ƒ Cat(name)
      ▶[[Prototype]]: Object
```

As you can see, in both cases the sayHello method is found via the [[Prototype]] link. There are just some minor differences. For example, with kiki the constructor points at a function, whereas for felix it points at a class. Also, the sayHello method on felix has a name, whereas for kiki it doesn't (because we defined sayHello using an anonymous function).

Note that if you want to access an object's [[Prototype]] property directly in code, it's available through the name __proto__:

```
kiki.__proto__;
▸ {sayHello: f, constructor: f}
```

Even though the property is technically called __proto__, we'll continue to call it the [[Prototype]] property, as that's how it shows up in the Chrome console.

Exploring Object.prototype

Any object that isn't created with an explicit constructor function is instead implicitly created with JavaScript's built-in Object constructor function. The prototype this constructor references, available as Object.prototype, contains basic methods that all objects should inherit. This prototype object marks the end of the line in the chain of prototype references. All objects eventually trace their origin back to Object.prototype.

For example, while our kiki object was created with the Cat constructor, its prototype, Cat.prototype, was never explicitly created with a constructor. Instead, JavaScript implicitly created this object using the Object constructor, so its prototype is Object.prototype. This is what the inner [[Prototype]] property within our view of kiki in the previous code listing is telling us. We can expand that inner [[Prototype]] property to examine Object.prototype:

```
▾ Cat {name: 'Kiki'}
   name: "Kiki"
   ▾[[Prototype]]: Object
    ▸ sayHello: f ()
    ▸ constructor: f Cat(name)
    ▾[[Prototype]]: Object
  ❶ ▸ constructor: f Object()
      ▸ hasOwnProperty: f hasOwnProperty()
      ▸ isPrototypeOf: f isPrototypeOf()
      ▸ propertyIsEnumerable: f propertyIsEnumerable()
      ▸ toLocaleString: f toLocaleString()
      ▸ toString: f toString()
      --snip--
```

Notably, this inner prototype object has a constructor property whose value is the Object function ❶, showing that it's the prototype property of JavaScript's built-in Object constructor. The remaining properties correspond to the many default methods that all objects inherit. For example, hasOwnProperty is a method that checks if an object has a property defined on itself, rather than on its prototype, and toString is a method that returns a string representation of the object.

When you create an object with an object literal, you aren't creating it with an explicit constructor function, so it, too, is created implicitly with the Object constructor and gets Object.prototype for its prototype. When we were inspecting objects in the console in Chapter 3 and saw they had a

[[Prototype]] property, that's what we were seeing. Let's take another look at one now:

```
let person = { name: "Nick", age: 39 };
person;
▼ {name: 'Nick', age: 39}
  age: 39
  name: "Nick"
  ▼[[Prototype]]: Object
    ▶ constructor: ƒ Object()
    ▶ hasOwnProperty: ƒ hasOwnProperty()
    ▶ isPrototypeOf: ƒ isPrototypeOf()
    ▶ propertyIsEnumerable: ƒ propertyIsEnumerable()
    ▶ toLocaleString: ƒ toLocaleString()
    ▶ toString: ƒ toString()
    --snip--
```

Here we declare a basic person object using an object literal, meaning it's created behind the scenes with the default Object constructor. Inspecting the object in the console, we can see that the contents of its [[Prototype]] property are exactly the same as the innermost [[Prototype]] of the kiki object. Both objects trace their roots to Object.prototype, kiki indirectly through its own prototype (Cat.prototype) and person directly.

Walking the Prototype Chain

When you ask for a property or method from an object, JavaScript first looks on the object itself. If it can't find the property there, it looks on the object's prototype. If JavaScript still can't find the property, it then checks the prototype's prototype, and so on, until it hits Object.prototype. This process is known as *walking the prototype chain*. Let's look up some properties and methods that will walk the prototype chain of our kiki object:

```
kiki.name;
'Kiki'
kiki.sayHello();
Miaow! My name is Kiki.
undefined
kiki.hasOwnProperty("name");
true
kiki.madeUpMethodName();
▶Uncaught TypeError: kiki.madeUpMethodName is not a function
    at <anonymous>:1:6
```

First, we access the name property, which is set directly on kiki itself. Second, we call the sayHello method, which is found on the kiki object's prototype. To call this method, JavaScript first checks on kiki and then, not finding it, checks on its prototype. Third, we call hasOwnProperty, a method from Object.prototype, which is the kiki object's prototype's prototype. (The method returns true, since the name property is set directly on kiki.) Finally, we call madeUpMethodName, a nonexistent method. After walking the entire prototype chain, from `kiki` to `Cat.prototype` to `Object.prototype`, JavaScript determines that the method can't be found and throws an error.

Figure 6-1 shows a visual representation of the `kiki` object's prototype chain and the associated constructor functions, `Cat` and `Object`.

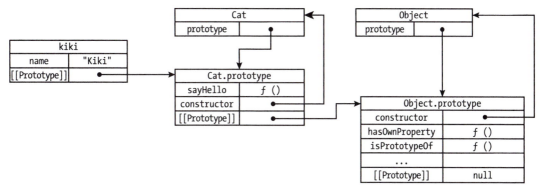

Figure 6-1: The prototype chain for kiki

Each box in the diagram represents an object, with the object's name as a heading. The left column of each box shows the names of the object's properties, and the right column shows the values of those properties. For example, the `kiki` object's `name` property has a value of `"Kiki"`, and the `Cat` `.prototype` object's `sayHello` property is a function, denoted by *f ()* (remember that a method is just a function that's a property of an object).

Some of the property values point at, or refer to, other objects. For example, all constructor functions have a `prototype` field that points to the object that will be used as the prototype for instances created with that constructor. Thus, the `Cat` constructor's `prototype` field points to `Cat.prototype`. Likewise, objects have a link to their prototype through their `[[Prototype]]` property. For example, the `[[Prototype]]` property of `kiki` links to `Cat.prototype`, since `kiki` was created with the `Cat` constructor. All prototype objects have a `constructor` field that links back to the constructor they belong to. As you can see, the `constructor` field for `Cat.prototype` connects back to `Cat`, and the `constructor` field for `Object.prototype` connects to `Object`. Instances like `kiki` don't have a `constructor` field defined directly on them. Instead, the constructor is looked up on the instance's prototype by walking the prototype chain.

As we saw in the `Dog` example, classes use the same prototype mechanism under the hood, so this technique of walking the prototype chain is also how properties and methods are looked up on instances of classes.

Overriding a Method

Understanding how JavaScript walks the prototype chain to locate an object's methods is important because it allows us to *override* the definition of a method that an object would otherwise inherit from its prototype. This technique is useful when we want an object to inherit most of its behavior from a prototype, but we want to give it some unique behavior as well. When you call a method, JavaScript uses the first definition it finds for that method as it walks the prototype chain, so if we define a method directly on an object, and that method has the same name as a method defined on the object's prototype, the method on the object itself takes precedence.

For example, say you want a new `Cat` object that says hello in a different way from the method defined on `Cat.prototype`. You could set a separate `sayHello` method directly on that new cat, like so:

```
let moona = new Cat("Moona");
moona.sayHello = function () {
  console.log(`HELLO!!! I'M ${this.name.toUpperCase()}!`);
};
moona.sayHello();
❶ HELLO!!! I'M MOONA!
kiki.sayHello();
❷ Miaow! My name is Kiki.
```

Here, we define a new instance with the `Cat` constructor and name it `moona`. Then we define a `sayHello` method on `moona` itself that logs a greeting in all caps. When we then call `moona.sayHello()`, we can see in the output that the `sayHello` definition set directly on `moona` takes precedence over the `sayHello` definition on `Cat.prototype` ❶. This is also known as *shadowing*, because the local method casts a kind of shadow over the prototype's method. Notice, however, that the original `sayHello` method on `Cat.prototype` remains intact, as you can see from the output when we call it on `kiki` ❷.

TRY IT YOURSELF

6-4. You can override a method on an instance of a class, just as you can on an instance created through prototype-based inheritance. Try creating a new instance of `Dog` called yappy, and modify its `sayHello` method to make it sound more yappy than other `Dog` instances.

6-5. Inspect the moona and yappy instances in the console. You should see that their `sayHello` methods are defined directly on the instances, whereas the `kiki` and `felix` instances have it defined on their respective prototypes.

Summary

In this chapter you learned about classes, which help you organize your code by sharing functionality between multiple objects. You learned how to create classes, how to use them to create instances, and how to extend classes by creating a hierarchy of subclasses and superclasses. You also learned about prototype-based inheritance, JavaScript's original system for allowing objects to inherit properties and methods. You explored how prototype-based inheritance compares to the newer class system, and you saw how to trace an object's chain of inheritance through the [[Prototype]] property in the console.

PART II

INTERACTIVE JAVASCRIPT

Now that you've learned the basics of the language, this second part of the book will show you how to use JavaScript to interface with a web browser. This will greatly open up the possibilities of the language, allowing you to write interactive, graphical web applications, such as games, an online shop, or even something like Facebook.

First you'll explore HTML and CSS, the two other pillars of web development besides JavaScript, and you'll see how to dynamically modify the contents and appearance of web pages using the DOM and JavaScript (Chapter 7). Next, you'll practice writing JavaScript code that responds to user-driven events in the browser, such as key presses and mouse clicks (Chapter 8). Finally, you'll learn how to use JavaScript and the Canvas API to generate static and animated graphics (Chapter 9).

7

HTML, THE DOM, AND CSS

To develop your own interactive web applications you'll need to learn some basic HTML and CSS, the languages used for creating web pages and changing how they look. A comprehensive introduction to these two languages would be beyond the scope of this book, but this chapter will teach you enough to get started. We'll also discuss the Document Object Model (DOM) and its application programming interface (API), which give us a way to modify web pages using JavaScript.

HTML

HTML stands for *HyperText Markup Language*. *Hypertext* is text that links to other text or documents, and *markup* is a system for annotating text in documents. Thus, HTML is a language for annotating text in documents that link to each other. In Chapter 1, I briefly introduced it as a language for describing web pages. From this perspective, the web pages are the documents that link to each other, and the annotations are instructions that tell a web browser how to display the pages.

HTML annotations take the form of *tags*. At its simplest, an HTML tag is a name enclosed in angle brackets. For example, the tag defining the body of the document, which identifies all the visible content of a web page, looks like this: <body>. Most tags come in pairs, with an opening tag and a closing tag: for example, <body> and </body>. A closing tag looks just like an opening tag but with a forward slash after the opening angle bracket.

Every pair of tags defines an *element*. Each HTML element represents some aspect of a web page, such as a heading, an image, or a paragraph. An HTML document contains a nested set of elements describing the document structure. In this context, *nesting* means that there are elements contained within other elements, which may in turn be contained within other elements, like matryoshka dolls.

Everything in between the opening and closing tags of an element is known as the *content* of that element. For example, Figure 7-1 shows a basic p element, short for *paragraph*, which represents a standard paragraph of text on a web page.

Figure 7-1: The anatomy of an HTML element

The content of the p element, located between the opening <p> tag and the closing </p> tag, is the actual text that will appear in the paragraph—in this case, Hello, World!

Creating an HTML Document

Let's create our first real HTML document. It will be a simple web page with a heading and a short paragraph of text. Open your text editor and create a new file called *helloworld.html* (refer to Chapter 1 if you need a refresher on creating new files). Enter the contents of Listing 7-1.

```
❶ <!DOCTYPE html>
❷ <html>
  ❸ <head>
       <title>Hello, World!</title>
     </head>
  ❹ <body>
       <h1>Hello!</h1>
       <p>Welcome to my document.</p>
     </body>
  </html>
```

Listing 7-1: A basic HTML document

The first line, the *doctype* ❶, specifies that this is an HTML document. This line is required for browsers to properly display these documents (even though we skipped it for our bare-bones HTML skeleton in Chapter 1). After this comes the opening <html> tag ❷. Everything else in this file is enclosed between this tag and the closing </html> tag. Every HTML document should have a single set of <html> and </html> tags defining one overarching html element. All other elements are nested within the html element.

Inside our html element are a head element ❸ and a body element ❹. Notice that our document follows the common convention of using indentation to indicate the nesting of elements within other elements. Since head and body are nested within the html element, their tags are indented. VS Code and many other text editors will apply this indentation automatically; as in JavaScript, it isn't required, but it helps with readability.

The head element contains *metadata*, or information about the page. In this case it contains a single element, title. Since it's nested inside head, by convention it receives a further level of indentation. The text content of the title element, Hello, World!, is the name of the web page. The name won't be displayed on the page itself, but it will appear as the tab title at the top of your browser when you load the page.

NOTE   *A* head *element can also contain links to scripts that will run on the page and stylesheets for modifying the look of the page, both of which we'll discuss later in this chapter.*

As mentioned earlier, the body element contains the visible content of the page, such as headings, images, text, and so on. Our body element contains two elements. The first, h1, is a top-level heading (HTML defines six heading levels, h1 through h6). Web browsers know to display the text content of an h1 element (in our case, Hello!) in large, bold text. As we've discussed, the second body element, p, will display as a standard paragraph of text. Our paragraph contains one sentence: Welcome to my document.

Open your web browser and load *helloworld.html.* You should see something like Figure 7-2.

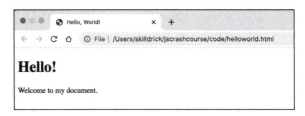

Figure 7-2: Our helloworld.html *document viewed in the browser*

As you can see, the text content of the title element is displayed as the title of the tab in the web browser. The h1 element is displayed as a heading on the page, with the text "Hello!" The p element is displayed as a standard paragraph below the heading, with the text "Welcome to my document."

Understanding Nested Relationships

An element that is directly nested within another element is called a *child*, while the element that contains the child is called a *parent*. For example, in *helloworld.html*, title is nested within head. We therefore say that title is a child of head, and head is the parent of title. An element that is either directly or indirectly contained within another element (by analogy, a child, grandchild, great-grandchild, or similar) is called a *descendant*. For example, h1 is a descendant of html, even though it isn't contained directly within html; instead, it's contained within body, which is itself contained within html. Conversely, the html element can be called an *ancestor* of the h1 element. Elements that have the same parent are called *siblings*. In our document, h1 and p are siblings because they both have body as a parent; similarly head and body are siblings.

The Document Object Model

When your web browser loads an HTML file, it creates an internal model of the elements known as the *Document Object Model*, or *DOM*. (Remember, *document* is just another word for a web page.) Unlike the HTML file itself, which is a static text file, the DOM is a dynamic model of the page, and you can modify it using JavaScript. To view the DOM for the *helloworld.html* document, open the JavaScript console and switch to the **Elements** tab. You should see something very similar to the HTML file, but with arrows to expand and collapse some of the elements. Expand them all and you should see the whole document, as in Listing 7-2.

```
<!DOCTYPE html>
<html>
  ▾<head>
    <title>Hello, World!</title>
  </head>
  ▾<body>
    <h1>Hello!</h1>
    <p>Welcome to my document.</p>
  </body>
</html>
```

Listing 7-2: The DOM of helloworld.html

To illustrate the dynamic nature of the DOM, try double-clicking the Hello! text in the h1 element within the Elements tab. Type in some new text and press ENTER. The web page's heading should change accordingly. Note, however, that you're not modifying the HTML file itself; rather, you're modifying the browser's model of the page.

Thanks to the DOM, you can update elements of a web page directly from the browser, and the results will be immediately displayed. Right now we're manually updating the DOM just to see how it works, but later in this chapter you'll learn how to use JavaScript to update the DOM programmatically. This allows you to write code that modifies what the viewer sees on the page. Ultimately, this is the key to creating dynamic web applications: JavaScript code that manipulates the DOM to change a web page's appearance as the user views and interacts with it.

The Elements tab in the browser provides one way to visualize the DOM. Figure 7-3 shows another way: we can think of the elements of our basic web page as a set of nested boxes.

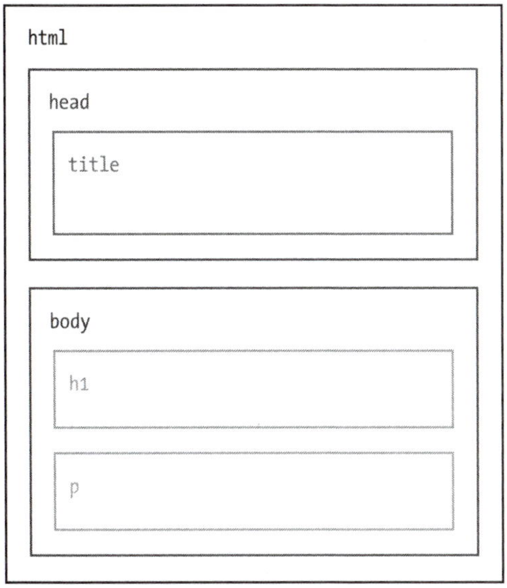

Figure 7-3: The DOM as nested boxes

The DOM doesn't really care about opening and closing tags, which are just how HTML describes the structure of the document in a textual format. From the browser's point of view, the important details are the elements and their parent, child, and sibling relationships. Figure 7-3 illustrates this more abstract view of the document structure. You can see right away that the h1 and p elements are nested within the body element, which is nested within the html element.

The DOM API

Web browsers allow you to modify the DOM using JavaScript with the *DOM API*. As mentioned at the start of this chapter, API stands for *application programming interface*, which is a way of interacting with a system or object via code. As you saw when you updated the h1 element, modifying the DOM modifies the web page, and any changes you make will, in general, be instantly visible. This means that the DOM API gives us a way to write code that will provide instant visual feedback to a viewer of our page.

The API provides a set of methods and properties for interacting with the DOM. A lot of these methods and properties are found on the document object, an object provided by the DOM API that represents the current document (that is, the web page). For example, document.title allows you to get and set the title of the current tab. Let's try that out now. Run the following code in the JavaScript console for *helloworld.html*:

```
document.title;
'Hello, World!'
document.title = "Hello, JavaScript!";
'Hello, JavaScript!'
```

When you run this, you should see the title change from Hello, World! to Hello, JavaScript! in the browser tab.

Element Identifiers

We can use the DOM API to modify any element in our page, and even to add new elements. To modify an element, we need a way of accessing it from our code. JavaScript offers many ways of accessing HTML elements. The simplest is to refer to an element by its id attribute.

HTML *attributes*, such as id, are key-value pairs we can add to HTML elements. The id attribute gives a unique identifier to an element. In an HTML document, attributes are always attached to the opening tag of an element; that is, they appear after the element name and before the closing angle bracket. Let's go back to the text editor and add an id attribute to the h1 element in our *helloworld.html* document. This will make the element easy to access with the DOM API. Update the document as shown in Listing 7-3. The unchanged code is grayed out.

```
<!DOCTYPE html>
<html>
  <head>
    <title>Hello, World!</title>
  </head>
  <body>
    <h1 id="main-heading">Hello!</h1>
    <p>Welcome to my document.</p>
  </body>
</html>
```

Listing 7-3: Adding an id attribute

We place the attribute after the opening tag name, h1. The attribute name and attribute value are separated by an equal sign, and the value should be wrapped in quotes. In this case, we're setting the id attribute to the value "main-heading".

If you reload the page, you should see no difference; the id attribute by default has no effect on the display of the element. To confirm that the page has been updated, right-click the "Hello!" heading and select **Inspect** from the menu. This will highlight the h1 element, including its new id attribute, in the Elements tab, as shown in Figure 7-4.

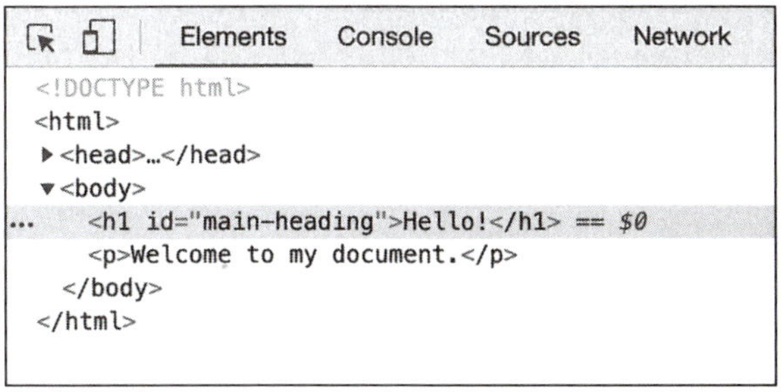

Figure 7-4: Chrome highlighting the h1 element in the Elements tab

Now that the h1 element has an ID, we can easily refer to it using Java-Script. In your web browser, switch to the **Console** tab for *helloworld.html* and enter the following:

```
let heading = document.getElementById("main-heading");
```

The method getElementById takes a string that corresponds to an HTML element's id attribute. It returns a representation of the HTML element with the specified ID. Here we store that element in the variable heading. Since identifiers are supposed to be unique, getElementById returns only one element. If the ID isn't found, the method returns null. If you break the rules and have more than one element with the same ID, browsers will usually return the first element with that ID, but this is an *undefined behavior*, meaning the behavior isn't specified and may change in the future.

Now let's ask the console for the value of heading:

```
heading;
  <h1 id="main-heading">Hello!</h1>
```

The console shows the HTML representation of the h1 element. In addition, if you hover over the output with your mouse, the browser highlights the element on the page, as you can see in Figure 7-5.

Now that we have the heading element bound to a variable, we can operate on it. For example, we can get and set the element's text as follows:

```
heading.innerText;
'Hello!'
heading.innerText = "Hi there...";
'Hi there...'
```

The innerText property represents the text of the element. As you can see in this example, it can be used both to get the text and to change it. When you update the value of innerText, the text of the heading element on the page updates as well. Again, though, keep in mind that this is just a change to the DOM—the browser's model of the web page—not the underlying HTML file itself. If you refresh the page, the browser will reload the original HTML file and your change will disappear.

Figure 7-5: Chrome highlighting the h1 element on the page

Writing code in the JavaScript console lets you instantly see the results in your browser when you update the DOM, but what if you want to update the DOM as someone else views a web page? You can't type code into the JavaScript console on other people's computers without physically being there, but you can embed JavaScript code directly into an HTML document, so anyone viewing your web page can see the results of that code. That's what we'll do next.

TRY IT YOURSELF

7-1. Give the p element of *helloworld.html* an ID and use it to update the text of that element from the console.

---

script Elements

If you want to include JavaScript in an HTML document, you have to use the script HTML element. There are two techniques for using script elements: either you include the JavaScript code as content between the opening and closing <script> tags, or you save the code in a separate JavaScript file and include the name of that file as a property of the script element. The advantage of including the JavaScript directly in the HTML file is that it keeps everything in one place. On the other hand, having the JavaScript in a separate file means you can use the same JavaScript file on multiple pages. Maintaining separate files can also be more manageable when your project has a lot of HTML and a lot of JavaScript.

You've already seen a script element with JavaScript content: I introduced this in Chapter 1 as a way to write JavaScript in an HTML file. Now let's look at the second technique. We'll create a page with an HTML file that includes a script element, and have that element point to a separate JavaScript file. In the JavaScript file, we'll write code to log a message to the console in order to prove that the script has been included in the web page.

Because our HTML and JavaScript are going to be in separate files, it will be easier to keep track of the two files if we put them in a new directory (or folder, in Windows jargon). Create a new directory called *chapter7* and make a new HTML file in that directory called *index.html*. This is the customary name for the main HTML file in a directory.

Enter the code shown in Listing 7-4 into *index.html*.

```
<!DOCTYPE html>
<html>
  <head>
    <title>Hello, JavaScript!</title>
❶ <script src="script.js"></script>
  </head>
  <body>
    <h1 id="main-heading">Hello, JavaScript!</h1>
  </body>
</html>
```

Listing 7-4: An HTML file with a script element pointing to a JavaScript file

We include a script element inside the head element ❶. We place it there by convention since the script won't be contributing to the visual content of the page, although it would technically be possible to put it in the body instead. The script element has a src attribute (short for *source*), which tells the browser the name of a JavaScript file to load. The browser looks in the same directory as the HTML file when a simple filename is given. You could also give a path to the JavaScript file, such as "/scripts/myscript.js", but as long as the HTML and JavaScript files are in the same directory, just the filename is enough.

Our HTML file won't work yet because we haven't created the referenced script file. Create a new file called *script.js* in your *chapter7* directory and enter the code shown in Listing 7-5.

```
console.log("Hello, HTML!");
```

Listing 7-5: A simple script.js file

Now open *index.html* in Chrome. When you open the JavaScript console, you should see the string Hello, HTML! printed to the console. If not, check the code carefully, and make sure that the filenames match exactly.

CSS

Modern web pages are made with three languages: HTML, JavaScript, and CSS. At a basic level, HTML defines the *content* of the page, JavaScript defines the *behavior* of the page, and CSS, short for *Cascading Style Sheets*, defines the *appearance* of the page. As we've seen, web browsers have default ways of displaying various HTML elements, such as headers and paragraphs. CSS gives us more control over the look of those elements, allowing us to override the default appearance of elements, like their size, color, and typeface.

Because this is a JavaScript book, we won't look at CSS in depth. However, knowing the basics of CSS will be helpful when we start making dynamic web pages. Additionally, some of the DOM API methods we'll be using rely on the CSS selector syntax, which we'll discuss shortly. Understanding where that syntax comes from will help you use those methods effectively.

link Elements

In this section we'll create a CSS file to include in our page and use that file to override some element styles. Including a CSS file is similar to including a JavaScript file, but you need to use a different HTML element, called link. The link element is a generic way of including an external resource on a page. To create a link to the CSS file we're about to write, open *index.html* in your text editor and add the line highlighted in Listing 7-6.

```
<!DOCTYPE html>
<html>
  <head>
    <title>Hello, JavaScript!</title>
    <script src="script.js"></script>
    <link href="style.css" rel="stylesheet">
  </head>
  <body>
    <h1 id="main-heading">Hello, JavaScript!</h1>
  </body>
</html>
```

Listing 7-6: Adding a CSS file with a link element

We set two attributes on the link element: href, short for *hypertext reference*, and rel, short for *relationship*. The href attribute works in the same way as the src attribute on script elements: you specify the linked file as the attribute's value. The rel attribute specifies the type of file you're linking to and how it relates to the document. Here we provide the string "stylesheet", which means the linked file should be interpreted as a stylesheet for the page, with information on how elements should appear.

Notice that unlike the HTML elements we've seen so far, the link element doesn't need a closing </link> tag. This is because while other elements may contain content, a link element never will. As such, there's no need for a closing tag to mark the end of the content.

Rulesets

A CSS file consists of one or more *rulesets* establishing how elements in a document should be styled. We'll write a basic ruleset now. Create a file called *style.css* in the *chapter7* directory and enter the contents of Listing 7-7.

```
h1 {
  color: red;
  font-style: italic;
}
```

Listing 7-7: Styling h1 elements in a style.css file

This piece of CSS says that h1 elements should be styled red and italic. Refresh *index.html* in your browser and you should see the style of the heading change.

A CSS ruleset such as this has two parts: a *selector* (h1 in this case) and a series of *declarations* between braces. The selector tells the browser which elements to operate on, and the declarations say what to do to those elements. Selectors *match* elements. That is, a selector is a pattern, and the browser checks to see which elements on the page match that pattern. In this case, h1 is a selector that matches all h1 elements. Our ruleset has two declarations for this selector, one for making the text red, and one for making the text italic. Each declaration consists of a property name followed by a colon, followed by a property value and a semicolon. For example, color is a property name, and red is that property's value.

Selectors

Our selector in Listing 7-7 targets all elements of a given type, but CSS also lets you create more specific selectors. To take advantage of them, we'll first have to add some more code to our HTML file. Update *index.html* as shown in Listing 7-8.

```
<!DOCTYPE html>
<html>
  <head>
    <title>Hello, JavaScript!</title>
    <script src="script.js"></script>
    <link href="style.css" rel="stylesheet">
  </head>
  <body>
    <h1 id="main-heading">Hello, <strong>JavaScript</strong>!</h1>
    <p class="highlight">This is my first <strong>paragraph</strong>.</p>
    <p>This is my second <strong>paragraph</strong>.</p>
    <h1>Here's another heading.</h1>
    <p class="highlight">This is my third <strong>paragraph</strong>.</p>
  </body>
</html>
```

Listing 7-8: Making our HTML more interesting

There are two new concepts in this expanded HTML. First, we wrapped some of the text in strong elements. This element marks its contents as being important somehow. By default, browsers make the content of strong elements bold. Second, we added a class attribute to two of the p elements. The class attribute is similar to the id attribute, but whereas IDs should be unique, you can apply the same class name to multiple elements. We use class when we want to treat a set of elements in the same way—for example, highlighting the text of certain paragraphs.

NOTE *The strong element is known as an* inline *element because you can apply it to part of a line rather than it defining a separate line.*

Refresh the page, and you should see the new text. The word *JavaScript* in the heading won't appear any different, because the h1 element is already styled bold by default, but the three instances of the word *paragraph* will all be bold thanks to the strong elements.

Our addition of the class attributes hasn't made a difference yet, but it will once we add some CSS targeting the highlight class. Let's do that now. Add the new code shown in Listing 7-9 to *style.css*, specifying some new CSS rulesets to target the new HTML with different kinds of selectors.

```
h1 {
  color: red;
  font-style: italic;
}

#main-heading {
  font-size: 48px;
}

strong {
  color: blue;
}

p strong {
  font-size: 24px;
}

.highlight {
  background-color: yellow;
}

.highlight strong {
  background-color: orange;
}
```

Listing 7-9: Adding more rulesets to style.css

This CSS code uses a few different kinds of selectors. The first new selector, #main-heading, is an ID selector. An *ID selector* picks out the HTML element with a specific id attribute. It uses a hash mark followed by the

ID you want to match, so #main-heading matches the element with id="main -heading". Here we use the selector to make our main heading larger than the default size for h1 elements. Note that numeric sizes in CSS require a unit; in this case we're using px, which means pixels.

The ruleset with the strong selector matches any strong element and sets its text to blue. The p strong selector is a bit more interesting. It's a *descendant selector*, which only matches the specified element if it's a descendant of some other specified element. In our example, p strong means "match any strong element that's a descendant of a p element." Thus, the selector will resize the text of the strong elements that are inside p elements, but ignore the strong text inside the h1 element.

If you want, you can chain multiple descendant selectors together. For example, html body p strong is a valid descendant selector (though a bit redundant, since all page content will be a descendant of html and body). This would match any strong element that's a descendant of a p element which in turn is a descendant of a body element which is itself a descendant of an html element.

Next comes a ruleset for .highlight, which is a *class selector*. This kind of selector matches all elements with a given class attribute. The class name is given after a period, so .highlight will match any element with class="highlight". Here we use the class selector to set a background color of yellow, creating a highlighting effect. Finally, .highlight strong combines a class selector with a descendant selector. It means "match any strong element that's a descendant of an element with the highlight class."

Anytime you have a class or ID selector, you can optionally include an element name before it, without a space. For example, p.highlight means "select any p elements with the highlight class," while .highlight means "select any elements with the highlight class." Likewise, h1#main-heading matches the h1 element with the id of main-heading. In this case, the element name is redundant because the id is unique, but you might want to include it to remind the reader that #main-heading is an h1 element. You also could apply your CSS file to two separate HTML files, where one has an h2 element with the id of main -heading, in which case h1#main-heading would only match on one of the pages.

Refresh the page in your web browser and you should see a hideous mix of styles, similar to Figure 7-6.

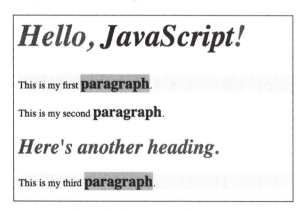

Figure 7-6: The result of our CSS styling experiments

We aren't going to win any design awards for this page, but it helps us see how the various CSS selectors work. Notice, for example, how all strong elements (selected with strong) have been colored blue, but only strong elements inside p elements (selected with p strong) are sized to 24 pixels. If this sizing had applied to *all* strong elements, the word *JavaScript* in the top heading would be smaller. Meanwhile, the first and third paragraphs, which were assigned to the highlight class, have a yellow background (selected with .highlight), except for the word *paragraph*, which has an orange background (selected with .highlight strong). The second paragraph, which isn't part of the highlight class, has no added background color.

TRY IT YOURSELF

7-2. Update the CSS to make it a bit more attractive. You can change the font with the font-family property; for example, font-family: Arial;. You can find other permissible color names by searching the web for "CSS colors."

Using CSS Selectors in JavaScript

As I mentioned earlier, some DOM API methods rely on CSS selector syntax to select elements from the DOM for manipulation. For example, the document.querySelectorAll method takes a string containing a CSS selector and returns an array-like object containing all the elements that match that selector. To get all the elements in our web page with the highlight class, you'd use document.querySelectorAll(".highlight");.

With *index.html* open in your browser, open the console and enter the following:

```
document.querySelectorAll(".highlight");
▸ NodeList(2) [p.highlight, p.highlight]
```

As you can see, the querySelectorAll method returns a NodeList with two elements. A NodeList is a kind of specialized array. For our purposes, we can just treat it like a regular array. If you click the arrow to expand the NodeList, you'll see the two p.highlight elements (the p elements with the class highlight) listed. Hover over each one in turn and you should see the corresponding element highlighted on the page.

Next, select the strong element in the main heading:

```
let strong = document.querySelectorAll("#main-heading strong");
strong;
▸ NodeList [strong]
```

Only one element matches the selector #main-heading strong. It's the strong element that's a descendant of the element with the main-heading ID. You therefore get a NodeList with a single element. Again, if you expand the list you can hover over the element to see it highlighted on the page. To get the text content of that element, you have to get element 0 from the NodeList using [0] and ask for its textContent property, as shown here:

```
strong[0].textContent;
'JavaScript'
```

In situations like this where you expect your selector to match only a single element, you can also use document.querySelector, which returns only the first element matching the selector, or null if no elements match.

TRY IT YOURSELF

7-3. Use document.querySelector to get the strong element in the main heading and change its text content.

7-4. We previously used document.getElementById("main-heading"), but you can also use querySelector to select a single element by its id. Do the two calls return the exact same result? Hint: you can use === to check equality.

7-5. Use document.querySelectorAll to select all the strong elements on the page. Next, try selecting just the strong elements that are contained within a p element with the highlight class.

7-6. Add some more elements with different class names and IDs and experiment with selecting them. For example, the em element is used for emphasizing text, and the pre element can be used for displaying code.

Summary

In this chapter you learned the basics of HTML and CSS, which define the content and appearance of a web page, respectively. HTML and CSS are both topics worthy of their own books, but we've covered enough ground for you to start building your own web pages. You can use the fundamentals from this chapter as a starting point for your own independent study of these two languages.

This chapter also introduced you to the DOM, the web browser's internal model of a web page. You've seen how to manipulate the DOM with JavaScript using the DOM API, and gotten a first look at how you can use JavaScript to create interactive web pages.

8

EVENT-BASED PROGRAMMING

When a user clicks a button, scrolls, or simply moves the mouse within a web page, that action creates an *event*. An event is the browser's way of signaling that an action happened in the DOM. Events allow us to create interactive web applications that respond to the user's actions. We do this by writing *handlers* for specific events: functions that are called when an event occurs. Using event handlers, we can change the color of an element when the user clicks it, move an element around the screen when the user presses a certain key, and much more.

In this chapter you'll learn how to write event handlers to respond to some common DOM events. In this way, you'll add interactivity to your web pages.

Event Handlers

Events are how the browser tells JavaScript that something has occurred in the DOM. It's almost as if every time the mouse moves over the window, or a key is pressed, the browser is shouting, "Hey, the mouse moved! A key was pressed!" These shouts happen all the time, but your JavaScript code can respond to them only if you explicitly tell it to listen for them. You do this by writing a JavaScript event handler that will perform some action when a certain type of event occurs.

An *event handler* is a function triggered by a specific event type on a specific element. For example, you could attach a handler to a particular h1 element that handles clicks on that element. Let's try that out now. We'll create a simple web page with a heading and use an event handler to log a message to the console when the heading is clicked.

First, you'll need an HTML file. Create a new directory called *chapter8* and make a new file in that directory called *index.html*. Enter the content shown in Listing 8-1.

```
<!DOCTYPE html>
<html>
  <head>
    <title>Event Handlers</title>
  </head>
  <body>
    <h1 id="main-heading">Hello <em>World!</em></h1>
    <script src="script.js"></script>
  </body>
</html>
```

Listing 8-1: An index.html *file for exploring event handlers*

As usual, our HTML file has a single html element containing a head with some metadata and a body with some content. Specifically, the body contains an h1 element with an ID of main-heading, and part of the heading text is wrapped in an em element (short for *emphasis*), which by default italicizes that portion of the text. It also contains a script element with a link to the file *script.js*. In a moment, that's where we'll write the code for our event handler.

Overall, this file is very similar to the *index.html* file we created in Chapter 7, with one important difference: the script element is inside the body element, not the head element. This is a bit of a cheat to get around a problem with how web browsers read web pages. As described in the previous chapter, the browser builds a model of the page called the DOM. It builds the DOM incrementally by reading through the HTML file from top to bottom. Anytime the browser reaches a script element, it executes the whole script before continuing. That means that if we had our script element in the head, and we looked up the h1 element in that script, the h1 element wouldn't be in the DOM yet! By placing the script element at the end of the body, we can be sure that all the page content has been loaded into the DOM *before* we run our JavaScript.

Now create a file called *script.js* in the same directory as the HTML code, and enter the script shown in Listing 8-2. This script adds an event handler for when the user clicks the h1 element.

```
let heading = document.querySelector("#main-heading");

heading.addEventListener("click", () => {
  console.log("You clicked the heading!");
});
```

Listing 8-2: Creating an event handler in script.js

Using the DOM API's querySelector method, we get the element with the ID main-heading and save it as the variable heading. You may recall from Chapter 7 that this method returns the first element to match the selector. In our case, there's only one main-heading element, so we know this method will select the element we want. We then use the addEventListener method on the heading element to attach an event handler to that element. addEventListener tells JavaScript to watch for a particular event happening on the element, and to execute some function when it does.

NOTE *Although the DOM API uses the term* listener, *the term* handler *is more commonly used to describe a function that reacts to an event.*

The addEventListener method has two required arguments. The first is the event type. This is a string representing the type of event to respond to, such as "click" (for mouse clicks), "keydown" (for keyboard key presses), or "scroll" (for window scrolling). We've specified "click". The second argument is the function to execute when the specified event happens. This function is the event handler. It will be called anytime the event happens on the element addEventListener was called on. In this case, the function, which logs a message to the console, will be called anytime someone clicks the heading element.

NOTE *As explained in Chapter 5, when a function is passed as an argument to another function, it's known as a* callback function, *or simply a* callback. *All event handlers are callback functions, since they're passed as arguments to the add EventListener method.*

Open *index.html* in your browser and open the console. When you click the heading, you should see the message "You clicked the heading!" printed to the console. Congratulations: you've made your first interactive web page!

TRY IT YOURSELF

8-1. Add a p element to the page and attach a click event handler to it.

Event Bubbling

When an event is triggered on an element, it also gets triggered on all the element's ancestors (that is, the parent of the element, the parent's parent, and so on). For instance, when you clicked the h1 element in the previous example, you were also technically clicking the body element that contains the h1 element. This makes sense intuitively; if you click some text in a box, you're also clicking the box. Therefore, if you had a separate handler attached to the body element, it would also receive the click event. This progression of events from children to ancestors is known as *event bubbling*.

Let's harness bubbling by adding event handlers to the em and body elements in our web page. Like our h1 event handler, these new handlers will log a message to the console when their elements are clicked. Since em is a child of h1 and h1 is a child of body, a single click on em should trigger the handlers attached to all three elements.

Add the code in Listing 8-3 to the end of *script.js*.

```
--snip--
document.querySelector("em").addEventListener("click", () => {
  console.log("You clicked the em element!");
});

document.querySelector("body").addEventListener("click", () => {
  console.log("You clicked the body element!");
});
```

Listing 8-3: Adding more handlers to script.js

This snippet adds two handlers, one to the em element and one to the body element, but we do it slightly differently from how we created the main-heading handler in Listing 8-2. Instead of saving each element to a variable, we just call addEventListener directly on the result of the document.querySelector method. This technique of calling a method directly on the return value of another method is known as *method chaining*: we chain multiple method calls together, so that the result of the first link in the chain is used as the object for the next method call. I used the longer technique for Listing 8-2 because it makes it more explicit that addEventListener is being called on an element, but the chaining technique is often preferred because of its terseness.

Reload *index.html* and open the console. When you click the word *World!* you should see the following output:

```
You clicked the em element!
You clicked the heading!
You clicked the body element!
```

When you click the em element, the handler function on that element is the first to get called. After that, the handler function on the h1 element is called, followed by the one on the body element. This is because the event "bubbles up" through the DOM, from the innermost element to the outermost element. If you click the non-italic part of the heading, you'll see just the main-heading and body handlers triggered.

Event Delegation

One of the more common uses for event bubbling is *event delegation*, a technique where you use a single handler to respond to events on multiple child or other descendant elements. For example, imagine you have a list of words, where each list item is a separate HTML element, and you want to handle clicks on each item in the same way. By adding a single handler to the list items' parent element, you can catch events on each item with only a few lines of code.

To illustrate event delegation, we'll write a simple application that builds up and displays a sentence based on words that you click in a list. First, we'll update our HTML file to include a list of words and an empty p element that we'll populate dynamically with the words of your choice. Then, we'll write the necessary event handler with JavaScript to take clicked words and add them to the p element for display. Finally, we'll add some CSS rules to make the application easier to interact with.

There are two types of lists in HTML: ordered (numbered) lists and unordered (bulleted) lists. We'll use an unordered list, which is created with the ul (*unordered list*) element. Each individual item in the list is wrapped in an li (*list item*) element. Therefore, the event resulting from a click on any li element will bubble up to the parent ul element.

Update *index.html* as shown in Listing 8-4.

```
<!DOCTYPE html>
<html>
  <head>
    <title>Event Handlers</title>
  </head>
  <body>
    <h1 id="main-heading">Hello <em>World!</em></h1>

    <ul id="word-list">
      <li>The</li>
      <li>Dog</li>
      <li>Cat</li>
      <li>Is</li>
      <li>Was</li>
      <li>And</li>
      <li>Hungry</li>
      <li>Green</li>
    </ul>

    <p id="sentence"></p>

    <script src="script.js"></script>
  </body>
</html>
```

Listing 8-4: Adding a list to index.html

This adds an unordered list of words to the document, as well as an empty p element, which we'll be modifying with JavaScript.

Next, we'll write an event handler for the ul element to handle clicks on any of the list items. The handler will take the word that was clicked and add it to the p element, allowing you to build up a sentence one word at a time. Delete all the code in *script.js* and replace it with Listing 8-5.

```
let wordList = document.querySelector("#word-list");
let sentence = document.querySelector("#sentence");

wordList.addEventListener("click", ❶ event => {
❷ let word = event.target.textContent;
  sentence.textContent += word;
  sentence.textContent += " ";
});
```

Listing 8-5: Delegating events

First we look up the two elements we care about using document.query Selector: the ul with the word list, and the empty p element. Next, we add a click handler to the ul element. This example is a little different from our previous handlers because the callback function has a parameter, which we're calling event ❶. If we give a handler function a single parameter (in this case, event, but the exact name isn't important), the parameter represents an object through which the DOM API passes information about the event that just happened. That information, which includes the element that was clicked, the element's text content, and so on, then becomes available for use within the callback function.

In our example, we use the event object to determine what word was clicked and store it in the variable word ❷. We find out which specific element was clicked with the event object's target property. When you click one of the li elements, event.target will be the li element you clicked, not the ul (the ul element is available with the currentTarget property). Then we use the textContent property, which returns the text of that element. Putting it together, if you were to click on the first li element, then event.target.textContent would return the string "The", and that string would become the value of the variable word.

Now that we have the word the user clicked, we can add it to the sentence. We use the += operator to append the word to the text content of the sentence element. You may recall that sentence.textContent += word; essentially converts to sentence.textContent = sentence.textContent + word;. In other words, we're taking the sentence element's existing text content, adding the string stored in word to the end, and reassigning that text to the element's text content. Then, after adding the word to the sentence, we use the same += trick to append a space to the end of the sentence in preparation for the next word that gets added.

Open *index.html* again in your browser. You should see the list of words. You won't see the empty p element because it doesn't have any content yet. As you click words from the list, you should see them being added to the p element.

To finish off our application, we need to add a small amount of CSS. JavaScript and CSS often go hand in hand because the styling can give helpful tips to the user that certain elements are interactive. In this case we'll add two hints via CSS: we'll modify the list items to change the mouse pointer to a finger when it hovers over them, so they look more "clickable," and we'll give the element that's currently under the mouse pointer an underline so it's easier to tell which word you're about to click (which isn't always obvious when the mouse is in the vertical space between words).

Create a new CSS file called *style.css* and add the two CSS declarations shown in Listing 8-6.

```
li {
  cursor: pointer;
}

li:hover {
  text-decoration: underline;
}
```

Listing 8-6: Adding styling in style.css

To change the cursor for li elements, we use cursor: pointer. This changes the cursor from the default arrow to a hand with a finger when it is over an li element, as happens when you hover over a link on a web page. The li:hover selector uses the :hover pseudo-class. A *pseudo-class* is a kind of selector that applies only when an element is in a certain state: li:hover matches any li element that the mouse is currently hovering over. When the pointer is over an li element, we use text-decoration: underline to underline the text of that element.

To include this CSS on the page, add a link element to the head of the *index.html* file, as shown in Listing 8-7.

```
<!DOCTYPE html>
<html>
  <head>
    <title>Event Handlers</title>
    <link rel="stylesheet" href="style.css">
  </head>
--snip--
```

Listing 8-7: Including style.css *in* index.html

Now when you hover over one of the list items, the cursor will change, and the currently hovered word will be underlined, as shown in Figure 8-1.

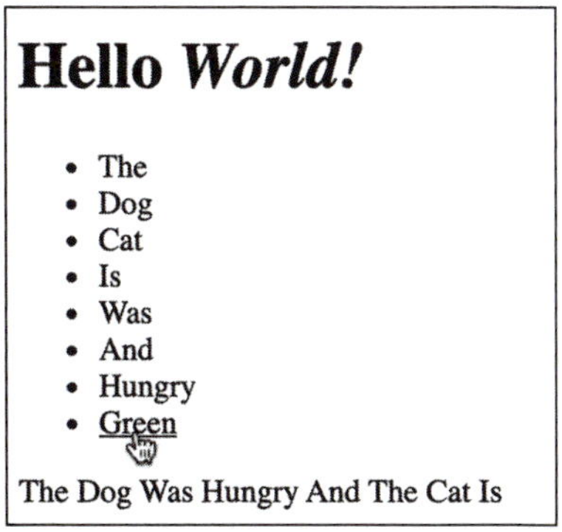

Figure 8-1: Using CSS to give hints to users

With that styling, our sentence-building application is complete! Event delegation simplified the JavaScript we wrote by letting us attach a single event handler, rather than using a separate handler for each list item.

Mouse Movement Events

The DOM produces events when the mouse moves, with the event name mousemove. These mousemove events are triggered on an element while the mouse moves over that element, and we can listen for them with the addEventListener method, just as we did for mouse clicks. Let's set up a simple mousemove handler to see it in action. The handler will log the mouse's position to the console as the mouse moves around the web page.

Still working within your *chapter8* project folder, add the code in Listing 8-8 to the end of *script.js*.

```
--snip--
document.querySelector("html").addEventListener("mousemove", e => {
  console.log(`mousemove x: ${e.clientX}, y: ${e.clientY}`);
});
```

Listing 8-8: A mousemove event handler

In this listing, we add a mousemove event handler to the html element. Since the html element encompasses the entire web page, this handler will respond to movements of the mouse anywhere in the browser window. The handler logs a message to the console including the clientX and clientY properties of the event, which tell us the x- and y-coordinates of the mouse relative to the browser window. In this example I'm using the shorter name e for the event parameter, rather than event, as in Listing 8-5. Remember, the name of the parameter doesn't matter; if the event handler callback function has a single parameter, that parameter will carry information about the event.

Refresh *index.html* in your browser and move the mouse pointer over the page. You should see messages similar to the following logged to the console:

```
mousemove x: 434, y: 47
mousemove x: 429, y: 47
mousemove x: 425, y: 48
mousemove x: 421, y: 51
mousemove x: 416, y: 51
mousemove x: 413, y: 54
mousemove x: 408, y: 55
```

There are two important things to note as you watch the console. First, the coordinates start at 0 in the top-left corner of the browser window, increasing as you go across and down. The x-coordinate increases as you move right, and the y-coordinate increases as you move down. This follows the standard convention for computer graphics.

Second, there are "gaps," or locations that the mouse appears to jump over. This is because mousemove events aren't triggered continuously, but some limited number of times per second. The exact number depends on the mouse, the browser, and the computer, but it tends to be in the low hundreds. Therefore, if you move the mouse fast enough, there will be locations on the screen that the mouse seems to skip over, because the events weren't triggering fast enough.

Now that you've seen mousemove events in action, we can try to do something slightly more interesting with them. In this next example, we'll make a box move around the page, following your cursor. To do that we'll need to modify our HTML, CSS, and JavaScript files. The HTML change is simple. Add the new line in Listing 8-9 to *index.html*.

```
--snip--
    <p id="sentence"></p>

    <div id="box"></div>

    <script src="script.js"></script>
  </body>
</html>
```

Listing 8-9: Adding a div to index.html

Here we're using a new HTML element called div, short for *content division*. It will become the movable box on our page. The div element is HTML's generic container element. This means that it's an element that can contain other elements, but by default has no appearance and no specific *meaning* (unlike ul, which means a list, or h1, which means a heading). We'll use CSS to give the div element an appearance next. Add the contents of Listing 8-10 to the end of *style.css*.

```
--snip--
#box {
  position: fixed;
  left: 0px;
  top: 0px;
  width: 10px;
  height: 10px;
  background-color: hotpink;
}
```

Listing 8-10: Styling the div with CSS

Here we're using #box to select the element with the ID box. There are a number of declarations within this ruleset. The first, position: fixed, tells the browser to put this element at the position specified next, by the left and top declarations. We indicate 0px for both, which tells the browser to put the element at the very top-left corner of the browser *viewport*, the part of the browser that shows the content. We specify the width and height of the element to be 10 pixels each. Finally, we give our 10×10 box a background color that's sure to jump out: hot pink.

Refresh the page now, and you'll see a small pink square appear in the top-left corner. Now it's time to write an event handler so you can move the square with your mouse. Modify *script.js* as shown in Listing 8-11.

```
let wordList = document.querySelector("#word-list");
let sentence = document.querySelector("#sentence");

wordList.addEventListener("click", event => {
  let word = event.target.textContent;
  sentence.textContent += word;
  sentence.textContent += " ";
});

let box = document.querySelector("#box");

document.querySelector("html").addEventListener("mousemove", e => {
  box.style.left = e.clientX + "px";
  box.style.top = e.clientY + "px";
});
```

Listing 8-11: Moving the div with JavaScript

The first addition here is to find the box using document.querySelector and save a reference to the element in the variable box. Next, we modify the mousemove event handler we wrote earlier. In order to move the box around, we're modifying its style property, which is an object representing the CSS applied to the element. For example, setting a value for box.style.left has the same effect as updating the value of left in the CSS file. In our handler, we set both the left and top values using the current position of the mouse.

As mentioned in Chapter 7, numeric values in CSS require a unit. We can't just assign a number, like box.style.left = 10. Instead, we have to provide a string including the units, like box.style.left = "10px". This is why we include + "px" at the end of each statement in our event handler. If e.clientX is 50, then e.clientX + "px" will give the string "50px", which gets assigned to the box.style.left property, updating the left position of the box. As the mouse moves, this handler will be called with e.clientX and e.clientY set to the current position of the mouse, and so the pink box will move around as your mouse moves. Refresh the page and give it a try!

TRY IT YOURSELF

8-2. What happens if you modify the values that set the box's position? For example, what would happen if you multiplied e.clientX by 2, or added 50 to e.clientY?

Keyboard Events

Keyboard events are triggered when keys are pressed on the keyboard. We'll focus on one keyboard event, called keydown, which is triggered when a key is pressed down. (As you might expect, there's a corresponding event called keyup that is triggered when a key is released.)

We'll add a handler to our web page that simply logs keydown events to the console as they happen. Add the code in Listing 8-12 to the end of *script.js*.

```
--snip--
document.querySelector("html").addEventListener("keydown", e => {
  console.log(e);
});
```

Listing 8-12: Logging keydown events

As in Listing 8-11, we're adding an event handler to the html element, meaning it will apply to the entire web page, but this time we're handling the keydown event. This event will be triggered whenever you press down a key on your keyboard. Our handler logs e to the console, meaning the entire event object will be logged when a key is pressed.

Try reloading the page to see the handler in action. You'll need to open the console, then click inside the document to give it *focus*. This just means that the key presses will get sent to your web page, instead of to the console's text input. As long as everything's set up correctly, you should see events being logged to the console as you type, as shown here:

```
▶KeyboardEvent {isTrusted: true, key: "h", code: "KeyH", location: 0, ctrlKey: false, ...}
▶KeyboardEvent {isTrusted: true, key: "e", code: "KeyE", location: 0, ctrlKey: false, ...}
▶KeyboardEvent {isTrusted: true, key: "l", code: "KeyL", location: 0, ctrlKey: false, ...}
▶KeyboardEvent {isTrusted: true, key: "l", code: "KeyL", location: 0, ctrlKey: false, ...}
▶KeyboardEvent {isTrusted: true, key: "o", code: "KeyO", location: 0, ctrlKey: false, ...}
```

Click the arrow next to one of the events to see the properties each event has. As you'll see, there are a lot, but we mostly care about which key was pressed, which we can find with the key property. We'll use this information next to move the pink box around using the keyboard.

In order to move the box around, we'll create two new variables to keep track of its x- and y-positions. Then we'll update those variables with an event handler when specific keys are pressed. Update *script.js* as shown in Listing 8-13. (Note that the mousemove handler has been removed in this listing.)

```
let wordList = document.querySelector("#word-list");
let sentence = document.querySelector("#sentence");

wordList.addEventListener("click", event => {
  let word = event.target.textContent;
  sentence.textContent += word;
  sentence.textContent += " ";
});
```

```
let box = document.querySelector("#box");

let currentX = 0
let currentY = 0

document.querySelector("html").addEventListener("keydown", e => {
  if (e.key == "w") {
    currentY -= 5;
  } else if (e.key == "a") {
    currentX -= 5;
  } else if (e.key == "s") {
    currentY += 5;
  } else if (e.key == "d") {
    currentX += 5;
  }

  box.style.left = currentX + "px";
  box.style.top = currentY + "px";
});
```

Listing 8-13: Using keydown events to move the box

We create two variables called currentX and currentY to store the location of the box. Then we modify our keydown handler to include an if...else statement that checks to see if the event's key property matches any of "w", "a", "s", or "d". If so, that indicates one of those four keys has been pressed (I'm using these keys as they're typically used for movement in games). Depending on which key has been pressed, we add or subtract 5 to or from currentX or currentY, corresponding to the box moving 5 pixels up, down, left, or right. After we update the appropriate variable, we update the style of the box with box.style.left and box.style.top, as we did in Listing 8-11. This time, however, we use the values of currentX and currentY to change the CSS.

When you reload the page, try pressing and holding down S or D to make the box move down or to the right. You should notice that holding the key down results in the box continuing to move, as the keyboard sends repeated keydown events. This is the normal behavior of a computer keyboard when you hold down a key. The exact repeat speed is controlled by your operating system.

TRY IT YOURSELF

8-3. The event object for a keydown event has a Boolean property called repeat that tells you if the current keydown was generated as a repeat from holding down the key. How could you modify the keydown handler to respond only to actual key presses, and not automatic repeats? Hint: one approach is to use the return keyword to return early from the handler function.

Summary

In this chapter you learned the basics of DOM events and event handling. DOM events are how the browser tells your code that something happened on your page. You can respond to these events with event handlers, JavaScript functions that are executed when a certain event happens to a certain DOM element. Event handlers allow you to create web pages that respond interactively to the user's actions. In particular, you saw how to write event handlers triggered by clicks, mouse movements, and key presses.

9

THE CANVAS ELEMENT

One of the more interactive elements in HTML is the canvas element. This element acts like a painter's canvas: it provides space for you to draw images within the browser window using JavaScript. What's more, by repeatedly erasing old images and drawing new ones, you can create animations on the canvas. In this sense, the canvas element is more like the screen at a movie theater, where the image is updated many times every second to create the appearance of motion.

In this chapter you'll learn how to create canvas elements and how to use the Canvas API, which gives you a way to manipulate the canvas via JavaScript. You'll write JavaScript to draw static images to the canvas. Then you'll build a simple interactive drawing application. Finally, you'll learn the basics of creating 2D animations on the canvas.

Creating a Canvas

To include a canvas element on a web page, you add it to the body element in the page's *index.html* file. All you need are the opening and closing HTML tags, <canvas></canvas>, as the canvas element doesn't have any required attributes. However, it's a good idea to give the canvas an id, so you can easily access it using JavaScript. It's also common to set the element's width and height attributes so you can establish the size of the canvas.

Images that appear in the canvas are generated using JavaScript, not HTML. Any HTML between the opening and closing tags will appear only if the browser doesn't support the canvas element, so this can be used as a fallback for older or text-only browsers.

Let's create an HTML file that includes a canvas element. We'll also include a script element linking to a JavaScript file, where we'll write code to generate images on the canvas. We'll use the same HTML file throughout the chapter to draw different kinds of images. Create a new directory called *chapter9*, and make a new file in that directory called *index.html*. Enter the content shown in Listing 9-1.

```
<!DOCTYPE html>
<html>
  <head>
    <title>Canvas</title>
  </head>
  <body>
    <canvas id="canvas" width="300" height="300"></canvas>
    <script src="script.js"></script>
  </body>
</html>
```

Listing 9-1: An index.html *file with a canvas element*

This is our familiar HTML template, similar to the *index.html* files we've created in previous chapters, but with a canvas element instead of an h1 element. The width and height attributes specify the size of the canvas in pixels. By default, the canvas is transparent, so you won't actually see anything yet if you load the page.

Making Static Drawings

Now that we have a canvas element, we're ready to draw on it using JavaScript and the Canvas API. We'll start by drawing a solid rectangle. Then we'll look at how to create other static drawings. Create a new file called *script.js* in the *chapter9* directory, and enter the code shown in Listing 9-2.

```
let canvas = document.querySelector("#canvas");
let ctx = canvas.getContext("2d");
ctx.fillStyle = "blue";
ctx.fillRect(10, 10, 200, 100);
```

Listing 9-2: Drawing a rectangle in script.js

First, we get a reference to the canvas element using the document .querySelector method. The canvas element has a method called getContext, which we use to get the canvas's *drawing context*. The drawing context is an object that provides the entire Canvas API as a set of methods and properties (like fillRect and fillStyle, respectively, both used in Listing 9-2). These methods and properties are what we'll use to draw images on the canvas. In this case, we pass the string "2d" to the getContext method to request the two-dimensional drawing context.

NOTE *You can draw 3D graphics on the canvas by passing the string "webgl" or "webgpu" to the getContext method instead of "2d", but both of those are much more complicated than 2D graphics and are outside the scope of this book.*

Next, we tell the drawing context that we want the fill color for new elements to be blue, using the fillStyle property. Finally, we draw a filled rectangle using the current fill color with the fillRect method. This method takes four arguments: the x- and y-coordinates of the top-left corner of the rectangle, and the width and height of the rectangle in pixels. The coordinates work the same way as the coordinates for the whole browser window: x values increase as you move from left to right across the canvas, and y values increase from top to bottom, with (0, 0) representing the top-left corner of the canvas.

Open *index.html* in your browser. You should see a solid blue rectangle, as shown in Figure 9-1.

Figure 9-1: The blue rectangle

Any subsequent calls to fillRect will use the same fillStyle, so they'll also produce blue rectangles (until you set a new fillStyle, that is). You can confirm this by drawing some more rectangles to the canvas.

TRY IT YOURSELF

9-1. Draw a 100-pixel square starting at (0, 0).

9-2. We set the canvas to be 300 pixels wide by 300 pixels tall. What happens if you draw a rectangle that's bigger than the canvas?

Drawing Outlined Rectangles

As well as fillRect for making a rectangle filled with a color, the Canvas API provides the strokeRect method for outlining (*stroking*) a rectangle. To try it out, modify *script.js* as shown in Listing 9-3.

```
let canvas = document.querySelector("#canvas");
let ctx = canvas.getContext("2d");
ctx.lineWidth = 2;
ctx.strokeStyle = "red";
ctx.strokeRect(10, 10, 200, 100);
```

Listing 9-3: Using strokeRect to outline a rectangle

First we specify the width of the outline with the lineWidth property, setting it to 2 pixels wide. Then we use strokeStyle and strokeRect, rather than fillStyle and fillRect, to create an outlined rectangle with no fill color. The strokeRect method takes the same arguments as fillRect: the x- and y-coordinates of the top-left corner, and the width and height of the rectangle.

When you reload *index.html*, you should see the rectangle is now outlined in red, with no fill, as shown in Figure 9-2.

Figure 9-2: A red-outlined rectangle

When you set styles on the drawing context, such as the line width or line color, those settings apply only to subsequent additions to the canvas. That is, they don't retroactively affect anything that's already been drawn. In this sense, the canvas really is very much like a physical canvas, where the current style is determined by the color of paint and type of brush you're using at the moment. To demonstrate, we'll draw several rectangles with different colors. Add the code in Listing 9-4 to the end of *script.js*, after the code for drawing the red rectangle.

```
--snip--
ctx.strokeStyle = "orange";
ctx.strokeRect(20, 20, 180, 80);

ctx.strokeStyle = "yellow";
ctx.strokeRect(30, 30, 160, 60);
```

```
ctx.strokeStyle = "green";
ctx.strokeRect(40, 40, 140, 40);

ctx.strokeStyle = "blue";
ctx.strokeRect(50, 50, 120, 20);
```

Listing 9-4: Drawing more rectangles

This code draws a series of nested rectangles, each offset by 10 pixels from the previous one and each 20 pixels smaller than the previous one. Before we draw each successive rectangle, we change the color of the outline by updating the strokeStyle property.

Refresh *index.html*, and you should see something like the image in Figure 9-3.

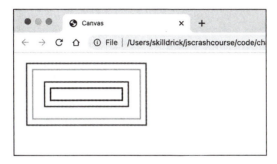

Figure 9-3: Concentric rectangles

Each rectangle is a different color, indicating that the style changes didn't impact anything that had already been drawn.

TRY IT YOURSELF

9-3. Rewrite the code to create the nested rectangles using a loop, so you only need to write the calls to ctx.strokeStyle and ctx.strokeRect once. Hint: think about how to manipulate the looping variable to (a) retrieve a stroke color from an array and (b) set the strokeRect arguments appropriately.

Drawing Other Shapes Using Paths

All other shapes besides rectangles are drawn on the canvas as *paths*. A path is a series of points connected by straight or curved lines, and then either stroked with an outline or filled in with a color. As an example, we'll draw a path between three different points and then fill it in to make a red triangle. Replace the contents of *script.js* with the code in Listing 9-5.

```
let canvas = document.querySelector("#canvas");
let ctx = canvas.getContext("2d");
ctx.fillStyle = "red";
ctx.beginPath();
ctx.moveTo(100, 100);
ctx.lineTo(150, 15);
ctx.lineTo(200, 100);
ctx.lineTo(100, 100);
ctx.fill();
```

Listing 9-5: Drawing a triangle with path methods

Drawing a path takes three steps. First, you declare that you want to start drawing a new path with beginPath. Then, you use various methods to define where the path will be. Finally, you use fill or stroke to fill or stroke the path.

In this case, we use two different methods to define the path: moveTo and lineTo. The moveTo method moves an imaginary pen to a particular point on the canvas defined by x- and y-coordinates, without drawing a line. We use this method to define the starting point of our path, (100, 100), which will be the bottom-left corner of the triangle. The lineTo method does the same as moveTo, but it draws a line as it moves. Thus, lineTo(150, 15) draws a line from (100, 100) to (150, 15), and so on. Finally, we fill the shape with the fill method. When you refresh the page, you should see a red triangle, as shown in Figure 9-4.

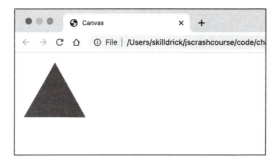

Figure 9-4: Drawing a filled triangle

Drawing circles follows a similar pattern, but uses a method called arc instead of moveTo and lineTo. The arc method draws an *arc*, a section of the circumference of a circle. You can produce any length of arc with the arc method, but here we'll use it to produce an entire circle.

Update *script.js* with the code in Listing 9-6. The first and third steps of the path drawing code are the same, but we replace the second step with the code for drawing a circle rather than a triangle.

```
let canvas = document.querySelector("#canvas");
let ctx = canvas.getContext("2d");
ctx.fillStyle = "red";
ctx.beginPath();
```

```
ctx.arc(150, 100, 50, 0, Math.PI * 2, false);
ctx.fill();
```

Listing 9-6: Drawing a circle with path methods

The arc method takes a whopping six arguments. The first two are the x- and y-coordinates of the center of the circle. In this case we're centering the circle at the coordinates (150, 100). The third argument is the circle's radius in pixels, which we set to 50. The next two arguments give the starting and ending angles of the arc in radians: we provide 0 for the starting angle and Math.PI * 2 for the ending angle to produce a full circle. The final argument specifies whether the arc should be drawn clockwise (false) or counterclockwise (true) from the starting angle to the ending angle. In this case, we pick clockwise, but since we're drawing a full circle, the direction is irrelevant.

NOTE   *Radians are a way of measuring angles. In degrees, a full revolution of a circle goes from 0 to 360. In radians, a revolution goes from 0 to 2π.*

When you refresh the page now, you should see a red circle, as shown in Figure 9-5.

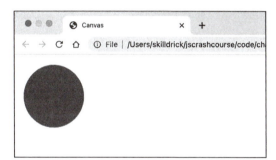

Figure 9-5: Drawing a filled circle

You can use the same technique to draw a stroked circle instead by using the stroke method rather than the fill method. What's more, you can make compound shapes like rounded rectangles by combining calls to the lineTo and arc methods. The Canvas API also allows for drawing more complex curves with the quadraticCurveTo and bezierCurveTo methods. Search the Mozilla Developer Network (MDN) Web Docs (*https://developer.mozilla.org*) for more details about these other methods.

Interacting with the Canvas

The canvas gets a lot more interesting when the user can interact with it. The canvas element itself doesn't have any notion of interactivity built in. However, we can add that interactivity with JavaScript by writing event handlers that listen for certain user actions and trigger Canvas API methods that update the canvas in response.

In this section, we'll build a very basic drawing application using a canvas element with a click handler. The handler will listen for clicks on the canvas, and call a method that draws a circle at the position where the click happened. We'll also create a slider so the user can set the opacity of the circles, and a button to clear the canvas.

First, let's add the necessary HTML elements to create a slider and a button. Make the modifications shown in Listing 9-7 to *index.html*.

```
<!DOCTYPE html>
<html>
  <head>
    <title>Canvas</title>
  </head>
  <body>
    <canvas id="canvas" width="300" height="300"></canvas>
    <div>
      <button id="clear">Clear</button>
      <input id="opacity" type="range" min="0" max="1" value="1" step="0.1">
      <label for="opacity">Opacity</label>
    </div>
    <script src="script.js"></script>
  </body>
</html>
```

Listing 9-7: Adding some additional elements to index.html

Here we add a new div element containing three other HTML elements. The div element is there to group the elements inside it together and to position them below the canvas (without the div they'd appear to the right of the canvas).

The first element inside the div is a button element. It creates a clickable button. Any content between the opening and closing tags will appear as text on the button, so our button will have the text *Clear*. Later, we'll write a JavaScript function that clears any circles on the canvas when the user clicks the button.

Next inside the div is an input element, which is used for taking values from the user. The input element doesn't allow any child elements, so it doesn't need a closing tag. In this case the input is of type range, which means it will display as a slider. This slider will be used to set the opacity of new circles drawn on the canvas. It has several attributes defining its functionality: min defines the minimum value the slider will produce, max defines the maximum value, value defines the initial value the slider is set to, and step is the size of each movement (enabling you to control the number of allowed values). This slider is set to range from 0 to 1 in steps of 0.1, and it starts at 1, which corresponds to full opacity.

The last element in the div is a label element, which applies a label to another element. The for attribute of the label determines which element the label should be applied to; its value has to match the id of another element. In this case, we assign the label to the slider by specifying opacity as the target id. This will cause the slider to be labeled *Opacity*, which is the text content of the label element. Thanks to the label element's for attribute, the browser understands that the label and input elements are related, and certain actions performed on the label will apply to the input. For example, if you hover over the label, the input will display as hovered, and if you click the label, the input will get keyboard focus (in this case, pressing the left or right arrow key will decrease or increase the value of the slider, respectively).

Load *index.html* in your browser, and you should see something similar to Figure 9-6 (the exact appearance of these elements may vary depending on your browser and operating system).

Figure 9-6: The new button and input elements

Now that we have the HTML elements, we can write the JavaScript that will make this application interactive. First, we'll add some general declarations and the code for drawing circles when the user clicks on the canvas. Update *script.js* with the code shown in Listing 9-8.

```
let canvas = document.querySelector("#canvas");
let ctx = canvas.getContext("2d");

let width = canvas.width;
let height = canvas.height;

let opacity = 1;

function drawCircle(x, y) {
❶ ctx.fillStyle = `rgba(0, 255, 0, ${opacity})`;
  ctx.beginPath();
  ctx.arc(x, y, 10, 0, Math.PI * 2, false);
  ctx.fill();
}

canvas.addEventListener("click", e => {
  drawCircle(e.offsetX, e.offsetY);
});
```

Listing 9-8: Drawing a circle on click

First we store the width and height of the canvas element in two variables, width and height. We'll need these variables later, in our function for clearing the canvas. The width and height properties of the JavaScript canvas object come straight from the HTML canvas element's width and height properties (which are both set to 300 in *index.html*). We also initialize the variable opacity to 1.

Next, we create a helper function called drawCircle. This function takes an x- and a y-coordinate and draws a filled circle at that location. We use the same path drawing methods demonstrated in Listing 9-6 to draw the circle. The x and y parameters determine the circle's center, and we set its radius to 10 pixels.

One key difference from the previous drawing examples is that we're setting fillStyle to an *RGBA* color instead of a named color like "red" or "blue" ❶. RGBA is a way of defining colors using four numbers corresponding to the red, green, blue, and alpha channels. The first three indicate the amount of each primary color of light. Their values can range from 0 to 255, and they can be combined to produce any color you might want. Setting all three to 0 produces black, and setting all three to 255 produces white. *Alpha* is another word for opacity, and it defines how opaque or transparent the color should be, ranging from 0 (completely transparent) to 1 (completely opaque).

In the Canvas API, you set RGBA colors using the string "rgba(...)" with the four values in the parentheses, separated by commas. For example, setting fillStyle to the string "rgba(0, 255, 0, 0.9)" would make bright green circles that are slightly transparent. In our case, we wrap the RGBA string in backticks so we can use a placeholder for the alpha value to allow the user to change the opacity with the slider.

Lastly, we add a click event handler to the canvas element using add EventListener. The handler calls the drawCircle function we just created, passing the offsetX and offsetY properties of the click event as the function's parameters. The offsetX and offsetY properties give the distance of the click event from the top-left corner of the clicked element itself (rather than from the top-left corner of the whole browser window), so they're ideal for determining exactly where on the canvas the click happened.

Reload *index.html* in your browser and try clicking on the canvas. Wherever you click, a small green circle should appear, as shown in Figure 9-7.

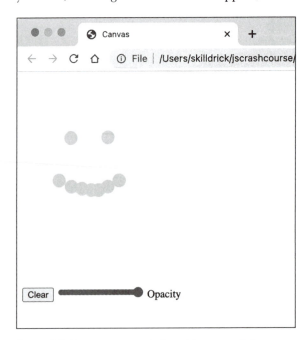

Figure 9-7: Drawing green circles with mouse clicks

To complete the drawing application, we need to wire up the Clear button and the Opacity slider. Add the code in Listing 9-9 to the end of *script.js*.

```
--snip--
document.querySelector("#clear").addEventListener("click", () => {
  ctx.clearRect(0, 0, width, height);
});

document.querySelector("#opacity").addEventListener("change", e => {
  opacity = e.target.value;
});
```

Listing 9-9: Wiring up the Clear and Opacity controls

First we add a `click` event handler to the Clear button. This calls a Canvas API method called `clearRect`, which clears a rectangular section of the canvas. Just like when drawing a rectangle, you define the rectangle to be cleared using the x- and y-coordinates of its top-left corner, followed by its width and height. Here we use (`0, 0, width, height`) to specify that we want to clear a rectangle that starts at the top-left corner of the canvas and is as wide and high as the canvas itself. Thus, `ctx.clearRect(0, 0, width, height);` clears the entire canvas.

Next, we add a `change` event handler to the Opacity slider. The `change` event is triggered on `input` elements when their value changes, so this handler will be called whenever the slider is set to a new position. We get the `input` element with `e.target` and get the element's current value with `.value`. Then we update the `opacity` variable with this value. Because the `drawCircle` function uses the value of `opacity` as the alpha component of the RGBA color, any new circles will use the latest value set with the Opacity slider.

Now when you reload *index.html* in your browser, you should have a fully functioning (if basic) drawing application! You can use the Opacity slider to change the opacity of new circles and the Clear button to clear the canvas and start drawing again. Try drawing overlapping circles with the Opacity slider set halfway to see how they overlay.

TRY IT YOURSELF

9-4. Add sliders for controlling the R, G, and B components of the color. These will need to range from 0 to 255. You could also add a Radius slider that controls the radius of the circle drawn in the `drawCircle` function.

9-5. Make a new function called `drawSquare` that draws a square centered on a point, and call that function from the `click` handler instead of `drawCircle`.

Animating the Canvas

As noted at the beginning of this chapter, you can animate the canvas by drawing on it and updating the image multiple times per second. In this section, we'll code a very simple animation to show the basics of how this works.

Animating the canvas generally follows this basic pattern:

1. Update state
2. Clear canvas
3. Draw image
4. Wait a short time
5. Repeat

State here means some variable(s) storing information about the current frame of the animation. This could be the current location of an object in motion, the direction the object is moving in, and so on. In our example, the state will be the x- and y-coordinates of a circle. When it's time to update the state, we'll increment the x- and y-coordinates by 1, meaning that the circle's position will gradually move diagonally down and to the right. Drawing the image will entail drawing a small circle centered at the updated x- and y-coordinates. We clear the canvas before drawing the circle to ensure that the image from the previous cycle is removed. We'll tackle the last two steps (waiting and repeating) by using the setInterval function to call our code every 100 ms, or 10 times a second.

We can continue to work with the same HTML and JavaScript files. The only change to make to *index.html* is to remove the div and its nested elements that we added in Listing 9-7, as they're not needed anymore. After removing those elements, update *script.js* based on the code in Listing 9-10.

```
let canvas = document.querySelector("#canvas");
let ctx = canvas.getContext("2d");

let width = canvas.width;
let height = canvas.height;

let x = 0;
let y = 0;

function drawCircle(x, y) {
  ctx.fillStyle = "rgb(0, 128, 255)";
  ctx.beginPath();
  ctx.arc(x, y, 10, 0, Math.PI * 2, false);
  ctx.fill();
}

function update() {
  x += 1;
  y += 1;
}
```

```
function draw() {
  ctx.clearRect(0, 0, width, height);
  drawCircle(x, y);
}

setInterval(() => {
  update();
  draw();
}, 100);
```

Listing 9-10: Creating an animation

We create two new variables, x and y, representing the location of the circle that we'll animate. These variables store the current state of the animation and will be updated at regular intervals. The drawCircle function itself is mostly unchanged, although the fillStyle is different. Now that we're not setting an opacity, we can use the simpler rgb(...)-format string for setting the red, green, and blue values. With "rgb(...)", the opacity of the color is always 100 percent.

After drawCircle we declare the update function, where we update the x and y variables, incrementing each by 1. Next we declare the draw function, which clears the canvas and then calls drawCircle to draw a circle at the current x- and y-coordinates. Finally, we call setInterval to orchestrate the animation. You may recall from Chapter 5 that setInterval takes a function and a time interval in milliseconds, and repeatedly calls that function once every time interval. Here we're calling an anonymous function every 100 ms. The anonymous function itself calls update and draw to create each frame of the animation.

Reload *index.html* in your browser, and you should see a small circle gradually move across the canvas from the top-left to the bottom-right corner. Even after the circle leaves the canvas, the x- and y-coordinates will keep increasing, but the canvas ignores anything drawn outside of its bounds.

TRY IT YOURSELF

9-6. Update the animation so the circle reappears at the top-left corner when it reaches the bottom-right corner. There are a few ways to do this. One option is to use the remainder operator (%), which evenly divides the first operand by the second and returns the remainder. For example, 325 % 100 gives 25. By passing x % width and y % height to the drawCircle function, you can ensure that the circle will always be drawn within the canvas. You can also use the %= operator to keep the x and y values within bounds in the update function, using x %= width and y %= height after incrementing their values. Try out both options.

(continued)

9-7. How could you make the circle start out at the left side of the canvas, move to the right, then move back, and so on? Hint: you'll need to declare another state variable to keep track of the direction, for example, `let forwards = true`, and use that variable to decide whether to increment or decrement x. You'll then need to update the new variable to be `false` when the x value gets past a certain point.

9-8. Try changing the time interval in the `setInterval` function. For example, what does the animation look like with an interval of 1,000 ms, or 10 ms, or 1 ms? Note that at a certain point, the browser won't be able to update as fast as you're asking it to, so it's unlikely that a 1 ms interval will run 10 times faster than a 10 ms interval.

Summary

In this chapter, you learned the basics of drawing on the canvas element, as well as some techniques for creating interactive applications and animations using the canvas. We'll build on some of these techniques later in this book as we learn how to make a canvas-based game.

PART III

PROJECTS

You've learned the basics of JavaScript and some powerful techniques for using JavaScript within web pages to create interactive applications. Now it's time to put these techniques to use by building some real projects!

This part of the book features three substantial projects that will help you practice what you've learned, show you how to develop and organize more sophisticated programs, and give you a taste of some of the many exciting things JavaScript can do. There are no dependencies between the projects, so you can work on them in any order you wish. Here's a little preview of each:

Project 1: Creating a Game

In this project, you'll extend your knowledge of data structures, conditionals, functions, and the Canvas API by making your own version of the classic game *Pong*. You'll develop two implementations of the game: one with standalone functions (Chapter 10) and one that uses classes and object-oriented design principles (Chapter 11). This will illustrate different ways of organizing your code.

Project 2: Making Music

This project introduces basic audio programming and sound synthesis techniques (Chapter 12), then harnesses those techniques to write a song using JavaScript (Chapter 13). You'll learn about the Web Audio

API and the Tone.js library, which simplifies the process of generating sounds. This will give you practice incorporating third-party JavaScript libraries into your applications.

Project 3: Visualizing Data

This project guides you through the process of developing interactive data visualizations with the popular D3 JavaScript library. You'll explore how to draw with Scalable Vector Graphics (SVG) and use D3 to organize SVG shapes into bar charts (Chapter 14). Then you'll build a dynamic visualization using data retrieved over the internet through the GitHub Search API (Chapter 15). Incorporating API requests into your applications is a very common programming task, so the project will prepare you to write code that interfaces with real-world data.

You can find the complete downloadable code for all of these projects, along with solutions to the Try It Yourself exercises, at *https://codepen.io/collection/ZMjYLO*.

PROJECT 1

CREATING A GAME

10

PONG

In this first project, you'll use JavaScript to re-create one of the first arcade video games: the classic *Pong* from Atari. *Pong* is a simple game, but it will teach you some important aspects of game design: a game loop, player input, collision detection, and score keeping. We'll even use some basic artificial intelligence to program the computer opponent.

The Game

Pong was developed in 1972 and was released that year as a hugely successful arcade machine. It's a very basic game, like table tennis, consisting of a ball and two paddles positioned on the left and right sides of the screen, which the players can move up and down. If the ball hits the top or bottom edge of the screen, it bounces off, but if it hits the left or right edge the player on the opposite side scores a point. The ball bounces off the paddles normally, unless it hits near the top or bottom edge of the paddle, in which case the angle of return changes.

In this chapter we'll make our own version of *Pong*, which we'll call *Tennjs* (like *Tennis* but with *JS*, get it?). In our game, the left paddle will be controlled by the computer and the right paddle will be controlled by a human player. In the original game, the paddles were controlled with rotating dial controllers, but in our version we'll use the mouse. The computer, rather than trying to anticipate where the ball will bounce, will just attempt to always match the vertical position of the ball. In order to give the human player a chance, we'll set an upper limit on how fast the computer can move the paddle.

Setup

We'll begin by setting up the project's file structure and creating a canvas for displaying the game. As usual, the project will require an HTML file and a JavaScript file. We'll start with the HTML file. Create a directory called *tennjs* and a file in that directory called *index.html*. Then enter the content shown in Listing 10-1.

```
<!DOCTYPE html>
<html>
  <head>
    <title>Tennjs</title>
  </head>
  <body>
    <canvas id="canvas" width="300" height="300"></canvas>
    <script src="script.js"></script>
  </body>
</html>
```

Listing 10-1: The index.html *file for our game*

This is almost exactly the same as the HTML file we created in Chapter 9, so there should be no surprises. The body element includes a canvas element, where we'll draw the game, and a script element referencing the file *script.js*, where our game code will live.

Next, we'll write some JavaScript to set up the canvas. Create the file *script.js*, and enter the code shown in Listing 10-2.

```
let canvas = document.querySelector("#canvas");
let ctx = canvas.getContext("2d");
let width = canvas.width;
let height = canvas.height;

ctx.fillStyle = "black";
ctx.fillRect(0, 0, width, height);
```

Listing 10-2: Setting up the canvas in script.js

This code should also be familiar. We first get a reference to the canvas with document.querySelector and get the canvas's drawing context. Then we save the width and height of the canvas to variables called width and height for easy access within the code. Finally, we set the fill style to black and draw a black square the size of the canvas. This way the canvas appears to have a black background.

Open *index.html* in your browser, and you should see something like Figure 10-1.

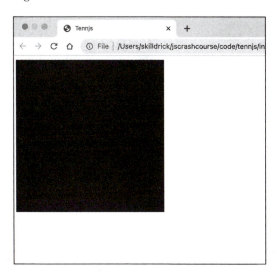

Figure 10-1: Our black square

We now have a blank, black canvas where we can create our game.

The Ball

Next, we'll draw the ball. Add the code in Listing 10-3 to the end of *script.js*.

```
--snip--
ctx.fillStyle = "black";
ctx.fillRect(0, 0, width, height);

const BALL_SIZE = 5;
❶ let ballPosition = { x: 20, y: 30 };

ctx.fillStyle = "white";
ctx.fillRect(ballPosition.x, ballPosition.y, BALL_SIZE, BALL_SIZE);
```

Listing 10-3: Drawing the ball

This code uses the fillRect method to draw the ball as a small white square near the top-left corner of the canvas. As in the original *Pong* game, the ball is a square rather than a circle. This gives the game a retro feel, and it will also simplify the task of detecting when the ball has collided with the walls or with a paddle. The size of the ball is stored in a constant called BALL_SIZE. We use the "true constant" all-caps style for the identifier name because the ball size won't change during the course of the program. We could just use the value 5 instead of the constant BALL_SIZE when we call the fillRect method to draw the ball, but we're going to end up needing to refer to the ball's size a lot more throughout the program. Giving the size a name will make it much easier to understand code that needs to know the size of the ball. The other good thing about this approach is that if we change our mind later and decide the ball should be bigger or smaller, we have to update the code in only place: the declaration of the BALL_SIZE constant.

We keep track of the ball's position with an object containing its x- and y-coordinates, created using an object literal ❶. In Chapter 9 we used separate variables for the x- and y-coordinates of the circle that was being drawn, but it's a bit tidier to store the two variables together as one object, especially since this program is going to be longer and more complex.

Refresh *index.html* and you should see the white ball sitting in the top-left corner of the canvas, as shown in Figure 10-2.

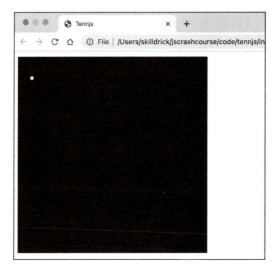

Figure 10-2: The ball

The ball is stationary for now, but soon enough we'll write code to make it move.

Refactoring

Next we're going to do a simple refactor. *Refactoring* is a software development term for modifying some code without changing its behavior, usually to make the code easier to understand or update. As the code for a project grows more complex, refactoring can help keep it organized.

In this case, I know that we're going to want to draw to the canvas multiple times, not just once. In fact, we'll eventually want to redraw the canvas once every 30 ms to give our game the appearance of motion. To make that easier to accomplish, we'll refactor so all the current drawing code becomes part of a function called draw. That way we can simply call the draw function anytime we want to redraw the canvas.

Update *script.js* with the changes shown in Listing 10-4.

```
let canvas = document.querySelector("#canvas");
let ctx = canvas.getContext("2d");
let width = canvas.width;
let height = canvas.height;

const BALL_SIZE = 5;
let ballPosition = { x: 20, y: 30 };

❶ function draw() {
    ctx.fillStyle = "black";
    ctx.fillRect(0, 0, width, height);

    ctx.fillStyle = "white";
    ctx.fillRect(ballPosition.x, ballPosition.y, BALL_SIZE, BALL_SIZE);
}

❷ draw();
```

Listing 10-4: Refactoring the drawing code

The only change here is to group all the drawing code into a single function called draw ❶, which we then immediately call ❷. Because it's a refactoring, nothing actually changes in the behavior of the program. You can refresh *index.html* to confirm that everything still looks as before.

The Game Loop

Almost all games contain a *game loop* that orchestrates everything that has to happen for each frame of the game. Game loops are similar to animation loops, like the one we looked at in Chapter 9, but with some additional logic. Here's the general shape of the game loop in most games:

1. Clear canvas
2. Draw image
3. Get player input
4. Update state
5. Check collisions
6. Wait a short time
7. Repeat

Getting and acting on input from a player (or players) is the main thing that distinguishes a game from an animation. *Collision detection* is another important aspect of most games: checking for when two objects in the game meet and responding accordingly. Collision detection is what stops you from walking through walls or driving through another car—and in this case, it's what will make the ball bounce off the walls and paddles. Apart from the player input and collision detection elements, the steps in the game loop are more or less the same as in an animation loop: we clear the canvas, draw the image, update the state of the game to move objects to their new positions, pause, and repeat.

Rather than trying to write the whole game loop at once, we'll build it up gradually. Update *script.js* with the content in Listing 10-5, which will be the beginnings of the game loop in our game. This code moves the ball (that is, updates the ball's state), redraws the canvas, pauses, and repeats.

```
--snip--
const BALL_SIZE = 5;
let ballPosition = { x: 20, y: 30 };

❶ let xSpeed = 4;
   let ySpeed = 2;

   function draw() {
     ctx.fillStyle = "black";
     ctx.fillRect(0, 0, width, height);

     ctx.fillStyle = "white";
     ctx.fillRect(ballPosition.x, ballPosition.y, BALL_SIZE, BALL_SIZE);
   }

❷ function update() {
     ballPosition.x += xSpeed;
     ballPosition.y += ySpeed;
   }

❸ function gameLoop() {
     draw();
     update();

     // Call this function again after a timeout
     setTimeout(gameLoop, 30);
   }

❹ gameLoop();
```

Listing 10-5: The game loop

The first change here is to initialize two new variables ❶, xSpeed and ySpeed. We'll use these to control the horizontal and vertical speed of the ball. The new update function ❷ uses these two variables to update the position of the ball. For every frame, the ball will move xSpeed pixels along the x-axis and ySpeed pixels along the y-axis. The two variables start out at 4 and 2, so every frame the ball will move 4 pixels to the right and 2 pixels down.

The gameLoop function ❸ calls the draw function followed by the update function. Then it calls setTimeout(gameLoop, 30), which will call the gameLoop function again after 30 ms. This is almost exactly the same as the setInterval technique we used in Chapter 9. You may recall that setTimeout calls its function only once after the timeout, while setInterval calls its function repeatedly. We're using setTimeout here so we have more control over whether or not to keep looping; later on we'll add some conditional logic to either call setTimeout or end the game.

Notice the line above the setTimeout call beginning with two slashes (//). This is an example of a *comment*, a note for yourself (or other people reading your code) embedded in the program file. When a JavaScript program executes, any text on a line following a // is ignored (anything on the line before the // is still evaluated as JavaScript code). Thus, you can use comments like this to explain how the code works, highlight important features, or make note of something you still need to do, without affecting the functionality of the program.

At the end of the script, we call the gameLoop function ❹ to set the game in motion. Since gameLoop currently ends with setTimeout, the result is that gameLoop will be repeatedly called once every 30 ms. Reload your page and you should see the ball move down and to the right, much like the animation from Chapter 9.

Bouncing

In the previous section you got the ball moving, but it just flew off the edge of the canvas. Next you'll learn how to make it bounce off the edge of the canvas at the appropriate angle—our first collision detection code. Update *script.js* with the code in Listing 10-6, which adds a checkCollision function to our game.

```
--snip--
function update() {
  ballPosition.x += xSpeed;
  ballPosition.y += ySpeed;
}

function checkCollision() {
❶ let ball = {
    left: ballPosition.x,
    right: ballPosition.x + BALL_SIZE,
    top: ballPosition.y,
    bottom: ballPosition.y + BALL_SIZE
  }

❷ if (ball.left < 0 || ball.right > width) {
    xSpeed = -xSpeed;
  }
❸ if (ball.top < 0 || ball.bottom > height) {
    ySpeed = -ySpeed;
  }
}

function gameLoop() {
  draw();
  update();
❹ checkCollision();
```

```
  // Call this function again after a timeout
  setTimeout(gameLoop, 30);
}

gameLoop();
```

Listing 10-6: Wall collision detection

The new function, `checkCollision`, checks to see if the ball has collided with one of the four walls of the canvas. If it has, it updates `xSpeed` or `ySpeed` as appropriate to make the ball bounce off the wall. First, we calculate values for the edges of the ball. We need to know where the left, right, top, and bottom edges are to determine if these edges have exceeded the bounds of the playing area. We group the values in an object called `ball` ❶ that has `left`, `right`, `top`, and `bottom` properties. Identifying the left and top ball edges is easy: they're `ballPosition.x` and `ballPosition.y`, respectively. To get the right and bottom edges, we add `BALL_SIZE` to `ballPosition.x` and `ballPosition.y`. This is one of those cases noted earlier where having access to the ball's size as a constant is helpful.

Next, we perform the actual collision detection. If the left edge of the ball is less than 0 or the right edge of the ball is greater than the width of the canvas ❷, we know that the ball has hit the left or right wall. In both cases, the math is the same: the new value of `xSpeed` should be the negative of the current value (that is, the value is *negated*). For example, the first time the ball hits the right edge, `xSpeed` will go from 4 to -4. Meanwhile, `ySpeed` remains unchanged. As a result, the ball continues moving down the screen at the same rate, but now it's moving to the left instead of to the right.

The same kind of check happens for the top of the ball colliding with the top wall or the bottom of the ball colliding with the bottom wall ❸. In either of these cases, we negate `ySpeed`, changing it from 2 to -2 when the ball hits the top edge, or from -2 to 2 when the ball hits the bottom edge.

The only other change to the code is to add a call to `checkCollision` to the list of things that happen in the `gameLoop` function ❹. Now when you refresh *index.html*, you should see the ball continuously bounce around the play area.

If you've been paying attention, you might have noticed that the ball isn't supposed to bounce off the left and right walls. Once we have moving paddles, we'll modify the collision detection code to only bounce off the paddles or the top and bottom walls, and to score a point for a side wall collision.

The Paddles

Our next task is to draw the two paddles. To do that we'll first introduce some new constants that establish the paddle dimensions and their horizontal position relative to the sides of the canvas, as well as some variables defining their vertical positions. (The paddles can only move up and down, not from side to side, so only their vertical positions need to be variables.) Update *script.js* with the changes in Listing 10-7.

```
--snip--
let xSpeed = 4;
let ySpeed = 2;

const PADDLE_WIDTH = 5;
const PADDLE_HEIGHT = 20;
const PADDLE_OFFSET = 10;

let leftPaddleTop = 10;
let rightPaddleTop = 30;

function draw() {
--snip--
```

Listing 10-7: Defining the paddles

First we set up the constants that define the paddles. PADDLE_WIDTH and PADDLE_HEIGHT define both paddles to be 5 pixels wide and 20 pixels tall. PADDLE_OFFSET refers to the distance of the paddle from the left or right edge of the playing area.

The variables leftPaddleTop and rightPaddleTop define the current vertical position of the top of each paddle. Eventually, leftPaddleTop will be controlled by the computer through a function we'll write to follow the ball, and rightPaddleTop will be updated when the player moves the mouse. For now, we're simply setting these values to 10 and 30, respectively.

Next, we update the draw function to display the paddles using the information we just defined. I've also added comments to the code to clarify what's happening at each step of the draw function. Modify the code as shown in Listing 10-8.

```
--snip--
function draw() {
  // Fill the canvas with black
  ctx.fillStyle = "black";
  ctx.fillRect(0, 0, width, height);

  // Everything else will be white
  ctx.fillStyle = "white";

  // Draw the ball
  ctx.fillRect(ballPosition.x, ballPosition.y, BALL_SIZE, BALL_SIZE);

  // Draw the paddles
❶ ctx.fillRect(
    PADDLE_OFFSET,
    leftPaddleTop,
    PADDLE_WIDTH,
    PADDLE_HEIGHT
  );
❷ ctx.fillRect(
    width - PADDLE_WIDTH - PADDLE_OFFSET,
    rightPaddleTop,
```

```
        PADDLE_WIDTH,
        PADDLE_HEIGHT
    );
}

function update() {
--snip--
```

Listing 10-8: Drawing the paddles

In addition to some extra comments to help document the program, the
new code features two calls to `fillRect`, one for drawing the left paddle ❶
and one for the right ❷. I've split the arguments over multiple lines because
the identifiers are so long. Remember that the parameters to `fillRect` are
`x`, `y`, `width`, and `height`, where `x` and `y` are the coordinates of the top-left corner
of the rectangle. The x-coordinate of the left paddle is `PADDLE_OFFSET` because
we're using that to mean the paddle's distance from the left edge of the canvas, while the y-coordinate of the left paddle is just `leftPaddleTop`. The `width`
and `height` arguments are the `PADDLE_WIDTH` and `PADDLE_HEIGHT` constants.

The right paddle is a bit more complicated to draw: to get the x-coordinate
of the paddle's top-left corner, we need to take the width of the canvas and
subtract the width of the paddle and the offset of the paddle from the right
edge. Given that the width of the canvas is 500, and the paddle width and
offset are both 10, that means the x-coordinate of the right paddle is 480.

When you refresh *index.html*, you should see the two paddles in addition
to the bouncing ball, as shown in Figure 10-3.

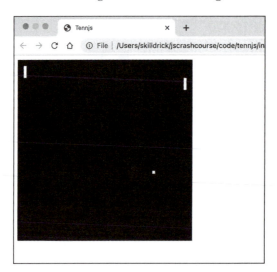

Figure 10-3: The paddles and ball

Note that the ball currently passes straight through the paddles, because
we haven't set up collision detection for the paddles yet. We'll get to that later
in this section.

Moving the Paddles with Player Input

The paddles are drawn at the vertical positions given by the variables leftPaddleTop and rightPaddleTop, so to make the paddles move up and down, we just have to update the values of these variables. Right now we're concerned only with the right paddle, which will be controlled by the human player.

To let the player control the right paddle, we'll add an event handler to *script.js* that listens for mousemove events. Listing 10-9 shows how it's done.

```
--snip--
let leftPaddleTop = 10;
let rightPaddleTop = 30;

document.addEventListener("mousemove", e => {
  rightPaddleTop = e.y - canvas.offsetTop;
});

function draw() {
--snip--
```

Listing 10-9: Adding an event handler to move the right paddle

This code follows the same pattern for event handling that you first saw in Chapter 8. We use document.addEventListener to check for mouse movements. When one is detected, the event handler function updates the value of rightPaddleTop based on the y-coordinate of the mousemove event (e.y). The y-coordinate is relative to the top of the page, not the top of the canvas, so we subtract canvas.offsetTop (the distance from the top of the canvas to the top of the page) from the y-coordinate. This way the assigned rightPaddleTop value will be based on the distance of the mouse from the top of the canvas, and the paddle will follow the mouse accurately.

Refresh *index.html*, and you should see the right paddle move vertically as the mouse moves up and down. Figure 10-4 shows how it should look.

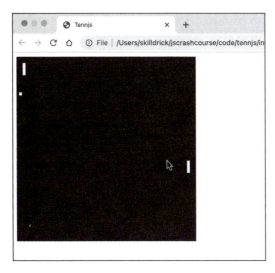

Figure 10-4: The right paddle moving with the mouse

Our game has now officially become interactive! The player has full control of the position of the right paddle.

Detecting Paddle Collisions

The next step is to add collision detection for the paddles. We need to know if the ball has hit a paddle and, if so, make the ball bounce off the paddle appropriately. This requires a lot of code, so I'll break it up over a few listings.

The first thing we have to do is create objects defining the four edges of the two paddles, as we did for the ball in Listing 10-6. These changes are shown in Listing 10-10.

```
--snip--
function checkCollision() {
  let ball = {
    left: ballPosition.x,
    right: ballPosition.x + BALL_SIZE,
    top: ballPosition.y,
    bottom: ballPosition.y + BALL_SIZE
  }

  let leftPaddle = {
    left: PADDLE_OFFSET,
    right: PADDLE_OFFSET + PADDLE_WIDTH,
    top: leftPaddleTop,
    bottom: leftPaddleTop + PADDLE_HEIGHT
  };

  let rightPaddle = {
    left: width - PADDLE_WIDTH - PADDLE_OFFSET,
    right: width - PADDLE_OFFSET,
    top: rightPaddleTop,
    bottom: rightPaddleTop + PADDLE_HEIGHT
  };

  if (ball.left < 0 || ball.right > width) {
--snip--
```

Listing 10-10: Defining the edges of the paddles

The leftPaddle and rightPaddle objects contain the edges of their respective paddles as four properties, left, right, top, and bottom. As in Listing 10-8, determining where the edges of the right paddle are requires a bit more math because we have to take into account the width of the canvas, the offset of the paddle, and the width of the paddle.

Next we need a function, which we'll call checkPaddleCollision, that takes the ball object and one of the paddle objects and returns true if the ball is intersecting with that paddle. The function definition is shown in Listing 10-11.

```
--snip--
function update() {
  ballPosition.x += xSpeed;
  ballPosition.y += ySpeed;
}

function checkPaddleCollision(ball, paddle) {
  // Check if the paddle and ball overlap vertically and horizontally
  return (
    ball.left   < paddle.right &&
    ball.right  > paddle.left &&
    ball.top    < paddle.bottom &&
    ball.bottom > paddle.top
  );
}

function checkCollision() {
--snip--
```

Listing 10-11: The checkPaddleCollision *function*

This function will be called with the ball and each of the paddle objects defined earlier. It uses a long Boolean expression made up of four subexpressions that are all &&'d together, so it returns true only if all four subexpressions are true. (I added spacing to each subexpression so the operands line up vertically; this is just to make the code easier to read.) In English, the subexpressions say:

1. The left edge of the ball must be to the left of the right edge of the paddle.
2. The right edge of the ball must be to the right of the left edge of the paddle.
3. The top edge of the ball must be above the bottom edge of the paddle.
4. The bottom edge of the ball must be below the top edge of the paddle.

If the first two conditions are true, the ball is intersecting horizontally, and if the last two conditions are true, the ball is intersecting vertically. The ball is truly intersecting with the paddle only if all four conditions are true. To illustrate this, see Figure 10-5.

The figure shows four possible scenarios we might check. In all the scenarios, the paddle has the following bounds: { left: 10, right: 15, top: 5, bottom: 25 }.

In Figure 10-5(a), ball has the bounds { left: 20, right: 25, top: 30, bottom: 35 }. In this case, ball.left < paddle.right is false (the left side of the ball is not to the left of the right side of the paddle), but ball.right > paddle.left is true. Likewise, ball.top < paddle.bottom is false and ball.bottom > paddle.top is true. The ball is neither vertically nor horizontally intersecting with the paddle.

In Figure 10-5(b), ball has the bounds { left: 20, right: 25, top: 22, bottom: 27 }. This time, ball.top < paddle.bottom and ball.bottom > paddle.top are both true, which means that the ball is vertically intersecting with the paddle, but not horizontally intersecting.

In Figure 10-5(c), ball has the bounds { left: 13, right: 18, top: 30, bottom: 35 }. In this case, the ball is horizontally intersecting with the paddle, but not vertically intersecting.

Finally, in Figure 10-5(d), ball has the bounds { left: 13, right: 18, top: 22, bottom: 27 }. Now the ball is both horizontally and vertically intersecting with the paddle. All four subexpressions are true, so check PaddleCollision returns true.

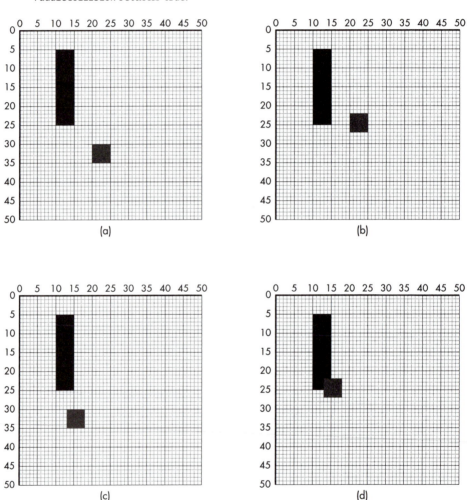

Figure 10-5: Collision detection conditions

Now it's time to actually call the checkPaddleCollision function from within the checkCollision function, once for each paddle, and handle the case where the function returns true. You can find this code in Listing 10-12.

```
--snip--
  let rightPaddle = {
    left: width - PADDLE_WIDTH - PADDLE_OFFSET,
    right: width - PADDLE_OFFSET,
    top: rightPaddleTop,
    bottom: rightPaddleTop + PADDLE_HEIGHT
  };

  if (checkPaddleCollision(ball, leftPaddle)) {
    // Left paddle collision happened
❶ xSpeed = Math.abs(xSpeed);
  }

  if (checkPaddleCollision(ball, rightPaddle)) {
    // Right paddle collision happened
❷ xSpeed = -Math.abs(xSpeed);
  }

  if (ball.left < 0 || ball.right > width) {
    xSpeed = -xSpeed;
  }
  if (ball.top < 0 || ball.bottom > height) {
    ySpeed = -ySpeed;
  }
}
--snip--
```

Listing 10-12: Checking for paddle collisions

Remember that checkPaddleCollision takes an object representing the ball and an object representing a paddle and returns true if the two are intersecting. If checkPaddleCollision(ball, leftPaddle) returns true, we set xSpeed to Math.abs(xSpeed) ❶, which has the effect of setting it to 4 because in our game xSpeed is only ever 4 (when moving to the right) or -4 (when moving to the left).

You might be wondering why we didn't just negate xSpeed, as we did with the vertical wall collision code earlier. Using the absolute value is a little trick to avoid multiple collisions that could send the ball bouncing back and forth "inside" the paddle. It's possible that if the ball hits at just the right point at the end of the paddle it will get bounced back, but the next frame will also result in a collision with the same paddle. If we were negating the xSpeed, then it would just keep bouncing. By forcing the updated xSpeed to be positive, we can ensure that a collision with the left paddle will always result in the ball bouncing to the right.

Following this, we do the same thing with the right paddle. In this case, if there's a collision we update xSpeed to -Math.abs(xSpeed) ❷, which in effect is -4, meaning that the ball will bounce to the left.

Refresh *index.html* again, and try to move the right paddle with your mouse so the ball hits it. You should now have ball-paddle bounces happening! At this point the ball can still safely bounce off the side walls, but we'll fix that soon.

Bouncing Near the Paddle Ends

I mentioned at the beginning of this chapter that in *Pong* you can change
the angle of the ball's bounce by hitting it near the top or bottom of the
paddle. We'll implement that functionality now. First we'll add a new function called adjustAngle immediately before checkCollision. It checks if the
ball is near the top or bottom of the paddle, and updates ySpeed if it is. See
Listing 10-13 for the code.

```
--snip--
function adjustAngle(distanceFromTop, distanceFromBottom) {
❶ if (distanceFromTop < 0) {
    // If ball hit near top of paddle, reduce ySpeed
    ySpeed -= 0.5;
❷ } else if (distanceFromBottom < 0) {
    // If ball hit near bottom of paddle, increase ySpeed
    ySpeed += 0.5;
  }
}

function checkCollision() {
--snip--
```

Listing 10-13: Adjusting the bounce angle

The adjustAngle function has two parameters, distanceFromTop and
distanceFromBottom. These represent the distance from the top of the ball to
the top of the paddle and from the bottom of the paddle to the bottom
of the ball, respectively. The function first checks if distanceFromTop is less
than 0 ❶. If so, that means the top edge of the ball is above the top edge
of the paddle at collision time, which is how we'll define being near the
top of the paddle. In this case, we subtract 0.5 from ySpeed. If the ball is moving down the screen when it hits near the top of the paddle, then ySpeed is
positive, so subtracting 0.5 reduces the vertical speed. For example, at the
start of the game, ySpeed is 2. If you align the paddle so the ball hits the top,
ySpeed will become 1.5 after the bounce, effectively reducing the angle of
bounce. However, if the ball is moving up the screen, then ySpeed is negative. In this case, subtracting 0.5 after a hit near the top of the paddle will
increase the ball's vertical speed. For example, a ySpeed of -2 will become -2.5.

If the ball hits near the bottom of the paddle ❷, the opposite happens.
In this case, we add 0.5 to ySpeed, increasing the vertical speed if the ball is
moving down the screen or decreasing the speed if the ball is moving up
the screen.

Next, we need to update the checkCollision function to call the new
adjustAngle function as part of the collision detection logic for the two paddles. Listing 10-14 shows the changes.

```
--snip--
  let rightPaddle = {
    left: width - PADDLE_WIDTH - PADDLE_OFFSET,
    right: width - PADDLE_OFFSET,
```

```
    top: rightPaddleTop,
    bottom: rightPaddleTop + PADDLE_HEIGHT
};

if (checkPaddleCollision(ball, leftPaddle)) {
  // Left paddle collision happened
  let distanceFromTop = ball.top - leftPaddle.top;
  let distanceFromBottom = leftPaddle.bottom - ball.bottom;
  adjustAngle(distanceFromTop, distanceFromBottom);
  xSpeed = Math.abs(xSpeed);
}

if (checkPaddleCollision(ball, rightPaddle)) {
  // Right paddle collision happened
  let distanceFromTop = ball.top - rightPaddle.top;
  let distanceFromBottom = rightPaddle.bottom - ball.bottom;
  adjustAngle(distanceFromTop, distanceFromBottom);
  xSpeed = -Math.abs(xSpeed);
}
--snip--
```

Listing 10-14: Calling `adjustAngle`

Within the `if` statement for each paddle, we declare `distanceFromTop` and `distanceFromBottom`, the arguments needed for the `adjustAngle` function. Then we call `adjustAngle` before updating `xSpeed` as before.

Now try out the game and see if you can hit the ball near the edge of the paddle!

TRY IT YOURSELF

10-1. Hitting the edge of the paddle can be tricky. To make it easier, try reducing the speed of the game by increasing the `setTimeout` interval—for example, from 30 ms to 60 ms. Another option is to expand what counts as "near the top" and "near the bottom" of the paddle. Instead of `distanceFromTop < 0` you could use `distanceFromTop < 5`, for example, which would check that the top of the ball is less than 5 pixels below the top of the paddle.

10-2. It isn't always obvious when a top or bottom hit has occurred, since the change to `ySpeed` is pretty small. To get some more feedback about what's actually happening when the ball hits the paddle, you can add logging to the `adjustAngle` function. For example, you could add the following line to the start of the function:

```
console.log(`top: ${distanceFromTop}, bottom: ${distanceFromBottom}`);
```

This way the console will show the ball's distance from the top and bottom of the paddle every time the ball hits a paddle. Another thing

(continued)

that might help is adding logging to the two conditionals within the adjustAngle function, like so:

```
if (distanceFromTop < 0) {
  // If ball hit near top of paddle, reduce ySpeed
  console.log("Top hit!");
  ySpeed -= 0.5;
} else if (distanceFromBottom < 0) {
  // If ball hit near bottom of paddle, increase ySpeed
  console.log("Bottom hit!");
  ySpeed += 0.5;
}
```

Now you'll get additional feedback indicating that the ball has hit the top or bottom of the paddle and that ySpeed is being adjusted.

Don't get carried away with logging, though. You should be careful about where you add logging in games, as it can quickly get very noisy and hard to read, and can also lead to performance problems. If you add logging in the checkCollision function, for example, then every frame of the game will produce a new log line! It's best to limit the logging to certain conditions that won't be true all the time: for example, logging only when a collision occurs, as we did here.

Scoring Points

Games are usually more fun when you can win or lose. In *Pong*, you score a point if you hit the wall behind the opposing player's paddle. When this happens, the ball gets reset to its starting position and speed for the next round of play. We'll deal with that part in this section too, but first, to keep track of the scores, we'll need to create some new variables. Update *script.js* with the code in Listing 10-15.

```
--snip--
let leftPaddleTop = 10;
let rightPaddleTop = 30;

let leftScore = 0;
let rightScore = 0;

document.addEventListener("mousemove", e => {
  rightPaddleTop = e.y - canvas.offsetTop;
});
--snip--
```

Listing 10-15: Variables to keep track of the scores

Here we declare two new variables, leftScore and rightScore, and set them both to 0. Later we'll add logic to increment these variables when points are scored.

Next, we'll add code for displaying the scores to the end of the draw function. Update the function as shown in Listing 10-16.

```
--snip--
  ctx.fillRect(
    width - PADDLE_WIDTH - PADDLE_OFFSET,
    rightPaddleTop,
    PADDLE_WIDTH,
    PADDLE_HEIGHT
  );

  // Draw scores
  ctx.font = "30px monospace";
  ctx.textAlign = "left";
  ctx.fillText(leftScore.toString(), 50, 50);
  ctx.textAlign = "right";
  ctx.fillText(rightScore.toString(), width - 50, 50);
}

function update() {
--snip--
```

Listing 10-16: Drawing the scores

This code uses some new canvas properties and methods we haven't seen yet. First, we use ctx.font to set the font of the text we're about to draw. This is similar to a CSS font declaration. In this case, we're setting the font to be 30 pixels tall and monospace style. *Monospace* means that each character takes up the same width, and is usually used for code, as in this book's code listings. It looks like this. There are many monospace fonts, but because operating systems can come with different fonts installed, we give only a generic font style (monospace), meaning the operating system should use the default font for that font style. In most operating systems, Courier or Courier New is the default monospace font.

Next, we use ctx.textAlign to set the alignment for the text. We choose "left" alignment, but because we want this to apply only to the left score, before drawing the right score we change the alignment to "right". This way if the scores get into double digits the numbers will extend toward the middle of the screen, keeping things visually balanced.

To display the left score, we use the ctx.fillText method. This method has three parameters: the text to be drawn, and the x- and y-coordinates at which to draw it. The first parameter must be a string, so we call the toString method on leftScore to convert it from a number to a string. We use 50 for the x- and y-coordinates to place the text near the top-left corner of the canvas.

NOTE *The meaning of the x-coordinate parameter for fillText depends on the text's alignment. For left-aligned text, the x-coordinate specifies the left edge of the text, whereas for right-aligned text it specifies the right edge.*

The right score is handled similarly to the left score: we set the text alignment, then call fillText to display the score. This time we set the x-coordinate to width - 50, so it appears as far from the right as the left score appears from the left.

When you refresh *index.html,* you should see the initial scores rendered, as illustrated in Figure 10-6.

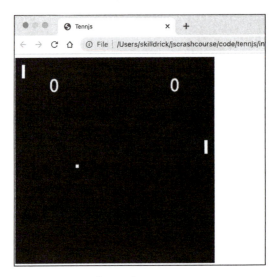

Figure 10-6: Displaying the scores

Now we have to handle the case where the ball hits the side walls. Instead of bouncing, the appropriate score should be incremented and the ball should be reset to its original speed and position. First we'll do another refactor and write a function that resets the ball. This also requires some changes to how the ball's speed and position variables are handled. Listing 10-17 shows the changes.

```
--snip--
const BALL_SIZE = 5;
❶ let ballPosition;

let xSpeed;
let ySpeed;

function initBall() {
❷ ballPosition = { x: 20, y: 30 };
   xSpeed = 4;
   ySpeed = 2;
}

const PADDLE_WIDTH = 5;
--snip--
```

Listing 10-17: The initBall *function*

Here we've separated the *declaration* of the ball state variables (ball Position, xSpeed, and ySpeed) from the *initialization* of those variables. For example, `ballPosition` is declared at the top level of the program ❶ but initialized in the new `initBall` function ❷ (short for "initialize ball"). The same goes for `xSpeed` and `ySpeed`. This is so we can reset the ball to its initial position and speed whenever we want simply by calling `initBall`, rather than by copy-pasting the values of the ball state variables all over the program. In particular, we can now call `initBall` at the start of the program to set up the ball for the first time, and we can also call it anytime the ball hits the left or right wall, to reset the ball to its original state.

Note that we can't both declare *and* initialize the ball state variables inside the `initBall` function—for example, by placing `let ballPosition = { x: 20, y: 30 };` within the function—because the `let` keyword defines a new variable *in the current scope*, which in that case would be the body of `initBall`. Thus, the variables would be available only within `initBall`. We want the variables to be available throughout the program, so we declare them with `let` at the top level of the program, outside the body of any functions. However, because we want to initialize the variables multiple times, we assign them their value in the `initBall` function, which can be called repeatedly.

Next we have to modify the collision detection code in the `checkCollision` function to increment the score and reset the ball when the left or right wall is hit. Listing 10-18 shows how.

```
--snip--
  if (checkPaddleCollision(ball, rightPaddle)) {
    // Right paddle collision happened
    let distanceFromTop = ball.top - rightPaddle.top;
    let distanceFromBottom = rightPaddle.bottom - ball.bottom;
    adjustAngle(distanceFromTop, distanceFromBottom);
    xSpeed = -Math.abs(xSpeed);
  }

❶ if (ball.left < 0) {
    rightScore++;
    initBall();
  }
❷ if (ball.right > width) {
    leftScore++;
    initBall();
  }

  if (ball.top < 0 || ball.bottom > height) {
    ySpeed = -ySpeed;
  }
}
--snip--
```

Listing 10-18: Scoring points on wall collisions

Previously, we checked for left and right wall collisions in a single `if` statement that made the ball bounce, but we have to handle the left and right walls individually, since a different player scores depending on which wall is hit. Therefore, we've split the if statement into two. If the ball hits the left wall ❶, rightScore is incremented and the ball is reset with a call to our new initBall function. If the ball hits the right wall ❷, leftScore is incremented and the ball is reset. The logic for collisions with the top and bottom walls remains the same.

Finally, since we've moved the initialization of the ball state variables to the initBall function, we need to call that function before the game loop starts in order to set the ball up for the first time. Scroll down to the bottom of *script.js* and update the code as shown in Listing 10-19, adding a call to initBall before the call to gameLoop.

```
--snip--
function gameLoop() {
  draw();
  update();
  checkCollision();

  // Call this function again after a timeout
  setTimeout(gameLoop, 30);
}

initBall();
gameLoop();
```

Listing 10-19: Calling initBall for the first time

Now when you refresh *index.html*, you should see the scores increment when the ball hits a side wall, and the ball should reset to its original speed and position after a side wall hit. Of course, it's pretty easy to beat the computer right now because it doesn't move its paddle yet!

Computer Control

Now let's add some challenge to this game! We want the computer-controlled opponent to move the left paddle and try to hit the ball. There are various ways to do this, but in our simple approach, we'll have the computer always try to match the current position of the ball. The logic for the computer will be very simple:

- If the top of the ball is above the top of the paddle, move the paddle up.
- If the bottom of the ball is below the bottom of the paddle, move the paddle down.
- Otherwise, do nothing.

With this approach, if the computer could move at any speed, then it would never miss. Since this would be no fun for us humans, we'll set a speed limit for the computer. Listing 10-20 shows how.

```
let canvas = document.querySelector("#canvas");
let ctx = canvas.getContext("2d");
```

```
let width = canvas.width;
let height = canvas.height;

const MAX_COMPUTER_SPEED = 2;

const BALL_SIZE = 5;
--snip--
```

Listing 10-20: Limiting the computer's speed

We declare the computer's speed limit as a constant, `MAX_COMPUTER_SPEED`. By setting it to 2, we're saying that the computer isn't allowed to move the paddle more than 2 pixels per frame of the game.

Next, we'll define a function called `followBall` that applies some very rudimentary artificial intelligence to move the computer's paddle. The new function is shown in Listing 10-21. Add it to your code between the `draw` function and the `update` function.

```
--snip--
function followBall() {
❶ let ball = {
    top: ballPosition.y,
    bottom: ballPosition.y + BALL_SIZE
  };
❷ let leftPaddle = {
    top: leftPaddleTop,
    bottom: leftPaddleTop + PADDLE_HEIGHT
  };

❸ if (ball.top < leftPaddle.top) {
    leftPaddleTop -= MAX_COMPUTER_SPEED;
❹ } else if (ball.bottom > leftPaddle.bottom) {
    leftPaddleTop += MAX_COMPUTER_SPEED;
  }
}

function update() {
  ballPosition.x += xSpeed;
  ballPosition.y += ySpeed;
❺ followBall();
}

--snip--
```

Listing 10-21: Computer-controlled paddle

Within the `followBall` function, we define objects representing the ball ❶ and the left paddle ❷, each with `top` and `bottom` properties representing their upper and lower bounds. Then we implement the paddle movement logic with two `if` statements. If the top of the ball is above the top of the paddle ❸, we move the paddle up by subtracting `MAX_COMPUTER_SPEED` from `leftPaddleTop`. Likewise, if the bottom of the ball is below the bottom of the paddle ❹, we move the paddle down by adding MAX_COMPUTER_SPEED to leftPaddleTop.

We call our new followBall function within the update function ❺. This way, moving the left paddle becomes part of the process of updating the state of the game that happens with each iteration of the game loop.

Reload the page and see if you can score a point against the computer!

Game Over

The final step in creating our game is to make it winnable (or losable). To do that, we have to add some kind of game over condition, and stop the game loop at that point. In this case, we'll stop the game loop once one of the players reaches 10 points, then display the text "GAME OVER."

First, we need to declare a variable for keeping track of whether or not the game is over. We'll use this variable to decide whether to continue repeating the gameLoop function. Listing 10-22 shows the changes to make.

```
--snip--
let leftScore = 0;
let rightScore = 0;
❶ let gameOver = false;

document.addEventListener("mousemove", e => {
--snip--

function checkCollision() {
--snip--
  if (ball.right > width) {
    leftScore++;
    initBall();
  }
❷ if (leftScore > 9 || rightScore > 9) {
    gameOver = true;
  }
  if (ball.top < 0 || ball.bottom > height) {
    ySpeed = -ySpeed;
  }
}
--snip--
```

Listing 10-22: Adding the gameOver variable

Near the top of *script.js*, we declare a variable called gameOver for recording whether the game is over ❶. We initialize it to false so the game doesn't end before it begins. Then, within the checkCollision function, we check to see if either of the scores has exceeded 9 ❷. If so, we set gameOver to true. This check could happen anywhere, but we do it in checkCollision to keep the logic that increments the scores and the logic that checks the scores together.

Next, we'll add a function for writing the text "GAME OVER," and we'll modify the game loop so it ends when gameOver is true. Listing 10-23 shows how.

```
--snip--
  if (ball.top < 0 || ball.bottom > height) {
    ySpeed = -ySpeed;
  }
}

❶ function drawGameOver() {
    ctx.fillStyle = "white";
    ctx.font = "30px monospace";
    ctx.textAlign = "center";
    ctx.fillText("GAME OVER", width / 2, height / 2);
}

function gameLoop() {
  draw();
  update();
  checkCollision();
❷ if (gameOver) {
    draw();
    drawGameOver();
❸ } else {
    // Call this function again after a timeout
    setTimeout(gameLoop, 30);
  }
}
```

Listing 10-23: Ending the game

We define the drawGameOver function after the checkCollision function ❶. It draws the text "GAME OVER" to the middle of the canvas in large, white text. To position the text in the middle of the canvas, we set the text alignment to "center" and use half the canvas width and height as the text's x- and y-coordinates. (With center alignment, the x-coordinate refers to the horizontal midpoint of the text.)

Within the gameLoop function, we've wrapped the call to setTimeout in a conditional statement that checks the value of the gameOver variable. If it's true ❷, the game is over, so we call the draw and drawGameOver functions. (The draw function is needed to display the final score; otherwise, the winning player would still be stuck with nine points.) If gameOver is false ❸, the game can continue: we keep looping as before by using setTimeout to call gameLoop again after 30 ms.

Once gameOver becomes true and the game loop ends, the game effectively stops. Nothing else will be drawn to the screen after the "GAME OVER" text—at least, not until the page is refreshed and the program starts again from the beginning. Go ahead and do that now: refresh *index.html* and see if you can beat the computer! Once one of you gets more than nine points you should see the "GAME OVER" text, as shown in Figure 10-7.

Figure 10-7: Game over

I hope you beat the computer, but don't worry if you didn't—the game is pretty hard. Here are some things you can do to make it easier for yourself:

- Increase the time between frames in gameLoop.
- Make the paddles taller.
- Reduce the computer's max speed.
- Make it easier to hit the edge of the paddle.
- Increase the effect on ySpeed of hitting the edge of the paddle.

Now that you have a working game, you can make any changes you want. If you're already a *Pong* pro, you might want to make it harder instead; the following exercises provide a few suggestions. You could also try customizing the appearance, or changing the size of the canvas—it's your game now.

TRY IT YOURSELF

10-3. Increase the speed of the game as the scores increase (note that you could do this either by increasing the xSpeed and ySpeed of the ball, or by reducing the setTimeout time in gameLoop).

10-4. Slow down the player's paddle—this will require something similar to the computer paddle movement, with the right paddle moving by some max amount each frame to try to reach the current mouse position.

10-5. Add a second, slower ball.

The Complete Code

For your convenience, Listing 10-24 shows the whole *script.js* file.

```
let canvas = document.querySelector("#canvas");
let ctx = canvas.getContext("2d");
let width = canvas.width;
let height = canvas.height;

const MAX_COMPUTER_SPEED = 2;

const BALL_SIZE = 5;
let ballPosition;

let xSpeed;
let ySpeed;

function initBall() {
  ballPosition = { x: 20, y: 30 };
  xSpeed = 4;
  ySpeed = 2;
}

const PADDLE_WIDTH = 5;
const PADDLE_HEIGHT = 20;
const PADDLE_OFFSET = 10;

let leftPaddleTop = 10;
let rightPaddleTop = 30;

let leftScore = 0;
let rightScore = 0;
let gameOver = false;

document.addEventListener("mousemove", e => {
  rightPaddleTop = e.y - canvas.offsetTop;
});

function draw() {
  // Fill the canvas with black
  ctx.fillStyle = "black";
  ctx.fillRect(0, 0, width, height);

  // Everything else will be white
  ctx.fillStyle = "white";

  // Draw the ball
  ctx.fillRect(ballPosition.x, ballPosition.y, BALL_SIZE, BALL_SIZE);

  // Draw the paddles
  ctx.fillRect(
    PADDLE_OFFSET,
    leftPaddleTop,
    PADDLE_WIDTH,
    PADDLE_HEIGHT
```

```
  );
  ctx.fillRect(
    width - PADDLE_WIDTH - PADDLE_OFFSET,
    rightPaddleTop,
    PADDLE_WIDTH,
    PADDLE_HEIGHT
  );

  // Draw scores
  ctx.font = "30px monospace";
  ctx.textAlign = "left";
  ctx.fillText(leftScore.toString(), 50, 50);
  ctx.textAlign = "right";
  ctx.fillText(rightScore.toString(), width - 50, 50);
}

function followBall() {
  let ball = {
    top: ballPosition.y,
    bottom: ballPosition.y + BALL_SIZE
  };
  let leftPaddle = {
    top: leftPaddleTop,
    bottom: leftPaddleTop + PADDLE_HEIGHT
  };

  if (ball.top < leftPaddle.top) {
    leftPaddleTop -= MAX_COMPUTER_SPEED;
  } else if (ball.bottom > leftPaddle.bottom) {
    leftPaddleTop += MAX_COMPUTER_SPEED;
  }
}

function update() {
  ballPosition.x += xSpeed;
  ballPosition.y += ySpeed;
  followBall();
}

function checkPaddleCollision(ball, paddle) {
  // Check if the paddle and ball overlap vertically and horizontally
  return (
    ball.left   < paddle.right &&
    ball.right  > paddle.left &&
    ball.top    < paddle.bottom &&
    ball.bottom > paddle.top
  );
}

function adjustAngle(distanceFromTop, distanceFromBottom) {
  if (distanceFromTop < 0) {
    // If ball hit near top of paddle, reduce ySpeed
    ySpeed -= 0.5;
  } else if (distanceFromBottom < 0) {
    // If ball hit near bottom of paddle, increase ySpeed
```

```
      ySpeed += 0.5;
    }
}

function checkCollision() {
  let ball = {
    left: ballPosition.x,
    right: ballPosition.x + BALL_SIZE,
    top: ballPosition.y,
    bottom: ballPosition.y + BALL_SIZE
  }

  let leftPaddle = {
    left: PADDLE_OFFSET,
    right: PADDLE_OFFSET + PADDLE_WIDTH,
    top: leftPaddleTop,
    bottom: leftPaddleTop + PADDLE_HEIGHT
  };

  let rightPaddle = {
    left: width - PADDLE_WIDTH - PADDLE_OFFSET,
    right: width - PADDLE_OFFSET,
    top: rightPaddleTop,
    bottom: rightPaddleTop + PADDLE_HEIGHT
  };

  if (checkPaddleCollision(ball, leftPaddle)) {
    // Left paddle collision happened
    let distanceFromTop = ball.top - leftPaddle.top;
    let distanceFromBottom = leftPaddle.bottom - ball.bottom;
    adjustAngle(distanceFromTop, distanceFromBottom);
    xSpeed = Math.abs(xSpeed);
  }

  if (checkPaddleCollision(ball, rightPaddle)) {
    // Right paddle collision happened
    let distanceFromTop = ball.top - rightPaddle.top;
    let distanceFromBottom = rightPaddle.bottom - ball.bottom;
    adjustAngle(distanceFromTop, distanceFromBottom);
    xSpeed = -Math.abs(xSpeed);
  }

  if (ball.left < 0) {
    rightScore++;
    initBall();
  }
  if (ball.right > width) {
    leftScore++;
    initBall();
  }
  if (leftScore > 9 || rightScore > 9) {
    gameOver = true;
  }
```

```
    if (ball.top < 0 || ball.bottom > height) {
      ySpeed = -ySpeed;
    }
  }

  function drawGameOver() {
    ctx.fillStyle = "white";
    ctx.font = "30px monospace";
    ctx.textAlign = "center";
    ctx.fillText("GAME OVER", width / 2, height / 2);
  }

  function gameLoop() {
    draw();
    update();
    checkCollision();

    if (gameOver) {
      draw();
      drawGameOver();
    } else {
      // Call this function again after a timeout
      setTimeout(gameLoop, 30);
    }
  }

  initBall();
  gameLoop();
```

Listing 10-24: The complete code

Summary

In this chapter you created a full game from scratch. The basics of game loops, collision detection, and rendering are broadly applicable, so with the knowledge you've acquired here you can start creating all kinds of 2D games. For example, you might try implementing your own version of *Breakout* or *Snake*. If you need some help with the logic, there are lots of tutorials online that you can follow. Have fun!

11

OBJECT-ORIENTED PONG

In the previous chapter we built our own version of the game *Pong*. Earlier, in Chapter 6, you learned about classes and object-oriented programming in JavaScript. You might be wondering why we didn't use any classes for our implementation of *Pong*. The main reason was that I wanted to keep the game code as simple as possible, without including any unnecessary concepts, to make it easier to see what the actual game is doing. As programs get larger and more complex, however, it helps to give them more structure, and one common way to do that is to use object-oriented programming.

To help you get a better understanding of how to design software in an object-oriented style, in this chapter we'll walk through an object-oriented version of *Pong*. There won't be any changes to the logic of the game, but the structure and organization of the code will be different. For example, the code for handling the ball will all live in a class called `Ball`. We'll use this class to keep track of the ball's position and to determine how the ball should bounce when it hits a wall or paddle. Similarly, all the code for handling the paddles will live in a class called `Paddle`. We'll be able to easily share common code that applies to both balls and paddles by making the `Ball` and `Paddle` classes inherit from a shared superclass.

This chapter will explore the general structure of the object-oriented *Pong* program, but we won't go into every single detail of the code; you should already have a pretty good idea of how it works from the last chapter. With that in mind, instead of building up the game incrementally, in this chapter we'll step through the full code in order, section by section. Because of that, the code won't run correctly or really *do* anything until you've entered it all. But before we get to the code itself, let's first look more broadly at how to approach designing an object-oriented computer program.

Object-Oriented Design

Writing code in an object-oriented way adds structure to computer programs by organizing the code into classes representing the various aspects of the program. This structure makes it easier for other programmers (and even a later version of you) to understand how your code works. A complete treatment of object-oriented design techniques would be beyond the scope of this book, but in this section we'll look at a few key principles at the heart of object-oriented programming.

An important first step in object-oriented design is modeling your domain, or world of your program. What are the different elements in the program, what do they need to be able to do, and how do they relate to and interact with each other? In this case, the domain is the game *Pong*, and there are several visible elements in the game: the ball, the paddles, and the scores. While there are two paddles, they mostly behave in the same way, so we can create a single `Paddle` class with two customized instances. Meanwhile, the ball is distinct enough to deserve its own class. We also have to model how these elements interact. For example, how do we model the ball colliding with a paddle? That code has to live somewhere. As you'll see, in my design, I decided that the code should live in the `Ball` class. In other words, the ball should "know" how to bounce off the paddles and the walls when it collides with them.

Another important aspect of object-oriented programming is *encapsulation*. This means hiding the inner details of a class from the rest of the program, and providing a simple interface for it to use to interact with the class. Encapsulating these details makes it easier to change them later without affecting the rest of the program. For example, the `Ball` class doesn't need to expose its speed or position to the rest of the program. If we decide to change how the speed is represented (for example, using `angle` and `speed` instead of xSpeed and ySpeed), we shouldn't have to change how any other part of the program works.

NOTE *Technically, xSpeed and ySpeed will be accessible outside of the Ball class, but we won't be accessing them, so we can treat them as encapsulated details. JavaScript does have a way to declare properties as* private, *meaning they can't be accessed outside of the class, but at the time of this writing it's a new feature and isn't available in all browsers.*

A final key aspect of object-oriented programming is *polymorphism*, the idea that if a method expects to receive objects of a certain class, then it can also receive objects that are instances of subclasses of that class. For example, in this chapter you'll see an Entity class that has a draw method and two subclasses: Paddle and Ball. In keeping with polymorphism, any code that uses the draw method should be able to receive any kind of Entity as an argument, without caring about whether we pass it a Ball or a Paddle.

In the end, object-oriented design is more of an art than a science, and there are a lot of different ways to do it. You should treat the design in this chapter as one possible way to approach the problem, rather than "the right way" to do things. With that in mind, let's dive into our object-oriented *Pong* code.

The File Structure

The HTML for the object-oriented version of *Pong* is exactly the same as in the previous chapter, but the JavaScript is completely different. If you want, you can make a copy of the *tennjs* directory, remove the *script.js* file, and create a new *script.js* file with the code shown in the following sections. Alternatively, you can just delete all the code in the *script.js* file in your existing *tennjs* directory and replace it with the new object-oriented code. Either way, the updated *script.js* file will consist of a series of class declarations, followed by some extra code to set the game in motion. We'll look at each section of the code in sequence.

The GameView Class

The first class we'll declare is called GameView. This class is responsible for the player's view of the game, or how the game is displayed. Because the game uses a canvas for rendering, the GameView class is responsible for the canvas and drawing context. This class is also responsible for drawing things to the canvas, such as the ball and paddles, and for displaying the "GAME OVER" text. See Listing 11-1 for the code.

```
class GameView {
❶ constructor() {
    let canvas = document.querySelector("#canvas");
    this.ctx = canvas.getContext("2d");
```

```
      this.width = canvas.width;
      this.height = canvas.height;
      this.offsetTop = canvas.offsetTop;
   }

❷ draw(...entities) {
      // Fill the canvas with black
      this.ctx.fillStyle = "black";
      this.ctx.fillRect(0, 0, this.width, this.height);

   ❸ entities.forEach(entity => entity.draw(this.ctx));
   }

❹ drawScores(scores) {
      this.ctx.fillStyle = "white";
      this.ctx.font = "30px monospace";
      this.ctx.textAlign = "left";
      this.ctx.fillText(scores.leftScore.toString(), 50, 50);
      this.ctx.textAlign = "right";
      this.ctx.fillText(scores.rightScore.toString(), this.width - 50, 50);
   }

❺ drawGameOver() {
      this.ctx.fillStyle = "white";
      this.ctx.font = "30px monospace";
      this.ctx.textAlign = "center";
      this.ctx.fillText("GAME OVER", this.width / 2, this.height / 2);
   }
}
```

Listing 11-1: The GameView class

The GameView constructor ❶ gets a reference to the canvas and its
drawing context and saves these as properties called canvas and ctx, respectively. It also stores some values that will be used for drawing: the width
and height of the canvas, and the offset of the canvas from the top of the
browser viewport.

The draw method ❷ uses rest parameters, introduced in Chapter 5. This
way, you can pass multiple arguments to draw, and all the arguments will be
collected into a single array called entities. Each argument will be an object
representing one of the elements in the game: the ball and the two paddles.
The method first draws a black rectangle to clear the canvas and then goes
through the array of elements, calling each element's own draw method
in turn ❸ and passing the drawing context as an argument. This will work
only if every object passed to GameView.draw has its own draw method; we'll see
how that's implemented in the next section. The draw method on GameView
has the ultimate responsibility for drawing to the canvas with each repetition of the game loop, but it delegates responsibility for actually drawing
the game elements to the objects representing those elements. In effect,
each element in the game "knows" how to draw itself, and GameView.draw just
orchestrates the calls.

The drawScores method ❹ takes an object containing the two scores and draws them to the canvas. It's much the same as the score drawing code from the previous chapter. The main difference is that instead of relying on a global variable for the width of the canvas, it's able to use the width property from the GameView class by referring to this.width.

The drawGameOver method ❺ is also mostly the same as the equivalent function in the previous chapter, but again, it gets the width and height from GameView rather than from global variables.

The Game Elements

Next we'll implement classes representing the three main game elements: the two paddles and the ball. We'll begin with a superclass called Entity that will be a parent to the subclasses Paddle and Ball. The Entity class exists to share the general code common to both the paddles and the ball. This includes code for keeping track of the sizes and positions of the elements, calculating the boundaries of the elements for collision detection, and drawing the elements. Since all the game elements are rectangles, all this code is the same whether we're dealing with a paddle or the ball. This shows the beauty of object-oriented programming: we can write all the common code once in the superclass, and let the subclasses inherit it.

Listing 11-2 contains the code for the Entity class.

```
class Entity {
❶ constructor(x, y, width, height) {
    this.x = x;
    this.y = y;
    this.width = width;
    this.height = height;
  }

❷ boundingBox() {
    return {
      left: this.x,
      right: this.x + this.width,
      top: this.y,
      bottom: this.y + this.height
    };
  }

❸ draw(ctx) {
    ctx.fillStyle = "white";
    ctx.fillRect(this.x, this.y, this.width, this.height);
  }
}
```

Listing 11-2: The Entity class

The Entity constructor ❶ takes an x- and a y-coordinate for the top-left corner of the entity, and a width and height for its size. These are saved as properties.

The boundingBox method ❷ returns an object with the left, right, top, and bottom bounds of the entity. In the previous chapter, we manually created these objects for each entity in the checkCollision function. The Entity superclass gives us a convenient way of generalizing this common calculation for both the ball and the paddles.

The draw method ❸ takes a drawing context and draws a white rectangle using the properties defined in the constructor. The objects passed into the draw method on GameView will all be subclasses of Entity, and it's the draw method on Entity that will be called for each item.

The Paddles

The Paddle class extends the Entity class. It's declared in Listing 11-3.

```
class Paddle extends Entity {
❶ static WIDTH = 5;
   static HEIGHT = 20
   static OFFSET = 10;

❷ constructor(x, y) {
     super(x, y, Paddle.WIDTH, Paddle.HEIGHT);
   }
}
```

Listing 11-3: The Paddle class

This class includes three *static properties*, which are properties assigned to the class itself rather than to an individual instance of the class. A static property's value will be shared across all instances of the class. In this case, while each instance of Paddle needs its own x- and y-coordinates, every Paddle object should have the same width and height, as well as the same offset from the left or right edge of the canvas. Thus, we define those values as the static properties WIDTH, HEIGHT, and OFFSET, which correspond to the PADDLE_WIDTH, PADDLE_HEIGHT, and PADDLE_OFFSET constants from the previous chapter.

NOTE
There's no straightforward way to define static constants in classes, which is why the constants from the previous chapter are now technically variables. Their names are in all caps to indicate that they should be treated as constants.

You declare a static property using the static keyword. For example, we declare the WIDTH static property using static WIDTH = 5 ❶. Static properties are accessed using dot notation, as with an instance's properties, except that you use the class name on the left side of the dot, rather than this or the name of the instance. For example, Paddle.WIDTH accesses the WIDTH static property.

The Paddle constructor ❷ has only two parameters: x and y. It uses super to call the constructor of its superclass (Entity), passing through the x and y parameters as well as Paddle.WIDTH for the width parameter and Paddle.HEIGHT for the height parameter.

The Ball

Next comes the Ball class. This is similar to the Paddle class in that it extends Entity, but Ball has its own logic for updating its position based on its speed, and for collision detection. Listing 11-4 shows the first part of the code for this class.

```
class Ball extends Entity {
❶ static SIZE = 5;

❷ constructor() {
     super(0, 0, Ball.SIZE, Ball.SIZE);
  ❸ this.init();
   }

❹ init() {
     this.x = 20;
     this.y = 30;
     this.xSpeed = 4;
     this.ySpeed = 2;
   }

❺ update() {
     this.x += this.xSpeed;
     this.y += this.ySpeed;
   }

❻ adjustAngle(distanceFromTop, distanceFromBottom) {
     if (distanceFromTop < 0) {
     // If ball hit near top of paddle, reduce ySpeed
     this.ySpeed -= 0.5;
     } else if (distanceFromBottom < 0) {
     // If ball hit near bottom of paddle, increase ySpeed
     this.ySpeed += 0.5;
     }
   }
}
```

Listing 11-4: The beginning of the Ball class

This class has a static property called SIZE that defines the width and height of the ball ❶. Next comes its constructor method ❷. Like the Paddle constructor, the first thing the Ball constructor does is call the constructor of its superclass, Entity, this time passing 0 for the x and y parameters and Ball.SIZE for the width and height parameters. The 0s are just placeholders; in fact, the ball starts each point at the same position, (20, 30). This positioning is handled by the Ball class's init method, which is called for the first time from the constructor ❸. The init method itself is defined to set the initial position and speed of the ball ❹, just like the initBall function from the previous chapter. This method will be called whenever the ball needs to be reset to its initial position (after a point is scored).

The next method, update, uses the ball's current speed to update its x- and y-position ❺. It's followed by the adjustAngle method ❻, equivalent to the adjustAngle function described in the previous chapter. It changes the ball's vertical speed (the angle of the bounce) depending on where the ball hits the paddle.

The Ball class definition continues in Listing 11-5 with the methods for collision detection.

```
class Ball extends Entity {
--snip--
  checkPaddleCollision(paddle, xSpeedAfterBounce) {
❶ let ballBox = this.boundingBox();
  let paddleBox = paddle.boundingBox();

  // Check if the ball and paddle overlap vertically and horizontally
❷ let collisionOccurred = (
    ballBox.left   < paddleBox.right &&
    ballBox.right  > paddleBox.left &&
    ballBox.top    < paddleBox.bottom &&
    ballBox.bottom > paddleBox.top
  );

  if (collisionOccurred) {
    let distanceFromTop = ballBox.top - paddleBox.top;
    let distanceFromBottom = paddleBox.bottom - ballBox.bottom;
❸ this.adjustAngle(distanceFromTop, distanceFromBottom);
❹ this.xSpeed = xSpeedAfterBounce;
  }
}

  checkWallCollision(width, height, scores) {
    let ballBox = this.boundingBox();

    // Hit left wall
❺ if (ballBox.left < 0) {
    scores.rightScore++;
    this.init();
  }
    // Hit right wall
❻ if (ballBox.right > width) {
    scores.leftScore++;
    this.init();
  }
    // Hit top or bottom walls
    if (ballBox.top < 0 || ballBox.bottom > height) {
❼ this.ySpeed = -this.ySpeed;
  }
  }
}
```

Listing 11-5: The rest of the Ball class

The checkPaddleCollision method has some overlap with the check
Collision and checkPaddleCollision functions from the previous chapter.
The method takes two parameters: an object representing one of the
paddles, and xSpeedAfterBounce. The latter represents the new value we
should set xSpeed to if a bounce off one of the paddles occurs, and it lets us

configure whether the ball is expected to always bounce to the right (from the left paddle) or to the left (from the right paddle). As in the previous chapter, we enforce that a collision with the left paddle makes the ball bounce right and vice versa to avoid weirdness where the ball could bounce around "inside" the paddle.

We use the boundingBox method from the parent Entity class to get the bounding boxes of the ball and the paddle ❶, storing them as ballBox and paddleBox. Next, we compare the various bounding box edges to determine if a collision has taken place between the ball and the paddle, saving the result in the Boolean variable collisionOccurred ❷. If collisionOccurred is true, we call the adjustAngle method with the appropriate distances as determined from the bounding boxes ❸, then set the ball's xSpeed to xSpeedAfterBounce ❹.

Finally, the checkWallCollision method checks to see if a collision has occurred between the ball and a wall. It takes the width and height of the playing area and an object representing the scores as parameters. If the ball hits the left wall ❺ or right wall ❻, the appropriate score is incremented, and the ball is reset with a call to the init method. If it hits the top or bottom wall, it bounces ❼.

The Scores and Computer Classes

The Scores class is a simple container for keeping track of the current scores. The Computer class contains the logic for following the ball. The code for these two classes is in Listing 11-6.

```
class Scores {
❶ constructor() {
    this.leftScore = 0;
    this.rightScore = 0;
  }
}

class Computer {
❷ static followBall(paddle, ball) {
    const MAX_SPEED = 2;
    let ballBox = ball.boundingBox();
    let paddleBox = paddle.boundingBox();

    if (ballBox.top < paddleBox.top) {
      paddle.y -= MAX_SPEED;
    } else if (ballBox.bottom > paddleBox.bottom) {
      paddle.y += MAX_SPEED;
    }
  }
}
```

Listing 11-6: The Scores and Computer classes

The Scores constructor ❶ sets the scores for the left and right players to 0. We could just use a plain object for the scores, but using a class keeps the structure of the code more consistent.

The Computer class has a single method called followBall, which updates the left paddle's position based on the ball's position. It's a *static method*, meaning it doesn't need an instance of the class to be called. We declare it as static using the static keyword ❷, similar to declaring a static property. Static methods are called using the class name rather than the instance name, like this: Computer.followBall(leftPaddle, ball).

NOTE *We create instances of a class when there are properties specific to that instance that need to be stored. The Computer class doesn't have any properties, so we don't need to create an instance of it. Since the Computer class is never instantiated, it also doesn't need a constructor.*

We could just as easily have created a standalone function to move the left paddle, but as with the Scores class, keeping the code as part of a Computer class maintains consistency.

The Game Class

We finally come to the Game class, which is where all the other classes get instantiated (where applicable) and are stitched together and orchestrated. See Listing 11-7 for the first part of the code.

```
class Game {
  constructor() {
    this.gameView = new GameView();
    this.ball = new Ball();
  ❶ this.leftPaddle = new Paddle(Paddle.OFFSET, 10);
  ❷ this.rightPaddle = new Paddle(
      this.gameView.width - Paddle.OFFSET - Paddle.WIDTH,
      30
    );

  ❸ this.scores = new Scores();
    this.gameOver = false;

  ❹ document.addEventListener("mousemove", e => {
      this.rightPaddle.y = e.y - this.gameView.offsetTop;
    });
  }

  draw() {
  ❺ this.gameView.draw(
      this.ball,
      this.leftPaddle,
      this.rightPaddle
    );

  ❻ this.gameView.drawScores(this.scores);
  }
```

Listing 11-7: The first part of the Game *class*

The Game constructor first instantiates the GameView, Ball, and Paddle classes. The leftPaddle instance is created with Paddle.OFFSET for its x-coordinate ❶. The right one uses Paddle.OFFSET, Paddle.WIDTH, and this .gameView.width to determine its x-coordinate ❷, similar to how we calculated the position of the right paddle in the previous chapter.

Instantiating other classes inside a class is a common feature of object-oriented code. This technique is called *composition*, because we're composing instances inside other instances

---

COMPOSITION AND INHERITANCE

Composition and inheritance both add structure to object-oriented programs. Composition is a way of modeling a "has a" relationship, as in the sentence "Game has a Ball." Inheritance, meanwhile, models an "is a" relationship, as in "Ball is an Entity."

For these two examples, it's pretty intuitive whether to use composition or inheritance—we know that the game has a ball, and that the ball is an entity—but the choice isn't always so clear. For example, you could argue that the methods in GameView are core to the Game class, and make Game inherit from GameView. It's a bit of a stretch to say that "Game is a GameView," but if you renamed GameView to ViewableGame it might make more sense.

When faced with a choice between composition and inheritance, a commonly followed design principle says to favor composition. This leads to greater flexibility and greater encapsulation. For example, if Game extended GameView, then all of the properties of GameView, like ctx, would also be present in Game. With the code as it's written now, these properties are confined to the GameView class itself, which encapsulates the logic better and increases flexibility: it's easier to make internal changes to the GameView class without having to worry about breaking the Game class.

Next, the Game constructor instantiates Scores ❸ and sets the gameOver Boolean to false. Finally, it sets up a mousemove event listener ❹ to update the right paddle's position when the user moves the mouse. An event listener set up in a class constructor works just like the other event listeners we've seen in the book: it will be available as long as the application is running, and it triggers its handler function whenever the event is detected.

After the constructor is the Game class's draw method, which has the top-level responsibility for drawing all the visual aspects of the game. First the method calls this.gameView.draw ❺, passing the three main game elements, this.ball, this.leftPaddle, and this.rightPaddle. This is a call to the draw method of the GameView class we saw in Listing 11-1, which took a variable number of objects as arguments and called the draw method on each one. The net result is that game.draw calls gameView.draw, which calls ball.draw, leftPaddle.draw, and rightPaddle.draw. It may seem a bit roundabout, but you'll often find cases like this in object-oriented code, where keeping the code in its logical place requires jumping through some hoops. In this case, game.draw is responsible for knowing *which* objects get drawn (because the Game class keeps track of all the game elements); gameView.draw is responsible for the drawing context, clearing the canvas, and calling the draw methods on the elements; and the draw method on each game element is responsible for knowing how to draw itself.

After it has drawn all the entities, the draw method calls this.gameView .drawScores, passing the this.scores object ❻.

The Game class continues with the rest of its methods in Listing 11-8.

```
class Game {
--snip--
  checkCollision() {
    this.ball.checkPaddleCollision(this.leftPaddle,
                                   ❶ Math.abs(this.ball.xSpeed));
    this.ball.checkPaddleCollision(this.rightPaddle,
                                   ❷ -Math.abs(this.ball.xSpeed));

  ❸ this.ball.checkWallCollision(
      this.gameView.width,
      this.gameView.height,
      this.scores
    );

  ❹ if (this.scores.leftScore > 9 || this.scores.rightScore > 9) {
      this.gameOver = true;
    }
  }

❺ update() {
    this.ball.update();
    Computer.followBall(this.leftPaddle, this.ball);
  }

❻ loop() {
    this.draw();
    this.update();
    this.checkCollision();

  ❼ if (this.gameOver) {
      this.draw();
      this.gameView.drawGameOver();
    } else {
      // Call this method again after a timeout
    ❽ setTimeout(() => this.loop(), 30);
    }
  }
}
```

Listing 11-8: The rest of the Game class

The Game class's checkCollision method coordinates all the collision detection logic. First it calls the ball's checkPaddleCollision method twice, to check for collisions between the ball and each of the paddles. Recall from Listing 11-5 that this method takes two arguments: a Paddle object and a new, post-bounce value for xSpeed. For the left paddle, we know that we want the ball to bounce right, so we make the new xSpeed positive by taking the Math.abs of the current xSpeed ❶. For the right paddle we want the ball to bounce left, so we make the new xSpeed negative by negating the result of Math.abs(xSpeed) ❷.

Next, the checkCollision method calls ball.checkWallCollision to handle wall collisions ❸. This method takes the width and height (because the Ball object doesn't know how big the playing area is) and the scores (so they can be incremented if a side wall is hit). Finally, the method checks to see if either score has exceeded the threshold ❹ and, if so, sets this.gameOver to true.

The Game object's update method ❺ controls the changes of state between each repetition of the game loop. It calls the ball's update method to move the ball, then tells the computer to move the left paddle based on the ball's new position using the Computer.followBall static method.

The last method of the Game class, loop, defines the game loop ❻. We call this.draw, this.update, and this.checkCollision in sequence. Then we check to see if this.gameOver is true. If so ❼, we call draw again to render the final score, and we call gameView.drawGameOver to render the "GAME OVER" text. Otherwise, we use setTimeout to call the loop method again after 30 ms ❽, continuing the game.

Starting the Game

The very last thing we have to do is start the game by instantiating the Game class and kicking off the game loop, as shown in Listing 11-9.

```
let game = new Game();
game.loop();
```

Listing 11-9: Starting the game

We must create the instance of the Game class at the top level of the program, outside any of the class definitions. All the other required objects are instantiated by the Game class's constructor, so creating a Game object automatically creates all the other objects as well. We could also have had the Game constructor call the loop method to set the game in motion as part of the Game class instantiation. However, placing the first call to game.loop at the top level of the program makes it easier to see exactly where the game gets going.

With this final listing, we now have all the code for the object-oriented version of our game! As long as you've entered all the code in order, it should now work, and gameplay should be exactly the same as in the version from the previous chapter.

Summary

In this chapter you created an object-oriented version of your *Pong* program, learning some strategies for object-oriented software design in the
process. None of the game's logic from the previous chapter changed; only
the code's organization differs. You may find one or the other of these two
versions easier to read and understand, depending on your preferences and
experience with object-oriented code.

Object-oriented design is a complex field, and it can take a lot of practice to decompose programs into individual objects that make sense on
their own. Even in this simple game, there are many ways you could split up
the game's components into objects and methods. For example, you might
decide that the GameView class is unnecessary and that Game can keep track of
the canvas, avoiding the need for the complex dance where draw calls draw
calls draw. The main thing is to arrange your code in a way that makes sense
and is easy for you and other programmers to understand and modify.

PROJECT 2

MAKING MUSIC

12

GENERATING SOUNDS

Now it's time for something completely different! In this next project, you'll create a
song using JavaScript and the Web Audio
API. You'll also learn some general tips about
sound synthesis and how electronic music is made.

This chapter will introduce the Web Audio API and Tone.js, a JavaScript
library built on top of it. This will be your first taste of the wide world of
third-party JavaScript libraries, which are collections of prewritten code
that you can harness to simplify complex tasks. Tone.js raises the level of
abstraction compared with the Web Audio API, allowing you to think about
and implement musical concepts in a more natural way. Once you're familiar with how it works, in Chapter 13 you'll put everything you've learned to
use to make a song that you can customize or even rewrite.

The Web Audio API

This section covers the basics of the Web Audio API, which provides a way to create and manipulate sounds in the browser using JavaScript. Google Chrome introduced the Web Audio API in 2011, and soon after that it was released as a W3C standard (the W3C, or World Wide Web Consortium, is an organization that develops standards for the web). To use it, you create nodes and then connect them together. Each *node* represents some aspect of a sound—one node might generate a basic tone, a second node might set its volume, a third might apply an effect such as reverb or distortion to the tone, and so on. With this scheme, you can produce almost any kind of sound you might want.

Setting Up

As always, we'll start with a simple HTML file. The file will give the user the ability to play a sound generated by the Web Audio API. Create a new directory called *music* and enter the content in Listing 12-1 into a new file called *index.html*.

```
<!DOCTYPE html>
<html>
  <head>
    <title>Music</title>
  </head>
  <body>
❶ <button id="play">Play</button>
❷ <p id="playing" style="display: none">Playing</p>
    <script src="script.js"></script>
  </body>
</html>
```

Listing 12-1: An index.html *file for exploring the Web Audio API*

This listing creates two visual elements: a Play button ❶ and a paragraph containing the text "Playing" ❷. The paragraph uses an inline style attribute, which allows us to add CSS declarations directly to the element from the HTML file. In this case, we're setting `display` to `none`, which hides the element. Later, we'll use JavaScript to remove the style and show the element when the audio is playing.

Next, we'll start writing the JavaScript. In many browsers, including Google Chrome, the Web Audio API won't play any sound until the user interacts with the page. We're using the Play button as our interactive element, which will trigger our audio code. Because we only need the button to be clicked once, we'll hide it after it's been clicked.

Create *script.js* in the same directory as the HTML file and add the content shown in Listing 12-2. This code hides the Play button and shows the "Playing" text when the user clicks the button. Note that we're not doing any Web Audio API code yet—this is just setting up the button.

```
❶ let play = document.querySelector("#play");
  let playing = document.querySelector("#playing");
❷ play.addEventListener("click", () => {
    // Hide this button
    play.style = "display: none";
    playing.style = "";
});
```

Listing 12-2: Switching the visibility of the elements on a mouse click

First, we get references to the two elements using the `document.query`
`Selector` method ❶. Then we add a `click` event listener to the Play button ❷.
When the user clicks it, our event listener adds an inline style attribute of
`display: none` to the button and sets the inline style of the paragraph to an
empty string, effectively removing the inline style set as an attribute in the
HTML file. The net effect of this code is that clicking the Play button will
hide the button and show the paragraph. This has two purposes: it lets the
user know that music should now be playing, and it removes the Play button
so it can't be clicked a second time.

Generating a Tone with the Web Audio API

With our setup out of the way, we can now write some Web Audio API code.
To get started, we'll just generate a single tone, the audio equivalent of
"Hello, world!" The code to generate the tone is shown in Listing 12-3. As I
mentioned earlier, the audio won't play unless it's triggered by a user event,
such as a mouse click, so all the audio code lives inside the click handler.

```
--snip--
play.addEventListener("click", () => {
    // Hide this button
    play.style = "display: none";
    playing.style = "";

❶ let audioCtx = new AudioContext();

❷ let oscNode = audioCtx.createOscillator();
  oscNode.frequency.value = 440;

❸ let gainNode = audioCtx.createGain();
  gainNode.gain.value = 0.5;

❹ oscNode.connect(gainNode);
  gainNode.connect(audioCtx.destination);

❺ oscNode.start(audioCtx.currentTime);
  oscNode.stop(audioCtx.currentTime + 2);
});
```

Listing 12-3: Playing a single tone with the Web Audio API

The first thing we do is create the *audio context* ❶. This is the object
through which we interact with the Web Audio API, similar to the drawing

context for the canvas element. Next, we create our first node, an oscillator ❷. In electronics and signal processing terms, an *oscillator* is a device that creates a signal that repeatedly goes up and down in a regular pattern. The default waveform a Web Audio API oscillator outputs is a sine wave, shown in Figure 12-1. When the wave oscillates fast enough, and is connected to a speaker, it creates an audible tone. In this example, we're setting the frequency to 440 Hertz (Hz), or 440 cycles per second. In other words, the oscillator is outputting a signal that transitions from 0 to 1 to –1 and back to 0 a total of 440 times every second. This means that one cycle of the wave lasts 1/440 of a second, or 2.27 ms. I used 440 Hz here because it's the standard reference pitch for tuning musical instruments. The frequency corresponds to the note A above middle C.

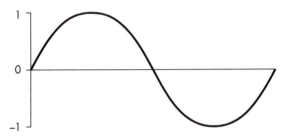

Figure 12-1: One cycle of a sine wave

Next, we create a gain node ❸ and set its value to 0.5. In signal processing, *gain* refers to an increase or decrease in a signal's amplitude, or its range of values. In practical terms, gain acts as a volume control. A gain of 2 doubles the amplitude, making the sound louder, a gain of 0.5 halves the amplitude, making the sound softer, and a gain of 1 (the default value of a gain node) has no effect on the amplitude. Applying a gain of 0.5 to the sine wave from Figure 12-1 would produce a sine wave with a maximum value of 0.5 and a minimum value of –0.5, as shown in Figure 12-2.

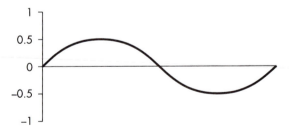

Figure 12-2: The sine wave from Figure 12-1, with a gain of 0.5 applied

So far we have two nodes: an oscillator node and a gain node. To actually apply the gain to the oscillator's signal, we need to connect the nodes together. We link the output of the oscillator node to the input of the gain node using the oscillator node's connect method ❹. Then, to be able to hear the result, we connect the output of the gain node to the main output, which is available to us through the audio context as ctx.destination. These connections mean that the oscillator signal is passed through the gain node and then passed to the output, which will ultimately go to your headphones or speakers, if the sound is turned on. Figure 12-3 illustrates these connections.

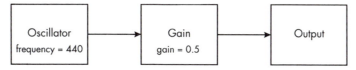

Figure 12-3: The graph of nodes

The oscillator node doesn't actually create a signal until we tell it to. To do that, we call the start method on the oscillator, passing audioCtx .currentTime as an argument ❺. The currentTime property corresponds to the amount of time in seconds that the audio context has been active. By passing audioCtx.currentTime to the start method, we're telling the oscillator to start playing immediately. Then we call the stop method, passing audioCtx .currentTime + 2. This tells the oscillator to stop two seconds after it started.

The effect of all of this code is that when you load the *index.html* page in your browser and click the Play button, a tone of 440 Hz should play for two seconds. If you don't hear anything, make sure sound is enabled on your computer and browser—for example, by playing a YouTube video. If it still doesn't work, check the console to make sure there aren't any errors.

TRY IT YOURSELF

12-1. Change the frequency, or pitch, of the tone by changing oscNode .frequency.value. Halving the frequency will lower the tone's musical pitch by an octave, and doubling it will raise its pitch by an octave.

12-2. Change the value of the gain node to alter the volume of the tone. For example, setting it to 0.25 will make it half as loud.

12-3. Change the duration of the tone by modifying the argument to the stop method. You can also add a delay between when the user clicks the Play button and when the tone starts by modifying the argument to the start method. For example, oscNode.start(audioCtx.currentTime + 0.5) would start playing the tone half a second after the button click.

You might be thinking that you just had to write a lot of code for a very simple example, and you'd be right! The Web Audio API is quite powerful, but you have to work at a very low level with extremely basic building blocks. To simplify things, next we're going to shift our focus to a popular, higher-level audio library called Tone.js.

The Tone.js Library

The Tone.js library is built on top of the Web Audio API. It's designed to make it easier to create music using the API. For example, instead of having to fiddle with oscillators and gain nodes, Tone.js lets you use electronic instruments with volume controls. Instead of using frequencies, you can use the names of musical notes. And instead of using seconds for controlling when events happen, you can use bars and beats.

The Tone.js website, *https://tonejs.github.io*, provides details on installing and using the library. The easiest option is to use a prebuilt file hosted on a content delivery network (CDN) like *https://unpkg.com*, which is what we'll do here. This way all you have to do to access the library is reference a URL directly from a script element in your HTML file. There's no need to download a copy of the library, as long as you have access to the internet while you're working.

Generating a Tone with Tone.js

Let's re-create our Web Audio API "Hello, world!" example using the Tone.js library instead. We can keep all the HTML the same, except for adding a new script tag for the library, as shown in Listing 12-4.

```
--snip--
    <p id="playing" style="display: none">Playing</p>
    <script src="https://unpkg.com/tone@14.7.77/build/Tone.js"></script>
    <script src="script.js"></script>
  </body>
</html>
```

Listing 12-4: Including Tone.js in the index.html *file*

We set the src of the new script element to an *unpkg.com* file containing the full Tone.js library as a single JavaScript file.

Next, we'll write the JavaScript. Since Tone.js uses the Web Audio API underneath, we still have the limitation that user input is required to start playing the audio. We therefore still need the click event handler, but everything else in *script.js* will change. Listing 12-5 shows the updated JavaScript file.

```
--snip--
play.addEventListener("click", () => {
  // Hide this button
  play.style = "display: none";
  playing.style = "";

  Tone.start();

  let synth = new Tone.Synth({
    oscillator: { type: "sine" },
    envelope: { attack: 0, decay: 0, sustain: 1, release: 0 },
```

```
  volume: -6
}).toDestination();

synth.triggerAttackRelease("A4", 2, 0);
});
```

Listing 12-5: Playing a single tone with Tone.js

The first thing we need to do is call `Tone.start`. This triggers the Tone.js library to start inside the click handler, ensuring that the browser will allow it to play audio. Next, we create a new `Tone.Synth` object. *Synth* is short for *synthesizer*, an electronic instrument, usually with a keyboard, that can generate (synthesize) all kinds of sounds. A `Tone.Synth` is a simple code version of such an instrument.

The `Tone.Synth` constructor takes an object as its argument that allows us to configure various aspects of the synthesizer. In this case, we're telling the synth to use an oscillator that generates sine waves. We're also giving the synth a simple amplitude envelope and a volume of -6. I'll explain what these settings mean in the following section, but for now, this is what we need to match the Web Audio API oscillator from Listing 12-3. After the constructor we chain the `toDestination` method, which connects the output of the synth to the audio context's output.

Finally, we tell the synth to play a single note using its `triggerAttackRelease` method. This method takes the note's name, the duration, and the time at which to play the note. We're passing "A4" for the note name, which is equivalent to 440 Hz, and telling it to play for two seconds, starting immediately. When you reload your browser and click the Play button, you should hear the same sound as when you ran Listing 12-3.

As you can hopefully see, using the Tone.js library simplifies the process of making music with the Web Audio API. Instead of having to create separate nodes for different aspects of a sound (pitch, gain, and so on), everything is unified under one `Synth` object. If you have any musical knowledge, you'll also find that the library uses concepts much closer to your understanding than the API does, for example, by using note names instead of frequencies. As you learn more about Tone.js, you'll see more examples of this.

Understanding the Tone.Synth Options

Let's take a closer look at the object we passed to the `Tone.Synth` constructor in Listing 12-5. The first property, `oscillator`, defines the options for the oscillator generating the signal. In this case, we're just setting the type of the oscillator to be a sine wave, using the `type` property.

The next property defines the options for the *amplitude envelope*, which determines how the volume of a note changes over the course of its duration. Most synthesizers, hardware and software, allow you to configure amplitude envelopes. The most common type of envelope is an *ADSR envelope*, short for *attack, decay, sustain, release*. The *attack* is the amount of time between the note being triggered (for example, when you press a key on a synthesizer) and the note reaching its maximum volume. The *decay* is the amount of time between the end of the attack and the sustain portion of the note. The *sustain* is a gain value that defines the volume the note will remain at after the attack and decay, for as long as the key is held down. Typically this is some fraction of the full volume achieved by the attack portion of the envelope. The *release* defines how long it will take for the note's amplitude to get back down to zero after the key is released. Figure 12-4 shows these different values graphically.

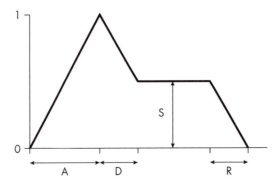

Figure 12-4: The parts of an ADSR envelope

ADSR envelopes are an approximation of how many real-world musical instruments work. For example, when you bow a violin, it takes some time for the note to get up to its full volume—that is, it has a long attack. By contrast, when you press a key on a piano, the attack is very short. Similarly, when you stop bowing a note on a violin it takes a little time for the string to stop vibrating, whereas the release of a piano note is more immediate. Synthetic ADSR envelopes are still pretty simplistic—they aren't a perfect simulation of real-life instruments—but they add a lot of expressivity to what would otherwise just be a boring tone.

That said, the ADSR envelope we've used for our synth is as boring as they come. We've set the attack, decay, and release values to 0 and the sustain to 1, meaning the tone is at full volume for its entire duration. This matches what we did with the simple Web Audio API oscillator from Listing 12-3, and it's part of why the resulting tone sounds so synthetic.

The final property of the synth options object, volume, sets the overall volume of the synthesizer in decibels (dB). Decibels are an alternative way to talk about gain, and in some ways they match the way we think about gain better. A setting of 0 decibels is equivalent to a gain of 1 (no change to the volume), –6 decibels is equivalent to a gain of 0.5, or half the volume, –12 decibels corresponds to a gain of 0.25, or a quarter of the volume, and so on; every +6 decibels doubles the volume, and every –6 decibels halves it. Our ears are attuned to the relative volume between sounds, so every time the level is halved or doubled, it sounds to us like it's going down or up by a fixed amount. This "fixed amount" is a fixed number of decibels that are added or subtracted, which is why decibels can be easier to use for setting volume. In this case, we're passing −6 dB to match the gain of 0.5 from Listing 12-3.

Now that you know what the options are, let's try playing with them! First, we'll modify the type of the oscillator. Currently the oscillator is set to generate a sine wave, but we're going to switch to a square wave instead. Figure 12-5 shows the waveform of a single cycle of a square wave.

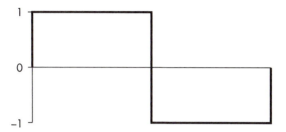

Figure 12-5: A square wave

Notice that a square wave has abrupt transitions between amplitude values, instead of the smooth curves of a sine wave. The code change to switch to a square wave oscillator is shown in Listing 12-6.

```
--snip--
  let synth = new Tone.Synth({
    oscillator: { type: "square" },
    envelope: { attack: 0, decay: 0, sustain: 1, release: 0 },
    volume: -6
  }).toDestination();
--snip--
```

Listing 12-6: Changing the oscillator type to a square wave

When you reload the code in your browser, you should hear a very different tone. The square wave is louder and brighter than the sine wave. Some other values you can try out for the oscillator type are "triangle" and "sawtooth". Figure 12-6 shows the waveforms of these two.

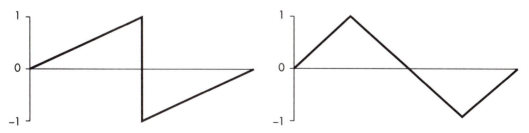

Figure 12-6: Sawtooth and triangle waves

Think about how these other oscillator types differ from "sine" and "square". The distinctive sound of each oscillator is known as its *color*, or *timbre*.

WHY DO DIFFERENT OSCILLATORS SOUND SO DIFFERENT?

Did you know that when you play a note on an instrument like a violin or piano, the resulting sound doesn't just contain the frequency of the note you're playing? It actually contains many frequencies at once. That's what the different oscillator types, like square, sawtooth, and triangle, are trying to simulate.

A sine wave is the simplest waveform—it contains only a single frequency. Other oscillator waveforms are in effect made up of a combination of many individual sine waves of various frequencies, where each frequency is a whole-number multiple of the original frequency. These multiples of the base frequency are known as *harmonics*, or *overtones*, while the base frequency is known as the *fundamental*. For example, a tone with a fundamental of 200 Hz has possible harmonics at 400 Hz (200 × 2), 600 Hz (200 × 3), 800 Hz (200 × 4), and so on. A sawtooth wave contains every harmonic (200, 400, 600, 800, . . .), while a square wave only contains every other harmonic (200, 600, 1000, . . .). However many harmonics a note has, the fundamental frequency is what we perceive as the note's pitch. The other harmonics simply add color to the sound.

With both square and sawtooth waveforms, the amplitude of the harmonics reduces the higher in frequency they get. A triangle wave has only every other harmonic, like a square wave, but the amplitude reduces more rapidly as the harmonics increase.

The presence of different harmonics, and their relative amplitude levels, is what causes the difference in sound between different oscillator types. Along with variations in amplitude envelope, they're also why a violin sounds different from a piano, for example. The triangle wave contains the same harmonics as the square wave, but the higher harmonics are quieter, which gives it a less harsh, more rounded sound. Because both of these waveforms contain only every other harmonic, they can sound a little hollow. By contrast, the sawtooth wave has all the harmonics, so it has a fuller sound.

Next, let's try changing the envelope. We intentionally used a very basic envelope in Listing 12-5 to match the Web Audio API example from Listing 12-3, which had no envelope. Now we'll set those values to something that sounds a little more musical, as shown in Listing 12-7.

```
--snip--
let synth = new Tone.Synth({
  oscillator: { type: "square" },
  envelope: { attack: 0.8, decay: 0.3, sustain: 0.8, release: 1 },
  volume: -6
}).toDestination();
--snip--
```

Listing 12-7: Changing the oscillator type to a square wave

The values of attack, decay, and release are all given in seconds, while sustain is a number between 0 and 1 representing the amplitude level to be sustained at. Here we're setting attack to 0.8 seconds, decay to 0.3 seconds, sustain to 0.8, and release to a whole second. When you reload the page and play the sound, you should hear the note slowly fade in to its max volume, then slightly reduce. After two seconds, the note is released and fades out over a second.

The final parameter to play with is the volume. As I explained earlier, every time you subtract 6 dB, the level is halved, and when you add 6 dB, it's doubled. Try out some different values here, for example, -12, -18, or -24. You can also go the other way, up to 0 dB.

Playing More Notes in Sequence

Our synthesizer is currently playing only a single note, but we can easily play more notes. Note frequencies in Tone.js can be given in Hz or with note names, like A4, as we did in Listing 12-5. These note names correspond to keys on a keyboard, as shown in Figure 12-7.

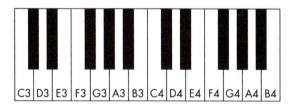

Figure 12-7: Note names on a keyboard

C4 is known as *middle C* and is located near the middle of most piano keyboards. Each octave on the keyboard from each C to the B above is given a number. For example, the leftmost key in Figure 12-7 is C3, and an octave above that is C4. As mentioned previously, 440 Hz corresponds to A4, which is the A above C4. The black notes are known as *accidentals* and are a semitone higher than the key to their left, or a semitone lower than the key to their right. For example, the black key to the right of C4 can be called C♯4 or D♭4 (♯ is the symbol for *sharp*, meaning a semitone higher, while ♭ is the symbol for *flat*, meaning a semitone lower). When writing note names in Tone.js, we use a hash mark (#) for sharp and the letter b for flat.

NOTE *There are no black keys between B and C or E and F because these notes are only a semitone apart.*

We're going to play a major scale from A3 to A4, which consists of the notes A3, B3, C♯4, D4, E4, F♯4, G♯4, and A4. Update your *script.js* to include the code in Listing 12-8 to implement this scale.

```
--snip--
  let synth = new Tone.Synth({
    oscillator: { type: "square" },
```

```
❶ envelope: { attack: 0.1, decay: 0.3, sustain: 0.8, release: 0.1 },
  volume: -6
}).toDestination();

synth.triggerAttackRelease("A3", 0.9, 0);
synth.triggerAttackRelease("B3", 0.9, 1);
synth.triggerAttackRelease("C#4", 0.9, 2);
synth.triggerAttackRelease("D4", 0.9, 3);
synth.triggerAttackRelease("E4", 0.9, 4);
synth.triggerAttackRelease("F#4", 0.9, 5);
synth.triggerAttackRelease("G#4", 0.9, 6);
synth.triggerAttackRelease("A4", 0.9, 7);
});
```

Listing 12-8: Playing a scale

This is very similar to Listing 12-5, except that we're triggering multiple notes, one after the other. Notice we've updated the envelope to have a shorter attack and release ❶. The release, in particular, needs to be shorter so the end of each note doesn't overlap with the start of the next.

As I mentioned earlier, the second argument to `triggerAttackRelease` is the duration of the note in seconds, and the third argument is the time at which to play the note, also in seconds. The first note, A3, is played for 0.9 seconds, starting at time zero (that is, immediately). The 0.1-second release happens after the 0.9-second duration, so each note will play for 1 second in total. The next note, B3, has the same duration, but the third argument of 1 means it will start a second later than the first note. The third note is programmed to start two seconds later than the first note, and so on for the rest of the notes. Play this in your browser, and you should hear a single octave of an A major scale.

Playing Multiple Notes at Once

The synthesizer we've been using so far is a *monophonic synth*, meaning it can play only a single note at a time. To play multiple notes at once, we'll need to create a *polyphonic synth* instead. In Listing 12-9, we update the code to create a new polyphonic synth and play two or three notes at a time.

```
--snip--
  Tone.start();

  let synth = new Tone.PolySynth(
    Tone.Synth,
    {
      oscillator: { type: "square" },
      envelope: { attack: 0.1, decay: 0.3, sustain: 0.8, release: 0.1 },
      volume: -6
    }
  ).toDestination();

  synth.triggerAttackRelease(["A3", "C#4"], 0.9, 0);
  synth.triggerAttackRelease(["B3", "D4"], 0.9, 1);
```

```
    synth.triggerAttackRelease(["C#4", "E4"], 0.9, 2);
    synth.triggerAttackRelease(["D4", "F#4"], 0.9, 3);
    synth.triggerAttackRelease(["E4", "G#4"], 0.9, 4);
    synth.triggerAttackRelease(["F#4", "A4"], 0.9, 5);
    synth.triggerAttackRelease(["G#4", "B4"], 0.9, 6);
    synth.triggerAttackRelease(["E4", "A4", "C#5"], 1.9, 7);
});
```

Listing 12-9: Creating and playing a polyphonic synth

Here we call new `Tone.PolySynth` instead of new `Tone.Synth` to create a polyphonic synth object. The `Tone.PolySynth` constructor takes two arguments: a monophonic synth (in this case, `Tone.Synth`) and an object with the options that would normally be passed to that monophonic synth's constructor (in this case, the same synth options we passed to the `Tone` `.Synth` constructor in Listing 12-8). The polysynth then creates multiple monophonic synths with the specified settings, effectively allowing it to play multiple notes at once.

Next, we play the same scale, but with additional simultaneous notes. This is achieved by passing an array of note names to the `triggerAttackRelease` method instead of a single note name—for example, we pass the array `["A3", "C#4"]` to play A3 and C♯4 at the same time. By default, you can play a maximum of 32 notes with a polysynth.

When you play this example, you should hear a harmonized scale with a nice major chord at the end.

The Tone.js Transport

Now that you've learned how to play notes, let's look at how to make songs. Although you could program a whole song by specifying the timing of every single note, as you did to play a scale in the last few examples, this technique quickly gets tedious. Fortunately, Tone.js has a concept called the *transport* that makes writing songs much easier. The transport keeps track of the current position in the song, as measured in bars and beats. This lets you schedule notes to play at certain points in the song in a musically intuitive way. The transport also allows you to have looped sequences of notes that start playing at a certain point along the transport and repeat over and over until you tell them to stop.

Western music tends to be structured around bars and beats, and it's most common to have four beats in a bar. The speed of the music is given in *beats per minute (BPM)*, and in our examples we'll be using the default Tone.js BPM of 120, which means a beat every 0.5 seconds. Beats are also known as *quarter notes* (because when there are four beats in a bar, one beat is a quarter of a bar). *Eighth notes* are half the duration of a quarter note, and *sixteenth notes* are half the duration of an eighth note, so there are four sixteenth notes per quarter note.

Positions along the transport are given as strings of three numbers separated by colons, like "0:0:0". The three numbers correspond to the current bar number, the current beat within that bar, and the current sixteenth note within that beat, respectively. Everything is zero-indexed. This means, for example, that "0:0:0" represents the beginning of the first bar, "1:1:0" represents the second beat of the second bar, and "6:3:2" refers to the third sixteenth note of the fourth beat in the seventh bar. We refer to these strings as *bars:quarters:sixteenths notation*.

Tone.Loop

The Tone.js transport gives us an easy way to define musical loops, including when they start and when they finish. The simplest of these, `Tone.Loop`, defines a way to constantly produce new notes. Let's try that out by playing a single note repeatedly every quarter note for four bars. Modify *script.js* with the code in Listing 12-10.

```
--snip--
  Tone.start();

❶ let synth = new Tone.Synth().toDestination();

❷ let loop = new Tone.Loop(time => {
❸   synth.triggerAttackRelease("C4", "16n", time);
  }, "4n");

❹ loop.start("0:0:0");
  loop.stop("4:0:0");

  Tone.Transport.start();
});
```

Listing 12-10: Looping

We start by creating a simple synth ❶. Notice we aren't passing an object to define the `oscillator`, `envelope`, or `volume` options, so the synth will be created using the library's default settings. Next, we create a new instance of `Tone.Loop` ❷, which has a constructor with two arguments. The first argument is some function that requires a time value, and the second argument is a duration indicating how often to call the function in the first argument. In this case, we pass the string "4n" as the second argument, which is Tone.js's notation for a quarter note ("4n" is short for "1/4 note"). This means the loop will repeat every beat.

NOTE *In our earlier listings we were passing numbers for durations, which give the duration in seconds. The advantage of using note length durations like "4n" for a quarter note or "16n" for a sixteenth note is that they will scale automatically if we change the BPM. For example, doubling the BPM will halve the duration of each quarter note.*

The body of the callback function we pass to `Tone.Loop` calls the `triggerAttackRelease` method on the synth to play the note C4 with a sixteenth note duration ❸. The third argument of the `triggerAttackRelease` method, time, represents the time to play a note. The `Tone.Loop` object will provide a new `time` value whenever it calls the callback function, filling it in with the appropriate location on the transport.

Finally, we call the `start` and `stop` methods on the loop returned by the `Tone.Loop` constructor ❹, passing the time when we want this loop to start and when we want it to stop, followed by a call to `Tone.Transport.start`, which starts the transport playing from the beginning. We start at `"0:0:0"`, the beginning of the first bar, and stop at `"4:0:0"`, the beginning of the fifth bar, meaning that this snippet will last four full bars with four beats each. Our loop repeats at every beat, playing one note each time, so we'll play a total of 16 notes. Try reloading the page and see! You can use the musician's trick of counting bars and beats like this: "*one* two three four, *two* two three four, *three* two three four, *four* two three four." Notice that Tone.js doesn't play a seventeenth note at time location `"4:0:0"` because the end of the loop isn't inclusive.

Listing 12-11 shows an alternative way of creating the same loop we wrote in Listing 12-10. This time we chain the start and stop methods directly to the `Tone.Loop` constructor.

```
--snip--
  let synth = new Tone.Synth().toDestination();

  new Tone.Loop(time => {
    synth.triggerAttackRelease("C4", "16n", time);
  }, "4n").start("0:0:0").stop("4:0:0");

  Tone.Transport.start();
});
```

Listing 12-11: Looping with fewer lines of code

With this notation, we don't need to create a variable to hold the `Tone.Loop` object, and we save a few lines of code by chaining the start and stop methods. We'll be using this pattern in the rest of this section.

`Tone.Loop` is basic, but it's also quite versatile. You can run any arbitrary code in the callback, so you can do more than play the same note over and over. For example, you could choose to play a new random note each time. Listing 12-12 shows how you could generate a short piece of music by randomly playing notes from a pentatonic, or five-note, scale (I chose a pentatonic scale here because any combination of notes in a pentatonic scale tends to sound pleasing).

```
--snip--
  Tone.start();

❶ let synth = new Tone.PolySynth(
    Tone.Synth,
    {
      oscillator: { type: "triangle" },
      volume: -9
    }
  ).toDestination();
```

```
❷ let notes = ["C4", "D4", "E4", "G4", "A4", "C5"];

  new Tone.Loop(time => {
    for (let i = 0; i < 3; i++) {
    ❸ if (Math.random() < 0.5) {
      ❹ let note = notes[Math.floor(Math.random() * notes.length)];
        synth.triggerAttackRelease(note, "32n", time);
      }
    }
  }, "8n").start("0:0:0").stop("8:0:0");

  Tone.Transport.start();
});
```

Listing 12-12: Using Tone.Loop to generate random music

For this example, we're switching to a polysynth ❶ so we can play multiple notes at once. The notes array contains one octave of a C major pentatonic scale, including the C from the next octave ❷. Inside the Tone .Loop callback, we use a for loop to run some code three times. Each time around, we call Math.random() ❸, which returns a random number between 0 and 1, to determine whether to play a note or not. If the value is less than 0.5, we play a note. Otherwise, that note is skipped. The note name is determined by picking a random index into the notes array, using the code Math .floor(Math.random() * notes.length) ❹.

The Tone.Loop object calls this code every eighth note ("8n") for eight bars ("0:0:0" to "8:0:0"). The effect of all this is that every eighth note, up to three notes from the array will be played (there's no guarantee of uniqueness, so the same note could be played two or three times at once, causing that note to be louder). For each of the three notes, there's a one in two chance it will be played, so overall there's a one in eight chance that no notes will be played on any given eighth note.

WEB AUDIO API TIME

Time in the Web Audio API, and by extension in Tone.js, can be tricky, because we're working with two independent clocks: the JavaScript clock and the Web Audio API clock. The JavaScript clock is what we use when we call a function like setTimeout and tell it to execute another function some number of milliseconds in the future. Unfortunately, this clock isn't very accurate: if you call setTimeout with a 100 ms timeout, the function may actually be called after 95 ms or 105 ms, and it may be delayed if the browser is busy doing something else. The Web Audio API, by contrast, has its own precise internal clock that keeps track of the number of seconds since the audio context was created. The current value of this clock is accessible through the currentTime property.

Using the Web Audio API's clock, you can schedule a sound to play at exactly 8 seconds (from the time when the context was created) and to stop playing at 10 seconds, and you know that it will be played for exactly 2 seconds. Instead of trying to execute a JavaScript callback at a specific time, we're using JavaScript to schedule future audio events, such as "start playing this oscillator at 8 seconds" and "stop playing this oscillator at 10 seconds." Once these events have been scheduled, there's no straightforward way to deschedule them. (Technically it's possible, but it would entail keeping a list of all the notes that have not been played yet and telling them not to play.)

Now, imagine that you're writing a song using Tone.js and it's made up of hundreds of notes all starting and stopping at different times. If you scheduled all these notes up front, there'd be no way to pause the song, jump to a specific point in time, or modify the song's BPM. To fix this, Tone.js aims to schedule notes *just in time*. For example, if you wanted to play a note at 12 seconds, Tone.js might aim to run the code that schedules the note when ctx.currentTime is 11.8 seconds. Running the code for scheduling a note at an arbitrary time requires using the JavaScript clock, because the Web Audio API clock can't be used to schedule code, just audio events.

The target amount of time between when something is scheduled and when it's executed is called the *lookahead*. In our example, we have a lookahead of 0.2 seconds. If the lookahead time is too short, then delays to the scheduling code could mean that the scheduled time is already in the past by the time the library is ready to schedule the notes. If the lookahead time is too long, then jumping around in the song or changing the BPM will be laggy. For a more detailed description of this problem, see Chris Wilson's "A Tale of Two Clocks" at *https://web.dev/audio-scheduling/*.

Tone.Sequence

In this section we'll look at another Tone.js helper, called Tone.Sequence. This lets you provide a list of note names to be scheduled to play at regular intervals. You can repeat the whole sequence as many times as you want. As an example, we'll create a repeating pattern of four notes: a G4 followed by three C4s. Update *script.js* with the code in Listing 12-13.

```
--snip--
  Tone.start();

  let synth = new Tone.Synth().toDestination();

  new Tone.Sequence(❶ (time, note) => {
    synth.triggerAttackRelease(note, "16n", time);
  }, ❷ ["G4", "C4", "C4", "C4"], ❸ "4n").start("0:0:0").stop("4:0:0");

  Tone.Transport.start();
});
```

Listing 12-13: Creating a repeating sequence with Tone.Sequence

This is very similar to our first Tone.Loop example (Listing 12-10), but with two important changes. First, the callback function takes two arguments, time and note ❶, instead of a single time argument. Second, there's an extra argument after the callback, which contains a list of notes ❷. Each time the callback is called, the next note in this list is passed as the note argument. It will keep cycling through the notes in the list over and over until it's time to stop. The third argument to Tone.Sequence gives the duration between each callback ❸. In this case we've used "4n", which means that a new note will be played every quarter note.

When you run this example, you should hear a pattern play for 4 bars, with 4 beats per bar, making 16 notes in total. If we wrote out all the calls to synth.triggerAttackRelease manually, instead of relying on Tone.Sequence to automate them, they would look like this:

```
synth.triggerAttackRelease("G4", "16n", "0:0:0");
synth.triggerAttackRelease("C4", "16n", "0:1:0");
synth.triggerAttackRelease("C4", "16n", "0:2:0");
synth.triggerAttackRelease("C4", "16n", "0:3:0");
synth.triggerAttackRelease("G4", "16n", "1:0:0");
synth.triggerAttackRelease("C4", "16n", "1:1:0");
--snip--
```

Here, I've just replaced the note and time arguments with what they would actually be for the first six calls of the callback. Notice how the second number is incrementing in the bars:quarters:sixteenths notation because of the "4n" we used as the duration between callbacks. (In practice, however, Tone.Sequence passes time as a number of seconds rather than using bars:quarters:sixteenths notation.)

If you want a sequence with some silent gaps (*rests* in musical terms), you can use null in place of a note name in the array of note names. Modify *script.js* with the code in Listing 12-14 to see this in action.

```
--snip--
  new Tone.Sequence((time, note) => {
    synth.triggerAttackRelease(note, "16n", time);
  }, ["C4", null, "B3", "C4", "G3", "A3", null, "B3"], "8n")
    .start("0:0:0")
    .stop("4:0:0");

  Tone.Transport.start();
});
```

Listing 12-14: Adding rests with null

Now we have a longer sequence of notes, with some nulls interspersed to insert pauses into the sequence. We've also changed the duration from "4n" to "8n", which means the notes will play twice as fast as before. When you play this updated example, you should hear a more interesting sequence of notes, including some rests.

Tone.Part

The last of the transport helpers we'll be looking at is Tone.Part. This is the most flexible of the helpers, as it allows us to specify the exact timing of every note played. With Tone.Part, instead of passing an array of note names, we pass an array of time/note pairs. For example, [["0:0:0", "C4"], ["0:1:0", "D4"], ["0:1:2", "E4"]] would play the three notes C4, D4, and E4 at the three times specified. This way, unlike with Tone.Loop and Tone.Sequence, the notes don't have to be played at equal time intervals. Also, by default Tone.Part doesn't loop, so the sequence of notes in the array is played only once. See the code in Listing 12-15 for an example.

```
--snip--
  Tone.start();
❶ let synth = new Tone.PolySynth(Tone.Synth).toDestination();

  new Tone.Part((time, note) => {
    synth.triggerAttackRelease(note, "16n", time);
  }, [
    ["0:0:0", ❷ ["C3", "E4"]],
    ["0:0:3", "D4"],
    ["0:1:0", "C4"],
    ["0:1:2", "D4"],
    ["0:2:0", ["E3", "E4"]],
    ["0:2:2", "E4"],
    ["0:3:0", "E4"],
    ["1:0:0", ["G3", "D4"]],
    ["1:0:2", "D4"],
    ["1:1:0", "D4"],
    ["1:2:0", ["E3", "E4"]],
    ["1:2:2", "G4"],
    ["1:3:0", "G4"]
❸ ]).start("0:0:0");

  Tone.Transport.start();
});
```

Listing 12-15: Playing a melody with Tone.Part

The first change we're making here is to the synth ❶. This time we're back to using a polyphonic synth, so we can play multiple notes at the same time. Other than the synth being different, the body of the callback function is the same. We're still calling synth.triggerAttackRelease and passing the note and `time` parameters, which `Tone.Part` will fill in automatically. Next comes the array of time/note pairs. You may notice that some of the notes are arrays themselves; for example, the first "note" in the list is `["C3", "E4"]` ❷. This pair of notes will be passed to the `triggerAttackRelease` method unchanged and will have the effect of playing two notes at once, just like our other polyphonic synth examples.

Finally, we call `.start("0:0:0")` ❸, which has the effect of playing this part immediately. If we used `.start("1:0:0")` instead, for example, then the melody would start after a bar's pause. The times given for each time/note pair are relative to the time passed to the `start` method.

When you play this example, you should hear the beginning of "Mary Had a Little Lamb."

TRY IT YOURSELF

12-5. See if you can extend the `Tone.Part` code to finish the "Mary Had a Little Lamb" melody. Hint: the next seven notes are the same as the first seven notes, but two bars later, so you can copy them and change the bar number in the time from a 0 to a 2. Just be sure to add a comma after the last time/note pair in Listing 12-15 before adding more notes.

Making Drum Sounds

Most electronic music has some kind of drum beat. The drum sounds used to make the beat can come from audio files, or they can be synthesized. We're going to be using the latter technique here. The core of a drum beat is built around three components: the kick drum (a "boom" sound), the snare drum (a "bah" sound), and the hi-hat (a "ti" sound). In this section, you'll learn techniques for synthesizing those sounds.

Hi-Hat Synthesis

A real-world hi-hat is made up of two cymbals facing each other. The top cymbal is connected to a pedal so the drummer can make the cymbals touch or move apart. We're going for a closed (cymbals touching) sound here. When you hit closed hi-hats with a drum stick, they make a high-pitched noise that quickly fades away.

We'll approximate this by using a different kind of synth, a `NoiseSynth`, to generate white noise instead of notes with pitches. In signal processing, *white noise* is a random signal that has equal-level components at all frequencies. We'll give the `NoiseSynth` an amplitude envelope that simulates the abrupt attacks of hitting the hi-hat with a stick. Finally, we'll pass the noise through a *filter*—a device that allows through some frequencies while reducing the level of others—to remove the low frequencies and make it sound higher and more cymbal-like.

First, we'll set up the `NoiseSynth` and envelope, and play the hi-hat sound in a loop. Update your *script.js* with the code in Listing 12-16.

```
--snip--
  Tone.start();

❶ let hiHat = new Tone.NoiseSynth({
    envelope: {
      attack: 0.001, decay: 0.1, sustain: 0, release: 0
    },
    volume: -6
  }).toDestination();

❷ new Tone.Loop(time => {
    hiHat.triggerAttackRelease("16n", time);
  }, "8n").start("0:0:0").stop("4:0:0");

  Tone.Transport.start();
});
```

Listing 12-16: The beginnings of a hi-hat sound

We create a new `NoiseSynth` ❶, passing an amplitude envelope and a volume of −6 dB. The envelope has a very short attack (1/1000 of a second) and a longer decay (1/10 of a second), which is supposed to mimic the amplitude envelope of a hi-hat being struck. Because sustain and release are both set to 0, the sound will be over immediately after the initial attack and decay periods (0.001 + 0.1 s). In particular, the sustain of 0 means the sound will sustain at 0 percent of its full volume, so even if the duration of the note is longer, you won't hear anything after the attack and decay.

Next, we use `Tone.Loop` to play a continuous stream of eighth-note hi-hats for four bars ❷. Note that the `triggerAttackRelease` method on `NoiseSynth` doesn't take a note name, because noise doesn't have any particular pitch. You have to specify only the duration and the time when the note should be played.

When you play this example, you should hear a stream of hi-hat sounds. It doesn't sound great yet, because we haven't added the filter. We'll do that in Listing 12-17.

```
--snip--
  Tone.start();

❶ let hiHatFilter = new Tone.Filter(15000, "bandpass").toDestination();

  let hiHat = new Tone.NoiseSynth({
    envelope: {
      attack: 0.001, decay: 0.1, sustain: 0, release: 0
    },
```

```
    volume: -6
❷ }).connect(hiHatFilter);

  new Tone.Loop(time => {
--snip--
```

Listing 12-17: Applying a filter to the hi-hat sound

First, we use `Tone.Filter` to create a *bandpass filter* ❶. This kind of filter lets through ("passes") only the frequencies at or around a frequency of your choice. In this case, we tell the filter to pass the band of frequencies around 15,000 Hz, or 15 kHz, while eliminating all others. The human range of hearing is roughly 20 Hz to 20 kHz, so our filter lets through only parts of the noise that are very high in pitch.

In Listing 12-16, we used `toDestination()` on the `NoiseSynth` to connect it directly to the output. In Listing 12-17, we're instead connecting the filter to the output ❶, and then connecting the synth to the filter ❷. This means that the synth's sound is run through the filter before being output through your speakers or headphones. As a result, when you play this example you should hear the same hi-hat sounds, but limited to high frequencies only, which sounds a bit more like a real hi-hat.

Snare Synthesis

In this section we'll synthesize a snare drum. A snare drum has a series of wires (known as the *snare*) resting against the bottom drumhead that rattle against the drumhead when the drum is hit. This gives it a relatively complex sound, composed of some noise and some more pitched sound. To mimic this, we'll use two separate sound sources: a noise synth and a regular synth with a fixed frequency. Both will have a short amplitude envelope to create a percussive feel, and we'll also pass the noise component of the sound through a bandpass filter to make the snare lower than the hi-hat. We'll create a new `Snare` class to encapsulate these details, as shown in Listing 12-18.

```
--snip--
  new Tone.Loop(time => {
    hiHat.triggerAttackRelease("16n", time);
  }, "8n").start("0:0:0").stop("4:0:0");

  class Snare {
    constructor() {
    ❶ this.noiseFilter = new Tone.Filter(5000, "bandpass").toDestination();
    ❷ this.noiseSynth = new Tone.NoiseSynth({
        envelope: {
          attack: 0.001, decay: 0.1, sustain: 0, release: 0
        },
        volume: -12
      }).connect(this.noiseFilter);
```

```
❸ this.synth = new Tone.Synth({
    envelope: {
      attack: 0.0001, decay: 0.1, sustain: 0, release: 0
    },
    oscillator: { type: "sine" },
    volume: -12
  }).toDestination();
  }

❹ triggerAttackRelease(duration, when) {
    this.noiseSynth.triggerAttackRelease(duration, when);
    this.synth.triggerAttackRelease("G3", duration, when);
  }
}

❺ let snare = new Snare();

❻ new Tone.Loop(time => {
    snare.triggerAttackRelease("16n", time);
  }, "2n").start("0:1:0").stop("4:0:0");

  Tone.Transport.start();
});
```

Listing 12-18: Synthesizing a snare drum

At a high level, the Snare class has two methods, constructor and trigger
AttackRelease. The constructor creates a filter and two synths. The trigger
AttackRelease method calls the triggerAttackRelease methods on the two
synths to play them simultaneously.

In the constructor, we start by creating the filter ❶ and noise synth ❷.
This is very similar to how we created the hi-hat, except we use a frequency
of 5,000 Hz for the bandpass filter, to reflect the lower sound of a snare
drum. Next, we create the pitched synth ❸, which uses a similar amplitude
envelope to the noise synth but with an even shorter attack to simulate the
sound of a snare drum (in a real snare drum, the snares are triggered by
the vibration of the drum skin, so they lag behind the sound of the drum
slightly). The synth is configured with a sine wave oscillator. Since we'll be
playing the two synths simultaneously, we give each one a volume of -12,
which results in an overall volume similar to the hi-hat.

The triggerAttackRelease method ❹ takes just a duration and a when
parameter. These are passed to the underlying synths' triggerAttackRelease
methods. When we trigger the pitched synth, we give it a note name of
"G3", which is the pitch I decided to tune the snare to. The inclusion of the
pitched synth is subtle but makes the drum sound a bit more realistic.

Next, we instantiate the class ❺, and finally we create a new Tone.Loop
object ❻. This loop is four times as long as the hi-hat loop ("2n" instead of
"8n", or a half note instead of an eighth note) and starts after one quarter
note. This means there will be a snare hit on the second and fourth beats
of every bar. When you play this example, you should hear the hi-hat every
eighth note and the snare every two quarter notes.

Kick Synthesis

The last drum sound to synthesize is the kick drum. A kick drum is much larger than a snare drum, and it doesn't have the rattling snare to make it sound noisy. The sound of a kick drum is fairly complex, but luckily Tone.js has a synth called a MembraneSynth that mimics it quite well. This synth takes a regular oscillator and lowers its frequency over a short period of time, which ends up sounding a lot like a kick drum when set up correctly. Listing 12-19 shows how this is done.

```
--snip--
  new Tone.Loop(time => {
    snare.triggerAttackRelease("16n", time);
  }, "2n").start("0:1:0").stop("4:0:0");

  let kick = new Tone.MembraneSynth({
❶ pitchDecay: 0.02,
    octaves: 6,
    volume: -9
  }).toDestination();

❷ new Tone.Loop(time => {
    kick.triggerAttackRelease(50, "16n", time);
  }, "2n").start("0:0:0").stop("4:0:0");

  Tone.Transport.start();
});
```

Listing 12-19: Synthesizing a kick drum

The options for the MembraneSynth include pitchDecay ❶, which specifies in seconds how quickly the frequency should change, and octaves, which specifies how many octaves to drop the frequency in that time. In our loop ❷, we trigger the synth with a frequency of 50 Hz. This loop has the same "2n" duration as the snare loop, but starting at time zero, which means that the kick and snare sounds will alternate every quarter note, giving a classic rock drum beat. When you play this example, you might recognize it as the basic drum pattern of a lot of songs.

Reverb

Reverb (short for *reverberation*) is an effect that makes music sound like it's being played in a room or larger enclosed space. The random echoes that real-world sounds make as they bounce around the walls of a room are what give this reverb effect. Reverb makes each sound take a little time to die away, and it will make our drums sound a bit more realistic. We can add reverb with Tone.Reverb, as you'll see in Listing 12-20.

```
--snip--
  Tone.start();

  let reverb = new Tone.Reverb({
    decay: 1,
```

```
  wet: 0.3
}).toDestination();

let hiHatFilter = new Tone.Filter(15000, "bandpass").connect(reverb);

let hiHat = new Tone.NoiseSynth({
  envelope: {
    attack: 0.001, decay: 0.1, sustain: 0, release: 0
  },
  volume: -6
}).connect(hiHatFilter);

new Tone.Loop(time => {
  hiHat.triggerAttackRelease("16n", time);
}, "8n").start("0:0:0").stop("4:0:0");

class Snare {
  constructor() {
    this.noiseFilter = new Tone.Filter(5000, "bandpass").connect(reverb);
    this.noiseSynth = new Tone.NoiseSynth({
      envelope: {
        attack: 0.001, decay: 0.1, sustain: 0, release: 0
      },
      volume: -12
    }).connect(this.noiseFilter);

    this.synth = new Tone.Synth({
      envelope: {
        attack: 0.0001, decay: 0.1, sustain: 0, release: 0
      },
      oscillator: { type: "sine" },
      volume: -12
    }).connect(reverb);
  }

  triggerAttackRelease(duration, when) {
    this.noiseSynth.triggerAttackRelease(duration, when);
    this.synth.triggerAttackRelease("G3", duration, when);
  }
}

let snare = new Snare();

new Tone.Loop(time => {
  snare.triggerAttackRelease("16n", time);
}, "2n").start("0:1:0").stop("4:0:0");

let kick = new Tone.MembraneSynth({
  pitchDecay: 0.02,
  octaves: 6,
  volume: -9
}).connect(reverb);
```

```
new Tone.Loop(time => {
  kick.triggerAttackRelease(50, "16n", time);
}, "2n").start("0:0:0").stop("4:0:0");

Tone.Transport.start();
});
```

Listing 12-20: Adding reverb

First we create our `Reverb` effect. The `decay` setting describes how long (in seconds) the reverberation will continue after the sound stops. The higher this number, the more echoey the effect. The `wet` setting specifies how much of the reverb sound is passed through compared with the original sound. In this case, `0.3` means that the output of this effect will be 30 percent reverb and 70 percent the original sound. The higher the `wet` setting, the more prominent the reverb effect will be.

The rest of the changes in Listing 12-20 replace any instances of `toDestination()` with `connect(reverb)`. This way all the drum sounds are passed through the reverb effect before the reverb effect is sent to the output. When you play this example, the drums should sound more like they're being played in a room. You can make the effect more pronounced by increasing the value of `wet` (to `0.6`, say) or by increasing the `decay` in the `Tone.Reverb` settings.

A Drum Loop

Now that we have our drum sounds set up, it would be nice to have an easier way to trigger them. Ideally, we would want to create a drum pattern by writing something like this:

```
kick:  x...x...
snare: ..x...x.
hiHat: xxxxxxxx
```

Then we can let JavaScript do the work of converting that notation into code that Tone.js can understand. Here, each x represents a note, each dot (.) represents a silence, and each column represents an eighth note. For example, in the first eighth note the kick and hi-hat play, in the second only the hi-hat plays, in the third the snare and hi-hat play, and so on. The pattern shown here matches the drum beat we built up in the previous sections.

To accomplish this, we'll make a helper function that will convert a string of x's and dots into an array of values that the `Tone.Sequence` transport helper can use. Recall that `Tone.Sequence` takes an array of note names and plays them repeatedly in sequence, with `null` being used for rests. Our function should convert dots to `null`s, while leaving x's the same.

NOTE *Since drum sounds don't have note names, any string can actually represent a drum hit to `Tone.Sequence` (we're just using x's for convenience). All that matters is that it isn't `null`.*

Listing 12-21 shows the definition of this function. Add it to your *script.js* file, before the current drum code.

```
--snip--
  Tone.start();

  // Converts a string to an array of notes or null.
  // Dots in the string become nulls in the array and are silent.
  function mkSequence(pattern) {
    return pattern.split("").map(value => {
      if (value == ".") {
        return null;
      } else {
        return value;
      }
    });
  }

  let reverb = new Tone.Reverb({
--snip--
```

Listing 12-21: The mkSequence helper function

The mkSequence function takes a string like "x...x..." and converts it to an array of strings and nulls, like ["x", null, null, null, "x", null, null, null], which is the format we need for Tone.Sequence. It splits the string into an array of individual characters using the split method and uses the array map method to create a new array by calling a function for each character. If the character is ".", then it replaces it with a null in the new array. Otherwise, it passes the character through unchanged.

Next, we'll create the strings that will be passed into this function, as shown in Listing 12-22. Add this code after the mkSequence function definition.

```
--snip--
  }

  let drumPattern = {
    kick:  "x...x...",
    snare: "..x...x.",
    hiHat: "xxxxxxxx",
  };

  let reverb = new Tone.Reverb({
--snip--
```

Listing 12-22: Defining drumPattern

We're storing the three strings in an object called drumPattern to keep them organized. I've added spaces to line up the strings so it's easier to see the pattern.

Finally, we'll use the helper and Tone.Sequence in place of our three existing calls to Tone.Loop, as shown in Listing 12-23.

```
--snip--
  }).connect(hiHatFilter);

  new Tone.Sequence(time => {
    hiHat.triggerAttackRelease("16n", time);
  }, mkSequence(drumPattern.hiHat), "8n").start("0:0:0").stop("4:0:0");

  class Snare {
--snip--
  let snare = new Snare();

  new Tone.Sequence(time => {
    snare.triggerAttackRelease("16n", time);
  }, mkSequence(drumPattern.snare), "8n").start("0:0:0").stop("4:0:0");

  let kick = new Tone.MembraneSynth({
    pitchDecay: 0.02,
    octaves: 6,
    volume: -9
  }).connect(reverb);

  new Tone.Sequence(time => {
    kick.triggerAttackRelease(50, "16n", time);
  }, mkSequence(drumPattern.kick), "8n").start("0:0:0").stop("4:0:0");

  Tone.Transport.start();
});
```

Listing 12-23: Using mkSequence with Tone.Sequence in place of Tone.Loop

Here, we replace each of the Tone.Loop calls with the new Tone.Sequence calls. In each case we call mkSequence, passing one of the strings from our drumPattern object, which will create an array of x's and nulls. The result of this call is passed to the Tone.Sequence helper, which we use to trigger the appropriate drum sounds. Again, Tone.Sequence will interpret any string, such as "x", as an appropriate note name for a drum hit, while the nulls represent silences. The last argument to Tone.Sequence, "8n", means that each dot or x in the drum pattern string represents an eighth note.

If you now reload the page, you should hear the same drum beat as before. This might seem like a lot of work to get the same output, but now we have a lot more flexibility to write different drum patterns, and we can easily modify them as we see fit. Try adding some extra snare or kick notes to the strings in drumPattern to see how it sounds.

Working with Samples

An important part of electronic music is *sampling*: using snippets of existing audio to build up a new piece of music. One common technique is to modify the playback speed of the samples to change their pitch, so a single sample can be used for multiple notes. If you've ever sped up a recording of someone's voice to make them sound high-pitched like a chipmunk, or slowed it down to make them sound low-pitched like a giant, it's the same principle.

Tone.js makes it easy to work with samples with the `Tone.Sampler` instrument. This instrument acts a lot like the synths we've seen so far, in that it has a `triggerAttackRelease` method that lets you play a certain note at a certain time. The difference is that instead of using an oscillator or noise generator as a source, it plays a snippet of an audio file, possibly pitch-shifted to the requested pitch.

To avoid any issues of copyright, I've sourced some samples from a free online sample database, *https://freesound.org*. I've reuploaded them to Amazon S3 (Simple Storage Service) in such a way that you can access them directly from your code without having to download them (if you want to know the technical details, the files are in a public S3 bucket with CORS headers enabling access from any origin). The samples are of three different trumpet notes, and are found at the following URLs:

- *https://skilldrick-jscc.s3.us-west-2.amazonaws.com/trumpet-c5.mp3*
- *https://skilldrick-jscc.s3.us-west-2.amazonaws.com/trumpet-d5.mp3*
- *https://skilldrick-jscc.s3.us-west-2.amazonaws.com/trumpet-f5.mp3*

If you enter any of these URLs into your web browser, the sample should play automatically.

Let's see how to load these samples into a new `Tone.Sampler` object. Tone.js lets you load all your samples from external URLs, such as our three S3 URLs, which we do in Listing 12-24. Insert the new sampler code at the end of *script.js*.

```
--snip--
  new Tone.Sequence(time => {
    kick.triggerAttackRelease(50, "16n", time);
  }, mkSequence(drumPattern.kick), "8n").start("0:0:0").stop("4:0:0");

  // Samples from freesound.org:
  // https://freesound.org/people/MTG/sounds/357432/
  // https://freesound.org/people/MTG/sounds/357336/
  // https://freesound.org/people/MTG/sounds/357546/
  const sampler = new Tone.Sampler({
    urls: {
      "C5": "trumpet-c5.mp3",
      "D5": "trumpet-d5.mp3",
      "F5": "trumpet-f5.mp3"
    },
    baseUrl: "https://skilldrick-jscc.s3.us-west-2.amazonaws.com/",
    attack: 0,
    release: 1,
    volume: -24,
    onload: () => {
      sampler.triggerAttackRelease(["C5", "E5", "G5"], "1n", 0);
    }
  }).toDestination();

  Tone.Transport.start();
});
```

Listing 12-24: Creating a sampler

We create the sampler by passing a configuration object to the `Tone.Sampler` constructor. In this example, the configuration object contains five properties. The first property, `urls`, contains an object mapping note names to filenames. For example, we're saying that the note name C5 corresponds to the filename *trumpet-c5.mp3*. Next, `baseUrl` defines the shared prefix of all the URLs, which saves us from having to write out the full URL for each sample. All the URLs are in the same S3 bucket, so we can use that as the base URL and then just provide the filenames in `urls`.

The sampler instrument doesn't apply a full ADSR envelope when it plays samples, but it does allow you to set the `attack` (fade-in speed) and `release` (fade-out speed). We use an instant attack (because the sample already has its own attack), and a long release of one second. We also set `volume` to –24 dB so the sampler isn't too loud. Finally, the `onload` property allows us to specify what happens once all the samples have been downloaded. In this example, we call `triggerAttackRelease` to play a three-note chord. Note that `Tone.Sampler` is by default polyphonic, so it can play multiple samples at once.

When you play this example, you'll still hear the drums. Once the samples load, you should also hear a C major chord played by the trumpet sampler. One interesting thing to note here is that although we provided a sample for the note C5, we didn't provide one for E5 or G5, the other pitches in the C major chord. When we tell the sampler to play these notes, it picks the closest provided sample and shifts its pitch by changing the playback speed. For instance, the closest sample to G5 has a pitch of F5, so this sample will be sped up slightly to sound like G5 instead. As long as the note we're trying to play isn't too far away from one of the provided samples, it will sound fine. If we push it too far, however, the result won't sound as realistic. For example, try raising the notes an octave by setting them to C6, E6, and G6 instead. They'll start to sound a bit silly now. Also, because the samples are being played back twice as fast, they're half the duration, so they won't last the full bar they're supposed to (the higher notes will finish earlier because they're played back faster). You can also go the other way and set the notes to C4, E4, and G4. This time the duration won't be a problem, since the samples are being played slower in order to shift them down in pitch, but the notes still won't sound as realistic.

Summary

In this chapter you learned about making sounds and music using the Web Audio API, and you saw how using a library like Tone.js can make your life much easier by hiding a lot of the lower-level details. You also learned a lot of tricks for sound synthesis and sampling using the Tone.js library. If some of the musical details went over your head, don't worry. The most important thing here was getting used to working with a new JavaScript API and library. We'll be putting all this to use in the next chapter, where we'll write an actual song using the instruments created in this chapter!

13

WRITING A SONG

You've now learned enough about the basics of Tone.js and sound synthesis to write a simple song. Our song is going to be made up of a few instruments: the drums we developed in the previous chapter, the trumpet sampler, two different synth bass parts, and some chords played on another synth.

Getting Organized

Our song will reuse a lot of the code from the previous chapter, but we'll reorganize it to make it easier to follow how the song is built. The *index.html* file will be exactly the same as in Chapter 12, but we'll start from scratch with a new *script.js* file, which we'll organize into four logical sections:

Instruments   For instantiating and setting up the instruments

Sequencing   For creating the looping sequences of notes to be played

Song   For scheduling the start and end of each sequence

Event Handling   The code that handles the `click` event that starts playing the song

We'll set off each of these four sections with a multiline comment to make the *script.js* file easier to navigate. Listing 13-1 shows what these comments look like. You can add them to the file now, in this order.

```
/////////////////
// Instruments //
/////////////////

////////////////
// Sequencing //
////////////////

//////////
// Song //
//////////

////////////////////
// Event Handling //
////////////////////
```

Listing 13-1: The comments delineating the main sections of script.js

Throughout the chapter, as we build up the song, I'll tell you to add each new piece of code to the end of a particular section. These comments will enable you to quickly find exactly where the new code should go.

Event Handling

Let's start by writing the Event Handling section of *script.js*. This code is almost identical to the code we wrote at the beginning of the previous chapter: it creates a `click` event listener that toggles the style of the Play button and "Playing" paragraph when the user clicks the button, and makes the Tone.js calls necessary to start playing the song. Enter the contents of Listing 13-2 in the Event Handling section of the code.

```
--snip--
////////////////////
// Event Handling //
////////////////////

let play = document.querySelector("#play");
let playing = document.querySelector("#playing");

play.addEventListener("click", () => {
  // Hide this button
  play.style = "display: none";
  playing.style = "";
```

```
  Tone.start();

  // Modify this to start playback at a different part of the song
❶ Tone.Transport.position = "0:0:0";
  Tone.Transport.start();
});
```

Listing 13-2: The event handling code

One important difference in this code compared to Listing 12-2 is that we use `Tone.Transport.position` to set the starting position of the transport before we call `Tone.Transport.start` ❶. Here we've set the starting position to `"0:0:0"`, which is the default, so this call isn't strictly necessary. However, including this line of code makes it easy to modify the starting position if you don't want to have to listen to the whole song every time you add a new element to it. For example, if you wanted to skip the first 20 bars, you could change the value of `Tone.Transport.position` to `"20:0:0"`.

Unlike in the previous chapter, all the code to create the instruments and sequences will live outside of the event handler. That code can all be executed before the user presses Play. Only the `Tone.start` call has to be inside the handler for the song to work correctly. We could even move the `Tone.Transport` lines outside of the handler if we wanted, but it feels more natural to have those come after `Tone.start`.

Making the Drumbeat

Now let's create the drumbeat to underlay the song. We'll use the same hi-hat, snare, and kick sounds we created in the last chapter. First we'll declare those instruments, as shown in Listing 13-3. Add this code to the Instruments section of *script.js*.

```
///////////////////
// Instruments //
///////////////////

❶ function mkDrums() {
    let reverb = new Tone.Reverb({
      decay: 1,
      wet: 0.3
    }).toDestination();

    let hiHatFilter = new Tone.Filter(15000, "bandpass").connect(reverb);

    let hiHat = new Tone.NoiseSynth({
      envelope: {
        attack: 0.001, decay: 0.1, sustain: 0, release: 0
      },
      volume: -6
    }).connect(hiHatFilter);
```

```
class Snare {
  constructor() {
    this.noiseFilter = new Tone.Filter(5000, "bandpass").connect(reverb);
    this.noiseSynth = new Tone.NoiseSynth({
      envelope: {
        attack: 0.001, decay: 0.1, sustain: 0, release: 0
      },
      volume: -12
    }).connect(this.noiseFilter);

    this.synth = new Tone.Synth({
      envelope: {
        attack: 0.0001, decay: 0.1, sustain: 0, release: 0
      },
      oscillator: { type: "sine" },
      volume: -12
    }).connect(reverb);
  }

  triggerAttackRelease(duration, when) {
    this.noiseSynth.triggerAttackRelease(duration, when);
    this.synth.triggerAttackRelease("G3", duration, when);
  }
}

let snare = new Snare();

let kick = new Tone.MembraneSynth({
  pitchDecay: 0.02,
  octaves: 6,
  volume: -9
}).connect(reverb);

❷ return { hiHat, snare, kick };
}

let drums = mkDrums();
--snip--
```

Listing 13-3: Declaring the drums

This code is identical to the code we wrote in the previous chapter, but to keep it a little more organized I've moved all of the drum setup code, including the reverb effect, into a single function called mkDrums (for "make drums") ❶. This function returns an object with the three drums ❷. We're using a new form of syntax for creating this object called *object literal shorthand syntax*. With this shorthand syntax, instead of typing out { hiHat: hiHat, snare: snare, kick: kick }, we just type { hiHat, snare, kick }. This works only if the property names are the same as the variable names.

Now that we've declared the drums, we'll create the actual drumbeat pattern. We'll use the same one-bar pattern that we developed in the previous chapter, with hi-hats on every eighth note and kick and snare sounds alternating every quarter note. Add Listing 13-4 to the Sequencing section of the code.

```
--snip--
///////////////////
// Sequencing //
///////////////////

// Converts a string to an array of notes or nulls.
// Dots in the string become nulls in the array and are silent.
❶ function mkSequence(pattern) {
  return pattern.split("").map(value => {
    if (value == ".") {
      return null;
    } else {
      return value;
    }
  });
}

❷ let drumPattern = {
  kick:  "x...x...",
  snare: "..x...x.",
  hiHat: "xxxxxxxx",
};

let hiHatSequence = new Tone.Sequence(time => {
  drums.hiHat.triggerAttackRelease("16n", time);
}, mkSequence(drumPattern.hiHat), "8n");

let snareSequence = new Tone.Sequence(time => {
  drums.snare.triggerAttackRelease("16n", time);
}, mkSequence(drumPattern.snare), "8n");

let kickSequence = new Tone.Sequence(time => {
  drums.kick.triggerAttackRelease(50, "16n", time);
}, mkSequence(drumPattern.kick), "8n");
--snip--
```

Listing 13-4: The drumbeat sequences

Again, this is identical to code we wrote in Chapter 12. We start with a helper function, mkSequence ❶, that takes in a pattern of x's and dots and turns it into note information that Tone.Sequence can use. Then we store the patterns we want in a drumPattern object ❷ and generate the sequences for each instrument with Tone.Sequence.

All that's left to do to create the drumbeat is to schedule the sequences to play on loop for most of the duration of the song, as shown in Listing 13-5. Add this code to the Song section of the *script.js* file.

```
--snip--
//////////
// Song //
//////////

hiHatSequence.start("0:0:0").stop("44:0:0");
snareSequence.start("0:0:0").stop("44:0:0");
kickSequence.start("0:0:0").stop("44:0:0");
--snip--
```

Listing 13-5: Scheduling the drumbeat sequences

Here we tell the drums to start at the beginning of the song and keep playing for 44 bars. Load the page and click **Play,** and you should hear the same drums as before, but for much longer. When you get tired of listening, reload the page to stop the drums playing.

Adding the Bass Lines

Next we're going to add a couple of bass synths and have them play two separate bass lines. First we'll create the synths, by adding the code in Listing 13-6 to the end of the Instruments section (just before the Sequencing section).

```
--snip--
let lowBass = new Tone.FMSynth({
  oscillator: {
  ❶ type: "triangle"
  },
  envelope: {
    attack: 0.0001, decay: 0.5, sustain: 0.3, release: 0.1
  },
  volume: -3
}).toDestination();

let highBass = new Tone.FMSynth({
  oscillator: {
  ❷ type: "square"
  },
  envelope: {
    attack: 0.0001, decay: 0.1, sustain: 0.3, release: 0.1
  },
  volume: -9
}).toDestination();
--snip--
```

Listing 13-6: Creating the bass instruments

Here we declare two bass instruments called lowBass and highBass. Both use a synth we haven't seen yet, called an FMSynth. *FM* is short for *frequency modulation*, and *FM synthesis* involves using one oscillator to modulate, or modify, the frequency of another oscillator. This kind of synthesis yields a richer sound than a plain oscillator, and it makes a good bass synth. There are a lot of parameters that can be modified in Tone.FMSynth (for example, the amount of modulation applied, the relationship between the frequencies of the two oscillators, the waveforms of the two oscillators, and so on), but we'll mostly stick to the default values. All we'll do is set the oscillator type ("triangle" for "lowBass" ❶ and "square" for highBass ❷), as well as the envelope and volume.

For generating the bass sequences, we're going to use a slightly different technique from our current mkSequence helper function. That helper is great for things like drums, where you need only a single character to determine whether a note is played or not, but it doesn't work for a bass line where we want to provide note names, which have at least two characters (like C3 or F#4). One notation we might choose for writing out a sequence could be something like:

```
"C3|  |  |C3|  |  |G2|B2"
```

The vertical pipe characters are used as divisions, and between each pair of pipes is either a note we want to play or a blank space, which represents a silence. (The sequence written out here is the start of the bass line for Ben E. King's "Stand by Me.")

Listing 13-7 gives the definition of mkPipeSequence, which we'll use for sequencing our bass lines. It takes a string like the one for "Stand by Me" and converts it into an array of note names and nulls. Insert this function into the Sequencing section of *script.js*, just after the definition of mkSequence.

```
--snip--
// Converts a string to an array of notes or nulls.
// Spaces between pipes in the string become nulls in the array and are silent.
function mkPipeSequence(pattern) {
  return pattern.split("|").map(value => {
❶ if (value.trim() == "") {
      return null;
    } else {
      return value;
    }
  });
}
--snip--
```

Listing 13-7: The mkPipeSequence function

This function uses split("|") to split the string by the pipe character. Using the "Stand by Me" example, this would give the array ["C3", " ", " ", "C3", " ", " ", "G2", "B2"]. We then map over each of these values. The trim method ❶ removes any whitespace from the start or end of a string, so " ".trim() results in "", an empty string. We replace any empty strings with nulls in the returned array and pass the note names through unchanged, resulting in a return value of ["C3", null, null, "C3", null, null, "G2", "B2"].

Next we want to create the actual sequences for the two bass lines (we won't be borrowing from "Stand by Me" here). Add the code in Listing 13-8 to the end of the Sequencing section.

```
--snip--
let lowBassSequence = new Tone.Sequence((time, note) => {
  lowBass.triggerAttackRelease(note, "16n", time, 0.6);
}, mkPipeSequence("G2|  |  |G2|G2|  |  | "), "8n");

let highBassSequence = new Tone.Sequence((time, note) => {
  highBass.triggerAttackRelease(note, "16n", time, 0.3);
}, mkPipeSequence("G3|F3|E3|D3|G2|D3|G3|D3"), "8n");
--snip--
```

Listing 13-8: The bass sequences

There are two bass parts here: the low one just plays three eighth notes per bar, while the high one plays eighth notes continuously.

Finally, we need to schedule these sequences against the transport, as shown in Listing 13-9. This code should be added to the end of the Song section.

```
--snip--
lowBassSequence.start("0:0:0").stop("47:3:0");
highBassSequence.start("4:0:0").stop("47:3:0");
--snip--
```

Listing 13-9: Scheduling the bass sequences

The low sequence starts at the beginning, and the high sequence starts after four bars. Both continue looping until partway through the 48th bar. This way, the bass parts will continue for a few bars after the drums stop.

If you now refresh the page and hit Play, you'll hear the beginnings of a song! Not only do we have drums and bass, but we have some very basic structure, with the second bass line coming in after four bars and the drums ending before the bass. That bass solo at the end is by far the most dramatic part of the song as it currently stands. To hear just that part, you can modify the value of Tone.Transport.Position in the Event Handling section of the code. If you set it to "40:0:0" and reload, you'll skip to the last eight bars of the song.

Adding Chords

Next we'll fill out the song with some chords. This song will have two separate chord sequences, which we'll schedule for different times in the song to give it some more structure and variety.

First we need to create the instrument that will play the chords. The code for this is in Listing 13-10; insert this at the end of the Instruments section.

```
--snip--
let chordSynth = new Tone.PolySynth(Tone.Synth, {
  oscillator: {
    type: "triangle"
  },
  volume: -12
}).toDestination();
--snip--
```

Listing 13-10: The chord synth

We need a PolySynth because the instrument will be playing more than one note at a time (that's what a chord is). The PolySynth is based on a regular Synth, using the default amplitude envelope and a triangle wave oscillator.

Next we'll create the sequencing code for the chords. Rather than writing a chord out manually each time we want to play it in a sequence, we'll create some named chords, and then create sequences using those chord names. Insert the code in Listing 13-11 at the end of the Sequencing section.

```
   --snip--
❶ let chords = {
    1: ["D4", "G4"],
    2: ["E4", "G4"],
    3: ["C4", "E4", "G4"],
    4: ["B3", "F4", "G4"],
  };

❷ function playChord(time, chordName) {
❸  let notes = chords[chordName];
    chordSynth.triggerAttackRelease(notes, "16n", time, 0.6);
  }

❹ let chordSequence1 = new Tone.Sequence((time, chordName) => {
    playChord(time, chordName);
  }, mkSequence("1...2...3..4...31...2...3..4.343"), "8n");

❺ let chordSequence2 = new Tone.Sequence((time, chordName) => {
    playChord(time, chordName);
  }, mkSequence("3...2...4..1.213"), "8n");
   --snip--
```

Listing 13-11: Sequencing the chords

The first thing we do is create an object called chords with the four chords that we'll be sequencing ❶. We could call them anything, but for simplicity I'm using the numbers 1, 2, 3, and 4 to refer to the chords (though note that because these are object keys, the numbers are interpreted as strings). Each chord number corresponds to an array of note names, which is the format our PolySynth requires. The two chord sequences will just be various orderings of these four chords.

Next comes a helper function for playing the chords ❷. This `playChord` function takes the time to play the chord and the name of the chord as a string (one of the numbers 1 through 4). Then it looks in the `chords` object and retrieves the array of notes keyed by the given chord name ❸. The function ends by calling `triggerAttackRelease` on the `chordSynth`, passing the array of note names. Because it's a `PolySynth`, our `chordSynth` instrument is able to play all the notes in the chord at once.

Finally, we make the two sequences, called `chordSequence1` ❹ and `chordSequence2` ❺. The callback for both of these sequences is our `playChord` function. We're also using the same `mkSequence` helper we used for sequencing the drums earlier, but in this case the values in the string are either dots (silence) or chord names. Unlike with our bass lines, `mkSequence` works here because each chord name is a single character, and we have our `playChord` function to reinterpret the chord names as pitches. As with the drums, we're passing `"8n"` as the last argument to `Tone.Sequence`, meaning that each dot or chord name is an eighth note. The first sequence is 32 eighth notes long, or 4 bars. The second sequence is 16 eighth notes long, or 2 bars.

Now we'll actually schedule the sequences against the transport. Add the code in Listing 13-12 to the end of the Song section.

```
--snip--
chordSequence1.start("8:0:0").stop("24:0:0");
chordSequence2.start("24:0:0").stop("32:0:0");
chordSequence1.start("32:0:0").stop("40:0:0");
--snip--
```

Listing 13-12: Scheduling the chord sequences

The first sequence starts playing after 8 bars and repeats through the end of bar 24, which is 16 bars, or four complete loops of the first sequence. Then the second sequence takes over and runs through bar 32; this is 8 bars, or four complete loops of the second sequence. Finally, the first sequence returns, playing through bar 40; this is also 8 bars, or two complete loops of the first sequence.

Try refreshing your browser and listening to the song again. Make sure to set `Tone.Transport.position` to `"0:0:0"` in the event handler to play from the beginning. If you don't want to wait eight bars for the chords to come in, set it to `"8:0:0"` to start playing where the chords start.

Playing a Tune

Now that we have drums, bass, and chords, the only thing our song is missing is a tune. We're going to use the trumpet sampler we created in the last chapter, and we'll sequence the notes using `Tone.Part`, which lets us easily schedule the timing of each note in the tune separately.

First we'll create the sampler, like we did in Chapter 12. Add the code in Listing 13-13 to the end of the Instruments section.

```
--snip--
// Samples from freesound.org:
// https://freesound.org/people/MTG/sounds/357432/
// https://freesound.org/people/MTG/sounds/357336/
// https://freesound.org/people/MTG/sounds/357546/
let sampler = new Tone.Sampler({
  urls: {
    "C5": "trumpet-c5.mp3",
    "D5": "trumpet-d5.mp3",
    "F5": "trumpet-f5.mp3"
  },
  baseUrl: "https://skilldrick-jscc.s3.us-west-2.amazonaws.com/",
  attack: 0,
  release: 1,
  volume: -24
}).toDestination();
--snip--
```

Listing 13-13: Declaring the trumpet sampler

Here we're creating a Tone.Sampler instrument with the same three samples as in the previous chapter. Note, however, that we're no longer using the sampler's onload property to tell it what to do once the samples have been downloaded. This is a bit of a cheat, but I know that the trumpets aren't going to play at the beginning of the song, and I'm banking on the fact that by the time they come in, the samples will have downloaded. The proper thing to do would be to hide the Play button until the samples have finished downloading, but that would add extra complexity to this project.

Listing 13-14 shows the code for sequencing the notes of the tune. Add this code to the end of the Sequencing section.

```
--snip--
let trumpetPart = new Tone.Part((time, note) => {
  sampler.triggerAttackRelease(note, "1n", time);
}, [
  ["0:0:0", "G5"],
  ["0:2:0", "C5"],
  ["1:0:0", "G5"],

  ["2:0:0", "D5"],
  ["2:2:0", "C5"],
  ["3:0:0", "B4"],

  ["4:0:0", "G5"],
  ["4:2:0", "C5"],
  ["5:0:0", "G5"],

  ["6:0:0", "D5"],
  ["6:2:0", "C5"],
  ["7:0:0", "B4"],
  ["7:2:0", "D5"],

  ["8:0:0", "C5"],
  ["8:2:0", "E5"],
```

```
    ["9:0:0", "F5"],
    ["9:2:0", "D5"],

    ["10:0:0", "C5"],
    ["10:2:0", "E5"],
    ["11:0:0", "D5"],

    ["12:0:0", "C5"],
    ["12:2:0", "E5"],
    ["13:0:0", "F5"],
    ["13:2:0", "D5"],

    ["14:0:0", "C5"],
    ["14:2:0", "E5"],
    ["15:0:0", ["B4", "G5"]]
]);
--snip--
```

Listing 13-14: Sequencing the tune

As a reminder, the Tone.Part constructor takes two arguments: a callback to play for each time/note pair, and a list of time/note pairs. Here, the callback plays a long note ("1n", or a whole bar) on the trumpet sampler for every time/note pair. The first note is played at "0:0:0" and the second is played two beats later, at "0:2:0". Because the notes are about four beats long, they will overlap—I did this intentionally to add some interest to the tune.

The tune won't play yet because we haven't said *when* to play it. Even though each note has a time, these times are relative to when the part is scheduled to begin. To schedule the part, we just have to add some code to the end of the Song section, as shown in Listing 13-15.

```
--snip--
trumpetPart.start("16:0:0");
--snip--
```

Listing 13-15: Scheduling the trumpet part

Unlike the sequences we scheduled so far, the part doesn't loop, so it doesn't need a stop time. We're telling Tone.js to start the trumpet part after 16 bars, which means that all the times given in the part are relative to "16:0:0". We can add the two times together to get the actual time when each note is scheduled (for example, "4:2:0" + "16:0:0" is "20:2:0").

Now you can listen to the complete song! Don't forget to reset Tone .Transport.position to "0:0:0" before you refresh the page.

TRY IT YOURSELF

13-1. Now that you've finished coding the song, try making it your own. Here are some ways you could modify it:

- Change the tempo (BPM) of the song by setting `Tone.Transport.bpm` `.value` to something other than 120.
- Change the drum pattern.
- Modify the Song section and update when the sequences are scheduled.
- Change the chords without changing the chord pattern.
- Change the chord pattern without changing the chords.

13-2. It's a little awkward that you have to reload the page to stop the song. Try adding a Pause button that calls `Tone.Transport.pause` and a Stop button that calls `Tone.Transport.stop`. You could also show the current position by displaying `Tone.Transport.position` on the page, using `setInterval` to update it regularly.

The Complete Code

We've been adding code all over the file, so just in case you got something mixed up, or if you just want to see how it should all look, Listing 13-16 gives the entire contents of *script.js*.

```
//////////////////
// Instruments //
//////////////////

function mkDrums() {
  let reverb = new Tone.Reverb({
    decay: 1,
    wet: 0.3
  }).toDestination();

  let hiHatFilter = new Tone.Filter(15000, "bandpass").connect(reverb);

  let hiHat = new Tone.NoiseSynth({
    envelope: {
      attack: 0.001, decay: 0.1, sustain: 0, release: 0
    },
    volume: -6
  }).connect(hiHatFilter);

  class Snare {
    constructor() {
      this.noiseFilter = new Tone.Filter(5000, "bandpass").connect(reverb);
      this.noiseSynth = new Tone.NoiseSynth({
        envelope: {
          attack: 0.001, decay: 0.1, sustain: 0, release: 0
        },
        volume: -12
```

```
      }).connect(this.noiseFilter);

      this.synth = new Tone.Synth({
        envelope: {
          attack: 0.0001, decay: 0.1, sustain: 0, release: 0
        },
        oscillator: { type: "sine" },
        volume: -12
      }).connect(reverb);
    }

    triggerAttackRelease(duration, when) {
      this.noiseSynth.triggerAttackRelease(duration, when);
      this.synth.triggerAttackRelease("G3", duration, when);
    }
  }

  let snare = new Snare();

  let kick = new Tone.MembraneSynth({
    pitchDecay: 0.02,
    octaves: 6,
    volume: -9
  }).connect(reverb);

  return { hiHat, snare, kick };
}

let drums = mkDrums();

let lowBass = new Tone.FMSynth({
  oscillator: {
    type: "triangle"
  },
  envelope: {
    attack: 0.0001, decay: 0.5, sustain: 0.3, release: 0.1
  },
  volume: -3
}).toDestination();

let highBass = new Tone.FMSynth({
  oscillator: {
    type: "square"
  },
  envelope: {
    attack: 0.0001, decay: 0.1, sustain: 0.3, release: 0.1
  },
  volume: -9
}).toDestination();

let chordSynth = new Tone.PolySynth(Tone.Synth, {
  oscillator: {
    type: "triangle"
  },
```

```
    volume: -12
}).toDestination();

// Samples from freesound.org:
// https://freesound.org/people/MTG/sounds/357432/
// https://freesound.org/people/MTG/sounds/357336/
// https://freesound.org/people/MTG/sounds/357546/
let sampler = new Tone.Sampler({
  urls: {
    "C5": "trumpet-c5.mp3",
    "D5": "trumpet-d5.mp3",
    "F5": "trumpet-f5.mp3"
  },
  baseUrl: "https://skilldrick-jscc.s3.us-west-2.amazonaws.com/",
  attack: 0,
  release: 1,
  volume: -24
}).toDestination();

/////////////////
// Sequencing //
/////////////////

// Converts a string to an array of notes or nulls.
// Dots in the string become nulls in the array and are silent.
function mkSequence(pattern) {
  return pattern.split("").map(value => {
    if (value == ".") {
      return null;
    } else {
      return value;
    }
  });
}

// Converts a string to an array of notes or nulls.
// Spaces between pipes in the string become nulls in the array and are silent.
function mkPipeSequence(pattern) {
  return pattern.split("|").map(value => {
    if (value.trim() == "") {
      return null;
    } else {
      return value;
    }
  });
}

let drumPattern = {
  kick:  "x...x...",
  snare: "..x...x.",
  hiHat: "xxxxxxxx",
};
```

```
let hiHatSequence = new Tone.Sequence(time => {
  drums.hiHat.triggerAttackRelease("16n", time);
}, mkSequence(drumPattern.hiHat), "8n");

let snareSequence = new Tone.Sequence(time => {
  drums.snare.triggerAttackRelease("16n", time);
}, mkSequence(drumPattern.snare), "8n");

let kickSequence = new Tone.Sequence(time => {
  drums.kick.triggerAttackRelease(50, "16n", time);
}, mkSequence(drumPattern.kick), "8n");

let lowBassSequence = new Tone.Sequence((time, note) => {
  lowBass.triggerAttackRelease(note, "16n", time, 0.6);
}, mkPipeSequence("G2|   |  |G2|G2|   |   | "), "8n");

let highBassSequence = new Tone.Sequence((time, note) => {
  highBass.triggerAttackRelease(note, "16n", time, 0.3);
}, mkPipeSequence("G3|F3|E3|D3|G2|D3|G3|D3"), "8n");

let chords = {
  1: ["D4", "G4"],
  2: ["E4", "G4"],
  3: ["C4", "E4", "G4"],
  4: ["B3", "F4", "G4"],
};

function playChord(time, chordName) {
  let notes = chords[chordName];
  chordSynth.triggerAttackRelease(notes, "16n", time, 0.6);
}

let chordSequence1 = new Tone.Sequence((time, chordName) => {
  playChord(time, chordName);
}, mkSequence("1...2...3..4...31...2...3..4.343"), "8n");

let chordSequence2 = new Tone.Sequence((time, chordName) => {
  playChord(time, chordName);
}, mkSequence("3...2...4..1.213"), "8n");

let trumpetPart = new Tone.Part((time, note) => {
  sampler.triggerAttackRelease(note, "1n", time);
}, [
  ["0:0:0", "G5"],
  ["0:2:0", "C5"],
  ["1:0:0", "G5"],

  ["2:0:0", "D5"],
  ["2:2:0", "C5"],
  ["3:0:0", "B4"],

  ["4:0:0", "G5"],
  ["4:2:0", "C5"],
  ["5:0:0", "G5"],
```

```
  ["6:0:0", "D5"],
  ["6:2:0", "C5"],
  ["7:0:0", "B4"],
  ["7:2:0", "D5"],

  ["8:0:0", "C5"],
  ["8:2:0", "E5"],
  ["9:0:0", "F5"],
  ["9:2:0", "D5"],

  ["10:0:0", "C5"],
  ["10:2:0", "E5"],
  ["11:0:0", "D5"],

  ["12:0:0", "C5"],
  ["12:2:0", "E5"],
  ["13:0:0", "F5"],
  ["13:2:0", "D5"],

  ["14:0:0", "C5"],
  ["14:2:0", "E5"],
  ["15:0:0", ["B4", "G5"]]
]);

//////////
// Song //
//////////

hiHatSequence.start("0:0:0").stop("44:0:0");
snareSequence.start("0:0:0").stop("44:0:0");
kickSequence.start("0:0:0").stop("44:0:0");

lowBassSequence.start("0:0:0").stop("47:3:0");
highBassSequence.start("4:0:0").stop("47:3:0");

chordSequence1.start("8:0:0").stop("24:0:0");
chordSequence2.start("24:0:0").stop("32:0:0");
chordSequence1.start("32:0:0").stop("40:0:0");

trumpetPart.start("16:0:0");

////////////////////
// Event Handling //
////////////////////

let play = document.querySelector("#play");
let playing = document.querySelector("#playing");

play.addEventListener("click", () => {
  // Hide this button
  play.style = "display: none";
  playing.style = "";

  Tone.start();
```

```
    // Modify this to start playback at a different part of the song
    Tone.Transport.position = "0:0:0";
    Tone.Transport.start();
});
```

Listing 13-16: The complete code

Summary

In this chapter, you coded a song in JavaScript! Now that you're used to working with Tone.js, you can use it to make your own song. Another fun thing to try is algorithmic music, where instead of writing out a fixed song, you write code that semirandomly produces new music each time it runs. One simple way to try this out is to come up with a list of nice-sounding chords, and then randomly choose which one to play on any given beat (you could use Tone.Loop to accomplish this, as we did in Listing 12-12 in the previous chapter).

PROJECT 3

VISUALIZING DATA

14

INTRODUCING THE D3 LIBRARY

Today's world is full of data, but raw data is basically impossible to understand without visualizing it in some way. Data visualizations can be incredibly simple, such as a chart on Wikipedia showing the average temperature each month in a particular city, or highly intricate, such as an animated infographic from a news organization illustrating the income mobility of tens of thousands of Americans. No matter the level of complexity, however, data visualizations always have the potential to give us more insight into the data we're exploring.

In this project you'll learn to use a powerful JavaScript library called D3.js (or D3 for short), which will enable you to create a whole range of data visualizations in the browser. The great thing about using JavaScript to make data visualizations is that they can be dynamic and interactive. *Dynamic* means the visualization can change over time; for example, they can be updated as new data comes in. *Interactive* means the user can manipulate the visualization, for example, by clicking to reveal more detail about a particular aspect. Also, because you're coding up the visualizations yourself, you're free to customize them in any way you want.

This chapter introduces you to the basics of working with D3, to prepare you for the next chapter, where you'll create an interactive visualization by loading data from an external API. D3 primarily uses a web graphics technology called Scalable Vector Graphics (SVG), so we'll start with a crash course in SVG before we dive into D3 itself.

The SVG Graphics Format

SVG is a way of defining images using points, lines, and curves, rather than pixels. These images are known as *vector graphics*. Because you're defining the *shape* of the image rather than the individual pixels themselves, you can resize or zoom in on an SVG image without it becoming pixelated (hence the *scalable* part of the name).

SVG is based on Extensible Markup Language (XML), a language for storing data that, like HTML, relies on a structure of nested elements with start and end tags. SVG XML looks similar to HTML, but it has its own set of tags that correspond directly to visual elements (in HTML, by contrast, the tags are used to define structure and content). SVG files can be standalone XML files, but SVG can also be embedded in an HTML file using the HTML svg element, making it easy to add SVG graphics to a web page.

One advantage of SVG over the Canvas API for rendering interactive graphics on the web is that each element of an SVG drawing is represented by a DOM element on the web page, which means you can style it with CSS and use JavaScript to add event handlers to respond to mouse events like clicks or hovers. On the other hand, Canvas-based graphics are faster to render, so applications like games that need a high frame rate tend to use the Canvas API rather than SVG.

Let's write our first SVG. Make a new directory called *svg* and create an *index.html* file in that directory containing the content of Listing 14-1. We'll embed our SVG in this HTML file. Also create two empty files in the same directory, called *style.css* and *script.js*—we'll fill those in later when we're ready to style the SVG and make it interactive.

```
<!DOCTYPE html>
<html>
  <head>
    <title>SVG</title>
    <link rel="stylesheet" href="style.css">
```

```
    </head>
    <body>
❶   <svg width="600" height="600"></svg>

      <script src="script.js"></script>
    </body>
</html>
```

Listing 14-1: An index.html *file for exploring SVG*

The code in Listing 14-1 follows our standard HTML template, with an empty svg element added ❶. The svg element is given a width and height of 600 pixels. When you load the page in your browser, it should be blank, because we haven't added content to our SVG yet.

Now let's add some graphics. We'll add a rectangle and some text to the svg element, as shown in Listing 14-2.

```
--snip--
  <body>
    <svg width="600" height="600">
❶   <rect width="95" height="20" x="5" y="5"
        stroke="red" fill="none"></rect>
❷   <text x="10" y="20" font-family="sans-serif">Hello, SVG!</text>
    </svg>

      <script src="script.js"></script>
--snip--
```

Listing 14-2: Adding graphics to the svg element

Everything inside the <svg> and </svg> tags is SVG XML, which has its own set of tag names. In this example, we use the rect ❶ and text ❷ elements. The rect element draws a rectangle, according to the specifications set through the element's attributes. We set the width and height to 95 pixels and 20 pixels, respectively, and its x- and y-coordinates (the location of the top-left corner of the rectangle) to (5, 5). We set the outline to red using the stroke attribute and give it no fill color (the default fill color is black). The rect element doesn't contain any content, so the opening tag is immediately followed by the closing tag.

Similarly, we use the text element to insert text into the drawing. The text element also uses x and y attributes to set its position, but in this case they refer to the start of the *baseline* of the text. In typography, the baseline is the invisible line that runs along the bottom of most letters, excluding those with descenders like *p* or *g*. By default, the x attribute gives the horizontal position of the start of the text. We set the font of the text to the default sans-serif font using the font-family attribute. The content of the text element is the actual text that will be drawn, in this case "Hello, SVG!"

When you reload the page, you should see this text surrounded by a red-outlined rectangle, as shown in Figure 14-1.

Figure 14-1: Our first SVG drawing

Try zooming in on the page (using CTRL-+ on Windows or Linux, or COMMAND-+ on macOS). The rectangle and text should remain sharp, even as you scale the image.

Grouping Elements

You can group multiple SVG elements together by nesting them inside a g (for *group*) element. This is useful because any attributes set on the g element itself will apply to all its child elements. To demonstrate, update the contents of your svg element as shown in Listing 14-3.

```
--snip--
<svg width="600" height="600">
❶ <g font-family="sans-serif" fill="blue">
    <text x="0" y="20">Always</text>
    <text x="0" y="40">Be</text>
    <text x="0" y="60">Coding</text>
  </g>
</svg>
--snip--
```

Listing 14-3: Grouping elements with the g element

In this example, we create a group with three child text elements, each containing a single word. The text elements have the same x-coordinate but different y-coordinates, so the words will be vertically stacked and left-aligned. The attributes of the parent g element (font-family and fill ❶) apply to all the child elements in the group. Reload the page and you should see that all three words are blue and in a sans-serif font.

Creating groupings with g elements also lets you apply *transformations* to all the child elements in a group. SVG supports several kinds of transformations, including translation, rotation, scaling, and skewing. We'll use translate to move all the elements by a fixed amount. Update *index.html* with the following change to the opening g element tag:

```
--snip--
  <g transform="translate(100, 50)" font-family="sans-serif" fill="blue">
--snip--
```

The `transform` attribute takes a list of transformations, separated by spaces. Here we're passing a single transformation: `translate(100, 50)`. This says to move all the elements in the group 100 pixels along the x-axis and 50 pixels down the y-axis.

We can also resize the group by adding a `scale` transformation after the `translate` transformation:

```
--snip--
  <g transform="translate(100, 50) scale(2, 3)" font-family="sans-serif" fill="blue">
--snip--
```

After the translation, the elements are now scaled horizontally by a factor of 2 and vertically by a factor of 3, as shown in Figure 14-2.

Figure 14-2: Transforming grouped elements

All the transformations are relative to the origin (0, 0), unless an earlier translation has moved the origin. This means the scaling affects the placement of elements, as well as their size. For example, when you scale a square with a top-left corner of (10, 10) and a bottom-right corner of (30, 30) by 2, the new corners will be at (20, 20) and (60, 60). The x- and y-coordinates relative to the origin are all doubled.

TRY IT YOURSELF

14-1. Try out some of the other transformations:

- `rotate(deg)` rotates around the origin by *deg* degrees.
- `rotate(deg, x, y)` rotates around the point (*x, y*) by *deg* degrees.
- `skewX(deg)` skews by *deg* degrees along the x-axis.
- `skewY(deg)` skews by *deg* degrees along the y-axis.

Drawing Circles

You can draw an SVG circle using the circle element. The attributes cx and cy set the coordinates for the center of the circle, and r sets the radius. To try it out, replace the content of the svg element with the code in Listing 14-4.

```
--snip--
<svg width="600" height="600">
❶ <circle fill="#faa0a0" r="100" cx="124" cy="130"></circle>

❷ <g stroke="#944e30" stroke-width="3">
     <rect width="8" height="100" x="120" y="90" fill="#e1704d"></rect>
     <circle fill="#acd270" r="18" cx="124" cy="150"></circle>
     <circle fill="#fdfce2" r="18" cx="124" cy="120"></circle>
     <circle fill="#f8c9dc" r="18" cx="124" cy="90"></circle>
  </g>
</svg>
--snip--
```

Listing 14-4: Drawing circles

In this example we're using the new circle element, as well as the g and rect elements. The first circle ❶ has a fill color of #faa0a0, or salmon pink, a radius of 100 pixels, and center coordinates (124, 130). Note that we're using *hex colors* here—see the "Hex Colors" box on the following page to learn more. Next, we use a group ❷ to apply a standard stroke color (chestnut brown) and width (3 pixels) to a rectangle and three smaller circles, with fill colors green, yellow, and rose. The effect of all this is a cute illustration of some Japanese *hanami dango* (a sweet treat popular in Japan during cherry blossom season), as shown in Figure 14-3.

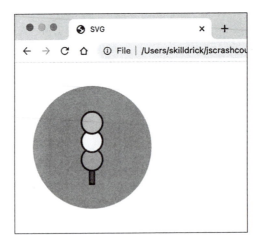

Figure 14-3: An illustration of hanami dango using SVG circles

Notice that the order in which elements are declared defines the order in which they're drawn. The three small circles are declared from bottom to top, so in places where they overlap, the upper circle appears on top.

Likewise, since the large circle is declared first, it's treated as a background for the rest of the illustration.

HEX COLORS

Hexadecimal color syntax, or *hex colors* for short, is a way of specifying RGB color values in CSS and other web graphics technologies like SVG and the Canvas API. Hex colors are written using the base-16 hexadecimal number system, in which digits range from 0 to f (a through f correspond to the decimal numbers 10 to 15). In decimal numbers, the rightmost digit represents units, the second-rightmost digit represents 10s, the third represents 100s, and so on. In hexadecimal numbers, the rightmost digit represents units, the second represents 16s, the third 256s, and so on. One hex digit can convey 16 different values, and two hex digits can convey 256 different values. Hexadecimal is often used in programming because 1 byte can contain 256 different values, so using the hex digits 00 through ff gives us a convenient way to encode bytes in text.

Hex colors generally use three pairs of hex digits to represent an RGB color, preceded by a hash mark. For example, in the hex color #944e30, red has a value of 94, green has a value of 4e, and blue has a value of 30. These three values correspond to the decimal values 148, 78, and 48, which together form a chestnut brown color. (To demonstrate how the conversion works, 94 in hexadecimal is nine 16s and four units, so $9 \times 16 + 4 = 148$ in decimal.) If both digits of each color component are the same, you can also use a shorthand three-digit form, combining the duplicate digits into one. For example, #000000 (black) can also be written as #000.

Defining Paths

The path element is the most powerful SVG element of all, allowing you to create custom shapes by drawing straight or curved lines ("paths") between different points. The d attribute of a path element (short for *data*) is a string containing the path definition, which is a list of path commands. The syntax of this string is optimized to be as compact as possible, so complex paths can be represented using relatively short strings. This is good for computers, but not good for humans; don't expect these strings to be easily readable.

In the next example we're going to re-create the HTML5 logo with path elements, starting with the outer shield shape. Replace the content of the svg element in *index.html* with the code in Listing 14-5.

```
--snip--
<svg width="600" height="600">
  <path fill="#e44d26" d="M 0 0 H 182 L 165 185 L 90 206 L 17 185 Z"/>
  <path fill="#f16529" d="M 91 15 H 165 L 151 173 L 91 190 Z"/>
</svg>
--snip--
```

Listing 14-5: Drawing the HTML5 logo shield

Before we dive deep into the path definition, it'll help to know what the result is supposed to look like. Reload the page, and you should see the shield design shown in Figure 14-4.

Figure 14-4: The HTML5
logo shield

This design is made of two paths, one for the darker main shield shape, and one for the lighter highlight on the right half of the shield shape. Let's look at the path definition for the darker part:

M 0 0 H 182 L 165 185 L 90 206 L 17 185 Z

There are six instructions here:

- M 0 0
- H 182
- L 165 185
- L 90 206
- L 17 185
- Z

Think of these commands as moving an imaginary pen around the screen to draw lines. The M command takes a position as an (x, y) coordinate pair and moves the pen to that position without drawing anything. The H command takes an x-coordinate and draws a horizontal line from the current pen position to that value of x. The L command takes an (x, y) coordinate pair and draws a line from the current position to that position. Finally, the Z command closes the path, drawing a line from the current position back to the start of the path. In English, the commands in the path say, "Move to (0, 0), draw a horizontal line to (182, 0), draw a line to (165, 185), draw a line to (90, 206), draw a line to (17, 185), then draw a line back to (0, 0) to close the path." The second path uses the same technique to draw the inner highlight on the shield, using a different fill color.

These commands define the points to move to using *absolute positions*, exact x- and y-coordinates. However, there's an alternative version of each command that takes a relative position instead, meaning the next point is defined in relation to the current position of the pen. The absolute commands all use uppercase letters, and the relative ones use the same letters but lowercase. For example, the path definition we just looked at could be rewritten using relative path commands like this:

```
m 0 0 h 182 l -17 185 l -75 21 l -73 -21 z
```

In this case, the move command is the same because there's no previous position to be relative to. The command h 182 says to draw a horizontal line 182 units to the right of the current position. The command l -17 185 says to draw a line 17 units to the left and 185 down from the current position, and so on. The Z and z commands do the same thing and are just included in the SVG spec for completeness.

In fact, this relative path definition can be written even more compactly:

```
m0 0h182l-17 185-75 21-73-21z
```

Spaces are needed only to avoid ambiguity between two numbers, but are otherwise optional in SVG paths. Thanks to all the negative numbers, we're able to remove almost all the spaces here. Also, if the same command is used multiple times in a row, you can include it once and then just keep providing numbers. For example, l-17 185-75 21-73-21 is the compact version of l -17 185 l -75 21 l -73 -21.

NOTE *The SvgPathEditor (https://yqnn.github.io/svg-path-editor/) is a very helpful tool for experimenting with and manipulating paths, and for converting between absolute and relative commands (it's what I used here to convert between the two forms). SVG has several additional path commands, mostly for drawing various types of curves. We won't go into those here, but you can find a full list on MDN at https://developer.mozilla.org/SVG.*

Now that you understand how path definitions work, we can add more paths to fill in the rest of the HTML5 logo. Update the content of the svg element as shown in Listing 14-6 (though I won't think any less of you if you decide this is too much typing!).

```
--snip--
<svg width="600" height="600">
  <path fill="#e44d26" d="M 0 0 H 182 L 165 185 L 90 206 L 17 185 Z"/>
  <path fill="#f16529" d="M 91 15 H 165 L 151 173 L 91 190 Z"/>
  <path fill="#ebebeb" d="m 34 38 h 57 v 23 h -32 l 2 24 h 30 v 23 h -51 z"/>
  <path fill="#ebebeb" d="m 41 118 h 23 l 2 18 l 25 7 v 24 l -47 -13 z"/>
  <path fill="#fff" d="m 148 38 h -57 v 23 h 55 z"/>
  <path fill="#fff" d="m 143 85 h -52 v 23 h 28 l -3 30 l -25 5 v 24 l 47 -13 z"/>
</svg>
--snip--
```

Listing 14-6: Completing the HTML5 logo

I used relative path commands here partly for variety, and partly because the relative numbers were smaller and made for shorter lines. When you reload the page, you should see the complete HTML5 logo, as shown in Figure 14-5. The two paths with the fill color #ebebeb (light gray) draw the two parts of the left side of the 5, and the two paths with the fill color #fff (white) draw the two parts of the right side of the 5.

Figure 14-5: The complete HTML5 logo

In general, you won't have to manually type out your own path definitions when you're creating data visualizations. D3 will create them for you. Still, it's helpful to understand the syntax so you can tell what's going on when you're debugging.

Styling Elements with CSS

When you embed SVG in your HTML file, each SVG element becomes part of the DOM, so it can be styled with CSS. To see how this works, we'll draw some SVG shapes and give them all class names. Replace the content of the svg element with the code in Listing 14-7.

```
--snip--
<svg width="600" height="600">
  <circle class="boring" r="40" cx="50" cy="50"></circle>
  <rect class="boring" x="120" y="10" width="80" height="80"></rect>
  <path class="boring" d="M 230 90 l 40 -80 l 40 80 z"></path>"

  <circle class="fun" r="40" cx="50" cy="180"></circle>
  <rect class="fun" x="120" y="140" width="80" height="80"></rect>
  <path class="fun" d="M 230 220 l 40 -80 l 40 80 z"></path>"
</svg>
--snip--
```

Listing 14-7: Some SVG elements with class names

Here we're drawing a circle, a square, and a triangle, and then another circle, square, and triangle. Notice that the triangles are drawn as paths—there's no dedicated triangle element like rect or circle. The first three shapes have the class name boring, and the second three have the class name fun. When you reload the page you should see two rows of three shapes, all with the same default black fill, as shown in Figure 14-6.

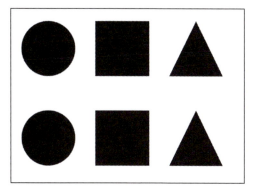

Figure 14-6: SVG shapes, without style

Now we'll style the shapes. Because they all have class names, we can select them in CSS, just like we'd select HTML elements. Add the code in Listing 14-8 to your *style.css* file.

```
.boring {
  fill: none;
  stroke: black;
  stroke-width: 3px;
}

.fun {
  fill: hotpink;
  stroke: greenyellow;
  stroke-width: 5px;
  stroke-dasharray: 10,5;
  stroke-linejoin: round;
}
```

Listing 14-8: Styles for the shapes

In this listing, we're giving different styles to the two classes: .boring gets a simple black outline, and .fun gets a pink fill and a thick dashed green-yellow outline. Note that the property names for styling SVG elements aren't the same as for HTML elements. For example, HTML elements use background-color and border-color, while SVG elements use fill and stroke.

It's worth noting that you could also apply these styles directly to the SVG elements as attributes in the *index.html* file. The advantage of using CSS is twofold: first, it means that all your styling information is in one place, so it's easily updatable, and second, to style several elements the same way you only need to add a class name to each element, as opposed to copying all the attributes from one element to another.

When you reload the page, you should notice that your shapes now have some style, as shown in Figure 14-7.

Figure 14-7: SVG shapes, with style

It's also possible to use pseudo-classes like :hover on SVG elements. Add the code in Listing 14-9 to the end of *style.css* to try this out.

```
--snip--
.fun:hover {
  fill: greenyellow;
  stroke: hotpink;
}
```

Listing 14-9: Adding a hover effect

Here we're swapping the fill and stroke color when the mouse hovers over one of the .fun elements. Reload the page and see for yourself!

This is one of the great advantages of SVG over the Canvas API: the browser knows about the SVG elements, and it knows, for example, when the mouse is hovering over them. Compare this with the canvas, where the browser just knows that some colored pixels have been drawn, and any mouse hover effects have to be explicitly coded in JavaScript.

Adding Interactivity with JavaScript

We can use JavaScript to add interactivity to our SVG elements, just as we can use CSS to style them. Again, this is possible because each SVG element embedded in the HTML becomes part of the DOM. To start with, we'll just write a script that selects the elements and logs them to the console, as a refresher on JavaScript DOM methods. Add the code in Listing 14-10 to the currently empty *script.js*.

```
document.querySelectorAll(".fun").forEach(element => {
  console.log(element);
});
```

Listing 14-10: Selecting the .fun elements

In this listing, we're using the querySelectorAll method to select all the elements with the class name fun. We then use the forEach method to iterate over the selected elements and log them to the console. When you run this code, you should see the three elements logged to the console on separate lines. If you hover over each element in the console, that element should also be highlighted on the web page.

Now we can add some interactivity. The changes to *script.js* in Listing 14-11 will make it so when you click one of the elements, that element will move to the right, and when you hold down SHIFT and click, the element will move to the left.

```
document.querySelectorAll(".fun").forEach(element => {
❶ element.setAttribute("data-offset", 0);

❷ element.addEventListener("click", event => {
  ❸ let offset = Number(event.target.getAttribute("data-offset"));

    if (event.shiftKey) {
      offset -=5;
    } else {
      offset +=5;
    }

  ❹ event.target.setAttribute("data-offset", offset);
  ❺ event.target.setAttribute("transform", `translate(${offset}, 0)`);
  });
});
```

Listing 14-11: Moving SVG elements on click

Inside the forEach method call, we're doing two things to each element. First, we set something called a *data attribute* on each element. Data attributes are HTML or SVG attributes that are just used for storing data in the DOM; their names all start with the string "data-". Specifically, we create the data-offset data attribute, which we'll use to keep track of how to position each element, and set its value to 0 ❶. Note that DOM attributes are always stored as strings, so the number 0 will be converted to the string "0".

Next, we attach a click event handler to each element ❷. The first thing the handler does is extract the data-offset attribute from the clicked element, using getAttribute, and store its value in the variable offset ❸. The clicked element is available as the target property on the event object. Note that we use the Number function here to convert the string into a number. The first time this handler is called, the variable offset will be set to 0, as that is the initial value we stored in the data-offset attribute ❶.

We use the shiftKey property on the event to determine if the SHIFT key was pressed when the mouse was clicked. If it was, we subtract 5 from offset. Otherwise, we add 5 to offset. We then assign the updated value to the data-offset attribute using setAttribute ❹. Finally, we use the setAttribute method again, but this time to set the transform SVG attribute ❺. As you saw earlier in this chapter, we can use transform to translate an element by some distance, with the string translate(x, y). Here we're setting the x value of the translation to the value of `offset` and the y value of the translation to 0. This means that if `offset` is a positive value the element will move to the right, and if it's a negative value the element will move to the left.

When you reload the page, the colorful SVG elements should now move when you click them. If you right-click one of the elements and select Inspect, you'll see that element in the Elements panel. As you click different elements in the browser viewport, you should see the `data-offset` and `transform` attributes update in the Elements panel.

The D3 Library

Now that you have an understanding of the basics of SVG, you can start to learn about the D3 library, which leverages SVG and JavaScript to create data visualizations. *D3*, short for *Data-Driven Documents*, gives you the ability to create documents whose contents are driven by data. It does this through a technique called *data binding*, where individual parts of the underlying data you want to visualize are linked to individual elements on the page. This way, if the data changes, the elements change as well. You'll see how that works later in this section.

Setup

We'll create a new set of files to explore D3. Make a new directory called *data*, containing an empty *script.js* file and an *index.html* file with the content in Listing 14-12.

```
<!DOCTYPE html>
<html>
  <head>
    <title>Data</title>
  </head>
  <body>
❶ <svg width="600" height="600">
    <circle cx="50" cy="50" r="10"></circle>
    <circle cx="100" cy="50" r="10"></circle>
    <circle cx="150" cy="50" r="10"></circle>
  </svg>

❷ <script src="https://unpkg.com/d3@7.4.4/dist/d3.js"></script>
    <script src="script.js"></script>
  </body>
</html>
```

Listing 14-12: A new index.html for working with D3

First we create an svg element ❶ and draw three circles. Then we use a script element to link to a copy of the D3 library hosted on *https://unpkg .com* ❷, much like we did with Tone.js for the music project. Now you'll be able to use code from D3 in your *script.js* file. When you load the page, you should see three black circles. Soon we'll manipulate those circles with D3.

Selections

One of D3's basic building blocks is the *selection*, a way to pick out a group of elements so you can apply certain operations to those elements. Let's use D3 to select the three SVG circles and change their fill color to hot pink. Add the code in Listing 14-13 to *script.js*.

```
d3.selectAll("circle").attr("fill", "hotpink");
```

Listing 14-13: Selecting the circles

The `d3.selectAll` method takes a CSS selector, in this case the element name `circle`, and returns a D3 selection, on which you can chain more method calls. Those chained method calls will apply to all the elements matching the selector. Here we're setting the `"fill"` attribute of every element in the selection to `"hotpink"`. When you reload the page, you should see that the black circles are now pink.

It's also possible to use a function instead of a value when updating elements in a selection. When you do this, the function is called and its return value is used as the value for updating these elements. This gives you the ability to modify elements dynamically. Update the *script.js* code with the changes in Listing 14-14 to see how it works.

```
d3
  .selectAll("circle")
  .attr("fill", "hotpink")
❶ .attr("r", (d, i) => 10 + i * 5);
```

Listing 14-14: Computing values with functions

With long method chains like this, it's common to split the code across multiple lines for readability. As before, we're selecting all the circles and setting their fill color to hot pink, but this time we're also updating each circle's radius ❶. The function used for generating the value here has two parameters, `d` and `i`. We'll cover the `d` parameter, short for *datum*, in the next section. `i`, short for *index*, is the index of the element in the selection (the first circle will have an index of `0`, the second `1`, and so on). We're using the code `10 + i * 5` to give each circle a different radius, based on their index numbers. Specifically, the circles will have radii of 10, 15, and 20. When you reload the page, you should see the three circles are now all different sizes.

NOTE *D3 selection modification methods like `.attr` return the selection itself. This lets us keep chaining modification methods, as we do with the two `.attr` calls in Listing 14-14.*

If you want to select a single element rather than a group, use the `d3.select` method instead of `d3.selectAll`. For example, to insert an `h1` element into the `body` element of your HTML, you could add the code in Listing 14-15 to the end of your *script.js* file.

```
--snip--
d3
  .select("body")
  .insert("h1", "svg")
  .text("Hello, D3!");
```

Listing 14-15: Using select to select a single element

In this example, we first select the body element. We then call insert on this selection, passing two arguments, "h1" and "svg". The first argument is the type of element to insert, and the second is the element before which to insert it. The insert method returns a new selection containing the inserted element, and the text method adds text content to elements in that selection (in this case, the single h1 element). When you reload the page, you should see a heading above the SVG element with the text "Hello, D3!" This example also illustrates the fact that D3 selections can apply to both HTML and SVG elements.

Data Binding

Perhaps the most important feature of D3 is its concept of data binding. In a D3-based application, you'll have some data that you're attempting to visualize. Each individual piece of the data, called a datum, will be bound to an individual element on the page (usually an SVG element). You use the datum to set some attribute of the element it's bound to, so the element visually reflects the datum.

To start with, we'll look at how to bind data to preexisting SVG elements. Keep the circles in *index.html*, but replace the content of *script.js* with the code in Listing 14-16.

```
let numbers = [3, 2, 1];

d3
  .selectAll("circle")
❶ .data(numbers)
  .attr("r", (d, i) => d * 5);
```

Listing 14-16: Binding data to our circles

We first create an array of numbers to use as data. Then we create a selection of all the circle elements. The data method ❶ binds the array of numbers to the selection of circles, one by one, so the first circle element has the value 3 bound to it, the second 2, and the third 1. Finally, we use the attr method to set the radius of each circle to a computed value based on the bound data. As you saw in the previous section, if you use a function instead of a value to set an attribute, that function will be called to compute the value for each element in the selection. The d parameter of the function corresponds to the datum bound to the current element.

When you reload the page, you should see three black circles that get smaller from left to right. To confirm that everything is working as expected, right-click the first circle and select **Inspect** to show the element in the Elements panel. You should see its r attribute set to 15, which is what we'd expect from d * 5 where d is 3.

It's also possible to directly see the datum set on an element using the Inspect tool, which can be very helpful for debugging, especially when your data is more complex than simple numbers. All you need is a reference to the element, which is easy to get through the Chrome console. Again, right-click the first circle and select **Inspect**. You should see something like Figure 14-8.

```
▼<body>
   ▼<svg width="600" height="600">
...      <circle cx="50" cy="50" r="15"></circle> == $0
         <circle cx="100" cy="50" r="10"></circle>
```

Figure 14-8: Selecting a `circle` element in the Elements panel

At the end of the selected line you should see the text == $0. This is an indication that a reference to the circle element is stored under the global variable named $0. To verify that this is the case, open the JavaScript console and enter $0:

```
$0
<circle cx="50" cy="50" r="15"></circle>
```

The console prints the circle element you selected, indicating that $0 is indeed a reference to that element. Now that you have that reference, you can see the datum bound to it using the __data__ property:

```
$0.__data__
3
```

This tells you the circle is bound to the value 3, the first number from our array, just as we'd expect. $0 always references the currently selected element, so if you right-click and inspect a different circle, entering $0.__data__ in the console again will give you the datum bound to that other circle.

Data Joins

You don't always know exactly how long your data is going to be, so it would be difficult to always have exactly the right number of SVG elements ready to bind to your data. D3 solves this problem with the concept of *joins*. In D3, you use a join to add or remove the necessary elements to match the data being bound.

We can extend our example from Listing 14-16 with a join so that SVG circle elements will be added or removed as needed, depending on the length of the numbers array. Update the *script.js* file as shown in Listing 14-17.

```
❶ let numbers = [3, 2, 1, 2, 3];

d3
❷ .select("svg")
```

```
    .selectAll("circle")
    .data(numbers)
❸ .join("circle")
    .attr("r", (d, i) => d * 5);
```

Listing 14-17: Joining in extra elements

Here we've create a longer array of numbers ❶. We've also added a line to select the svg element ❷ before selecting the circle elements within it. This is necessary because D3 will need to add new circle elements, and it needs to know which containing element to add them to. Finally, we've added a call to the join method ❸. This method takes the name of the element from the selection to add or remove to match the data. In this case, we're saying that if there aren't enough circle elements in the svg element for all the items in data, then D3 should add more (or conversely, if there are too many, D3 should remove some).

If you reload the page, you'll see this doesn't quite work as you probably expected. The new circles all end up in the top-left corner of the drawing area. That's because these new circles don't have their cx or cy attributes set, unlike the initial three circles that were defined in *index.html*. To fix this, we need to set these two attributes using D3, as shown in Listing 14-18.

```
let numbers = [3, 2, 1, 2, 3];

d3
  .select("svg")
  .selectAll("circle")
  .data(numbers)
  .join("circle")
  .attr("cx", (d, i) => (i + 1) * 50)
  .attr("cy", 50)
  .attr("r", (d, i) => d * 5);
```

Listing 14-18: Setting the cx and cy attributes

The cx attribute is based on the index of the data. The first element should be at 50, the second at 100, and so on. The calculation (i + 1) * 50 gives us the right values. Because the circles are all in a line, the cy attribute is just a constant value. Now when you reload the page you should see five circles in a line.

NOTE   *As mentioned previously, you can use the same join technique to remove elements when you have too many. If you change the array of numbers to contain only two elements and reload the page, you'll see only two circles.*

Now that we're using D3's join method to create new SVG elements as needed to suit the data, there's no reason to create them in the HTML file. Modify *index.html* as shown in Listing 14-19, removing all the circle elements, then reload the page.

```
--snip--
  <body>
    <svg width="600" height="600"></svg>

    <script src="https://unpkg.com/d3@7.4.4/dist/d3.js"></script>
    <script src="script.js"></script>
  </body>
</html>
```

Listing 14-19: Removing the circle *elements*

Everything should still work, because the join method adds in all the circle elements it needs. Note that the .selectAll("circle") line is still needed in *script.js* for the join to work correctly, even though the first time this is called there will be no circles to select.

Real-Time Updates

If the underlying data changes, we'll need to perform the join again to update the visualization. To do this, we'll move all the data binding and joining code into its own function, which we can call as needed. We can test this out by adding some buttons to the page that allow us to add random values to the start or end of our numbers array, or drop numbers from the array. Update *index.html* with the changes shown in Listing 14-20.

```
--snip--
  <body>
    <div>
      <button id="prepend">Prepend</button>
      <button id="append">Append</button>
      <button id="drop">Drop</button>
    </div>

    <svg width="600" height="600"></svg>
--snip--
```

Listing 14-20: Adding buttons to index.html

Reload the page and you should see the three new buttons at the top. Next, we'll move the code that updates the visualization into its own function. Replace the code in *script.js* with the content of Listing 14-21.

```
let numbers = [3, 2, 1];

❶ function update(data) {
    d3
      .select("svg")
      .selectAll("circle")
    ❷ .data(data)
      .join("circle")
      .attr("cx", (d, i) => (i + 1) * 50)
      .attr("cy", 50)
```

```
        .attr("r", (d, i) => d * 5);
}

❸ update(numbers);
```

Listing 14-21: Moving the update code into its own function

There's no functional change here—we're just creating an update function to do the SVG updating for us ❶, and then calling it ❸. Notice that we're passing data, the function's parameter, to the .data method ❷, rather than passing the numbers array directly.

Next we'll add the code for handling button clicks, which will insert a random floating-point number between 1 and 5 into the numbers array at the start or end, or drop the last element in the array. Add the code in Listing 14-22 to the end of *script.js*.

```
--snip--
update(numbers);

❶ function getRandomNumber() {
    return 1 + Math.random() * 4;
}

❷ d3.select("#append").on("click", () => {
    numbers.push(getRandomNumber());
    update(numbers);
});

❸ d3.select("#prepend").on("click", () => {
    numbers.unshift(getRandomNumber());
    update(numbers);
});

❹ d3.select("#drop").on("click", () => {
    numbers.pop();
    update(numbers);
});
```

Listing 14-22: Updating on button clicks

First we declare a helper function for generating a random number ❶, since there are two places where we need to do this. Then we declare the handlers for the three buttons. Notice that instead of using the regular DOM API methods for adding click handlers, as we've done previously in this book, we're using d3.select to select the buttons and the on method to add an event handler. The regular DOM API methods would work as well, but using D3 methods is more concise and more consistent with the other D3 code in this file.

The first handler is triggered by a click on the Append button ❷: it pushes a random number onto the end of the numbers array, then we call the update function to redraw the visualization with an extra circle. The second handler, triggered by a click on the Prepend button, causes a random number to be unshifted onto the front of the numbers array ❸. The third is triggered by a click on the Drop button; it pops the last number from the array ❹. After each of these actions we also call the update function.

Reload the page and try out the different buttons. You should see the elements being added and removed as needed.

Transitions and Key Functions

Instead of updating a D3 visualization abruptly with each change in the data, you can use *transitions* to allow elements to animate their attributes as they change. Transitions are a useful feature in D3 because, if done right, they allow you to see how data evolves. Let's add a transition to our update function to see how this works. Make the changes shown in Listing 14-23.

```
--snip--
function update(data) {
  d3
    .select("svg")
    .selectAll("circle")
    .data(data)
    .join("circle")
    .transition()
    .duration(500)
    .attr("cx", (d, i) => (i + 1) * 50)
    .attr("cy", 50)
    .attr("r", (d, i) => d * 5);
}
--snip--
```

Listing 14-23: Adding transitions

The transition method in a chain like this means that every following attribute change will animate from its current value to the new value. The duration method sets the length of the animation in milliseconds. This means that the position and radius of each circle will take half a second (500 ms) to animate from its current value to the new value. New circles start off with default values of 0 for each attribute, so they will transition in from the top-left corner of the SVG.

Unfortunately, the way we've coded our update function, the animation won't be quite as satisfying as you might want. Reload the page and click **Prepend** a few times. You should see some odd behavior. You might have expected the existing circles to move over to the right, making room for a new circle being added on the left. Instead, the existing circles all appear to resize in place, while a new circle flies in from the top-left corner and takes its place to the right of the existing circles. With this animation, it's actually very hard to see that an element is being *prepended* on the left. Rather, the animations suggest that an element is being *appended* on the right, and that all the elements are being resized. Clicking the Append button, on the other hand, does the correct thing: a new element animates in and appears at the end of the row, while the existing elements don't change.

The problem here is that when D3 updates an existing selection with a new array of data, it uses a default mode called *join-by-index*. This means that the first item in the array is joined with the first element in the selection (in this case, the leftmost circle), the second item in the array with the second element in the selection, and so on. If there are more items in the array than existing SVG elements, new elements are added at the end. Thus, when you click Prepend and add a new number to the start of the data array, every circle in the line is re-bound to a new datum. The first circle in the line is bound to the new number that's been added to the start of the array, so it appears to resize. The second circle is bound to what used to be the first number in the array, so it appears to resize as well, and so on. Finally, since there's now one more data item than there are SVG elements, a new circle is created and added at the end of the line.

The solution to making the animation more intuitive is to help D3 understand the *identity* of each element in the array of data. Instead of assuming that every index in the array will always map to the same index in the selection, we provide what D3 calls a *key function*. The key function allows us to specify something about each datum that identifies it uniquely. This way, each existing datum stays bound to the same SVG element even as new data is added, regardless of the ordering of the data.

The key function is passed as an optional second argument to the data method. Listing 14-24 shows the necessary change to the update function.

```
--snip--
  .selectAll("circle")
  .data(data, d => d)
  .join("circle")
--snip--
```

Listing 14-24: Adding a key function

The key function d => d here says that given a datum, the datum itself is the unique identifier. In this case, we're just using raw numbers, so the value of the number is as good as we can get for a "unique" identifier. Usually you'll be working with more complex data, and you can use the key function to expose an identifier that is actually unique. For example, if each datum were an object representing an employee with a unique employeeId property, then you could use a key function like d => d.employeeId.

Reload the page and click **Prepend**. You should now see all the circles slide to the right to accommodate the newly prepended element. This is because D3 now knows which item in the new array should map to which element in the selection when the array changes.

Advanced Joins

D3's join method has extra options that give you more control over how the visualization responds to changes in the data. When D3 joins new data to an existing selection, some elements may be updated, some may be added (for the case of a new datum with no existing element), and some elements may be removed. In our case, we've seen how clicking Prepend both adds a new element and updates all the other elements by shifting them to the right. Meanwhile, clicking Drop removes the last element. In D3 parlance, adding a new element is called an *enter*, removing an existing element is called an *exit*, and modifying an existing element is called an *update*.

You can customize the join method by passing it three functions that will be called for each of these three possible element changes. This way you're able to specify three different behaviors: one for entering elements, one for elements that are being updated, and one for exiting elements. To test this functionality, modify your update function as shown in Listing 14-25. To start, these changes result in the same behavior we got from the simple join method in the previous listing.

```
--snip--
  .data(data, d => d)
  .join(
    enter => enter.append("circle"),
    update => update,
    exit => exit.remove()
  )
  .transition()
--snip--
```

Listing 14-25: The join method with enter, update, and exit functions

This more advanced version of the join method takes three functions. The first function has a single parameter called enter, which is a selection of temporary placeholders for each of the entering elements. To get the same behavior as the simple .join("circle") version, we just use the append method to add a circle to each enter placeholder. Note that the enter place-holders themselves aren't elements in the DOM. They're just a handle for D3 to give you a place to append your new entering elements, before they get added to the DOM. For example, if there were five new elements need-ing to be entered, then enter.append("circle") would create five new circle elements and place them inside the svg element.

The second function has a single parameter called update, which is a selection containing all the existing elements that are already bound to a datum. To get the same behavior as before, we just return the selection unchanged.

The third function has a single parameter called exit, which is a selection containing all the elements that should be removed because they no longer have a corresponding datum. To get the same behavior as before, we call the remove method on the selection, which removes each exiting element from the DOM.

When you reload the page, you should see the same behavior as before; so far, this change doesn't have any functional impact. Now that we have it working, though, we can rework our animations to add some finesse. The current shift-right animation for elements in the updating selection is fine, but entering elements currently fly in from the top-left corner, and exiting elements just disappear. Let's instead make it so entering elements grow into place from their correct position, and exiting elements shrink away to nothing at their current position. The changes to implement that behavior are shown in Listing 14-26.

```
--snip--
function update(data) {
  d3
    .select("svg")
    .selectAll("circle")
    .data(data, d => d)
    .join(
      enter => enter
      ❶ .append("circle")
        .attr("cx", (d, i) => (i + 1) * 50)
        .attr("cy", 50)
        .transition()
        .duration(500)
      ❷ .attr("r", (d, i) => d * 5),
      update => update
        .transition()
        .duration(500)
      ❸ .attr("cx", (d, i) => (i + 1) * 50),
      exit => exit
        .transition()
        .duration(500)
      ❹ .attr("r", 0)
      ❺ .remove()
    );
}

update(numbers);
--snip--
```

Listing 14-26: Finessing the animations

In this updated code, we've moved all the transitions into the individual enter, update, and exit functions, instead of having a single transition call for all the elements. The enter function appends a circle element ❶ and then immediately sets its position (the cx and cy attributes), but not its radius. Once the position is set, we use the transition method to animate the radius from zero (the default value) to the value calculated from the datum ❷. The order here is important: anything that comes in the chain *before* the call to transition will happen immediately, and anything *after* the call to transition will be animated. This means that any new circles will appear in the right position immediately, and the change in size (from zero to the desired radius) will animate. This will arguably look more natural than the previous version, where all three attributes animated in from zero, leading to the circles flying in from the corner.

The update function has to animate only the cx attribute of the circle ❸ to slide it to its updated position. All other attributes should be unchanged for existing elements. Finally, the exit function animates the radius of the circle back to zero ❹ before removing it ❺. If remove is called after a call to transition, as it is here, the actual element removal won't take place until after the animations have completed.

When you reload the page, you should see the new and improved animations: new elements expand in at the appropriate position and removed elements shrink away.

<hr>

TRY IT YOURSELF

14-2. Try modifying the animations for entering elements. For example, right now the radius expands from the default value of 0, but what if you wanted the radius to start out big (say, 50) and then shrink to its correct value? Hint: you'll need to set the starting radius before the call to transition.

14-3. You can also animate color. For example, try starting the elements with a fill attribute of purple, and then animating them to red.

14-4. What if you wanted to animate the circles in from the top of the screen, with a fixed radius? Hint: move the setting of the radius to before transition, move the setting of cy to after transition, and add a starting cy value of something like -50.

<hr>

Creating a Bar Graph

Now that you've learned the basics of D3, let's put them to use in a small project: creating a bar graph that visualizes the frequency of characters in a text box. The bar graph will update as new text is typed or pasted into the box. Creating this visualization will let you practice data joins, teach you some new techniques like drawing axes to contextualize the data, and prepare you for the more substantial project in the next chapter.

Setting Up

To get started, make a new directory called *frequency* and add empty *script.js* and *style.css* files. Then create an *index.html* file and add the code in Listing 14-27.

```
<!DOCTYPE html>
<html>
  <head>
    <title>Character Frequency</title>
    <link rel="stylesheet" href="style.css">
  </head>
  <body>
    <div>
   ❶ <textarea rows="5" cols="70"></textarea>
    </div>
```

```
    <script src="https://unpkg.com/d3@7.4.4/dist/d3.js"></script>
    <script src="script.js"></script>
  </body>
</html>
```

Listing 14-27: The index.html *file for the character frequency project*

This HTML document follows the same pattern we've been using throughout the book. The only new addition is the textarea element ❶, which creates a multiline text input. The rows and cols attributes set the number of lines and the width (in fixed-width characters) of the text area.

Notice that the document doesn't contain an svg element. We're going to create it using JavaScript. This is because we'll need to refer to the svg element's width and height multiple times to determine the placement of elements in the visualization, so it makes sense to define those parameters in the JavaScript rather than in the HTML file. And since we'll be defining the width and height in the JavaScript, we may as well create the svg element itself in the JavaScript, too. We'll do that right now. Add the code in Listing 14-28 to *script.js*.

```
const width = 600;
const height = 600;

// Add an svg element to the page
let svg = d3
  .select("body")
  .append("svg")
  .attr("width", width)
  .attr("height", height);
```

Listing 14-28: Creating the svg element using JavaScript

We first declare constants for the width and height of the svg element. Then we use D3 to select the body element and append an svg element to it, setting the width and height attributes in the process. We save the result of creating the element into the variable svg because we're going to need it later.

Calculating Character Frequencies

Next, we'll add the code for reading the text from the text area and counting the number of occurrences of each character. This generates the underlying data for the visualization. Anytime the text changes, we'll need to update the data and redraw the chart. For now, though, we'll just read the text, figure out the character frequencies, and log the output to the console. Add the code in Listing 14-29 to the end of *script.js*.

```
--snip--
d3.select("textarea").on(❶"input", e => {
❷ let frequencies = {};

❸ e.target.value.split("").forEach(char => {
    let currentCount = frequencies[char] || 0;
```

```
    frequencies[char] = currentCount + 1;
  });

  console.log(frequencies);
});
```

Listing 14-29: Calculating character frequencies

The input event ❶ is triggered anytime the content of the text area changes, whether from typing, deleting, pasting, or some other action. The first thing we do in the event's handler function is initialize a new object for keeping track of the character frequencies ❷. This frequencies object will use characters for its keys and the number of appearances of that character for its values. We then get the target of the event (the text area), get its value (the text), and split it into its individual characters ❸. For each character, we determine the current count for that character, defaulting to 0 if it hasn't been seen yet. Then we add 1 to that count and store the new count back in the object. Once all the characters have been counted, we log the frequencies object to the console so we can check everything is working as expected. Note that we recalculate the frequencies object every time the text changes, rather than just trying to track added or deleted characters. This makes it much easier to handle cases where multiple characters are added or removed at once, for example, when text is pasted into the box.

Load the page, and you should see the text area (the svg element is invisible, but you can see it in the Elements panel if you want to check it's there). When you type text into the text area, you should see objects being logged to the console on every keystroke, each time containing the frequencies of the characters in the text area. For example, if you type in the word *hello*, you'll get this object after typing the final *o*:

```
{ "h": 1, "e": 1, "l": 2, "o": 1 }
```

A single object containing all the characters and their frequencies works well for logging to the console, but what we're going to want for rendering with D3 is an array of objects, each describing a single character and its associated frequency. This way, each entry in the array will be a datum bound to a bar in our bar chart. To make the chart easier to read, the array should be sorted alphabetically by character. Continuing with the word *hello*, instead of the object shown previously, we need something like this:

```
[
  { "char": "e", "count": 1 },
  { "char": "h", "count": 1 },
  { "char": "l", "count": 2 },
  { "char": "o", "count": 1 }
]
```

To put the data in this array format, change the end of *script.js* as shown in Listing 14-30.

```
--snip--
    frequencies[char] = currentCount + 1;
  });

❶ let data = Object.entries(frequencies).map(pair => {
    return { char: pair[0], count: pair[1] };
  });

❷ data.sort((a, b) => d3.ascending(a.char, b.char));

  console.log(data);
});
```

Listing 14-30: Converting the frequency data to an array

First, we use `Object.entries` to convert the frequencies object into an array
of two-element arrays ❶, where the first element is the key and the second
element is the value. We map this array into an array of objects, where the
key is stored under the property char and the value is stored under the property count. Next, we want to sort the data by character. The sort method ❷
orders the elements in an array by applying a comparison function to every
pair of elements a and b, to determine whether a should be sorted after b or
vice versa. Here we use the `d3.ascending` comparison function, passing a.char
and b.char, which means the array will be sorted into ascending alphabetical
order based on the char property of each object.

Reload the page, and you should now see this new data array being
logged as text changes in the text area.

Drawing the Bar Graph

Now that we have the data in the format we need, we can render it as a bar
graph. We're going to start out with a basic, naive rendering for now, where
we simply create SVG rect elements with widths proportional to the character frequencies. We'll gradually build from there to create a more informative visualization. Make the changes to *script.js* shown in Listing 14-31.

```
--snip--
// Add an svg element to the page
let svg = d3
  .select("body")
  .append("svg")
  .attr("width", width)
  .attr("height", height);

❶ function update(data) {
  svg
    .selectAll("rect")
    .data(data)
❷  .join("rect")
    .attr("width", (d, i) => d.count * 5)
    .attr("height", 10)
    .attr("x", 20)
```

```
      .attr("y", (d, i) => i * 20);
}

d3.select("textarea").on("input", e => {
--snip--

  data.sort((a, b) => d3.ascending(a.char, b.char));

❸ update(data);
});
```

Listing 14-31: Defining the update function

Here we declare an update function ❶, which gets called every time the text changes ❸. The function creates, updates, or deletes the SVG elements needed to render the data, according to the same pattern we learned earlier for binding data to a selection (using the data method) and joining in the necessary elements with the simple version of the join method.

The join method returns a selection containing all the current rect elements ❷, including any that were just added. Each rect is now bound to a single datum, which represents a single character and the number of occurrences of that character. We set the width, height, x, and y attributes as appropriate to create a horizontally oriented bar chart. The width attribute is set to 5 times the character count, so every new instance of a character makes the bar 5 pixels wider. The height attribute is a constant value of 10 (all bars are the same height), and the x attribute is a constant value of 20 (all bars start 20 pixels from the left of the SVG element). The y attribute is set to 20 times the index of the datum, meaning that there will be a bar every 20 pixels, giving 10 pixels of space between each bar.

Reload the page and type the word *hello* into the text area. As you type each letter, you should see bars appear or update in the SVG element, ending with something like Figure 14-9.

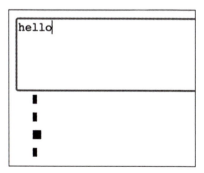

Figure 14-9: A basic bar chart

So far so good, but we still have a ways to go. There are two major issues here. First, there are no axes or labels, so we don't know what character each bar represents or what the width of the bar corresponds to. Second, there's no autoscaling of the bar widths and heights, meaning that we currently have a limit of 30 distinct characters and a count of 116 per character before the bars don't fit in the 600×600-pixel SVG element. Luckily, both of these problems are easy to fix using D3.

Scaling the Bars

A *scale* in D3 is a way of converting from some data value to a visual value. For example, earlier we set the width of the bars in our character frequency graph to be five times the data value, which is a simple form of scaling. In that case, we set the scale factor manually, but D3 can also determine the scaling automatically based on the minimum and maximum data values, known as the *domain*, and the minimum and maximum display values, known as the *range*.

For example, say you're plotting a graph of people's ages. Your data values range from 0 to 105, and the space for rendering those values ranges from 30 to 330 pixels from the left side of the SVG. Your domain is thus [0, 105], and your range is [30, 330]. A value of 0 in the data domain maps to 30 in the visual range, and a value of 105 maps to 330. See Figure 14-10 for a visual representation of this mapping.

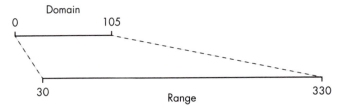

Figure 14-10: Scaling values from a domain of [0, 105] to a range of [30, 330]

The beauty of D3 scaling is that the scale factor can change dynamically based on changes in the domain. This way, the current maximum data value can always map to the full visual range, even as the maximum data value changes. To implement this dynamic scaling for our bar graph, we need to keep track of the maximum count value among all the data, and use that as the upper value of the domain. As a result, if the maximum count increases, the bars that aren't at the maximum count will all scale down accordingly, while the bar at the maximum count will continue to occupy the full horizontal range. For example, say that our visual range for the bars is [0, 500], and we have the following data:

```
[
  { "char": "a", "count": 1 },
  { "char": "b", "count": 1 },
  { "char": "c", "count": 2 }
]
```

The domain of our data would be [0, 2]. The "c" bar would be 500 units wide, and the "a" and "b" bars would each be 250 units wide. If we then added another two c's, the "c" bar would still be 500 units wide, but now the "a" and "b" bars would each be 125 units wide.

Let's implement that dynamic horizontal scaling now. Modify your script with the code shown in Listing 14-32.

```
--snip--
// Add an svg element to the page
let svg = d3
    .select("body")
    .append("svg")
    .attr("width", width)
    .attr("height", height);

let margin = { top: 20, right: 10, bottom: 20, left: 50 };

function update(data) {
❶ let xScale = d3.scaleLinear()
      .domain([0, d3.max(data, d => d.count)])
      .range([margin.left, width - margin.right]);

  svg
    .selectAll("rect")
    .data(data)
    .join("rect")
❷ .attr("width", (d, i) => xScale(d.count) - xScale(0))
    .attr("height", 10)
❸ .attr("x", xScale(0))
    .attr("y", (d, i) => i * 20);
}
--snip--
```

Listing 14-32: Creating a scale for the bar widths

First, immediately before the update function definition, we create an object describing the margins of our bar chart diagram. These values indicate how far from the edges of the SVG element the main body of the diagram will be. As Figure 14-11 shows, when the time comes we'll use these margins to determine where to draw the bars and the axes.

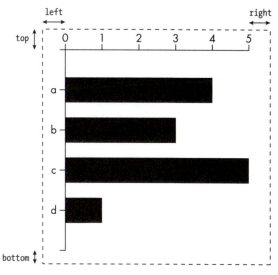

Figure 14-11: How margins can be used to position a diagram in an SVG element (the dotted line)

Inside the update function, we use the d3.scaleLinear method to create a scale ❶. This means that input values map linearly to output values (as opposed to logarithmically, for example). We set the domain from zero to the max count, using the D3 max helper. This helper takes an array of data and a function that returns a value from the datum, and returns the maximum value. In this case, it's returning the maximum count value. The range is set from margin.left to width - margin.right and gives us the position of the right side of the longest bar.

The scaleLinear helper gives us a function that maps from the data domain to the visual range, which we assign to the variable xScale. (As discussed in Chapter 5, it's possible for a higher-order function to return another function, as scaleLinear is doing here.) We modify our width attribute setting to call that xScale function, passing the count from each datum ❷. Here, xScale(0) gives the horizontal position of the left side of the bar, which corresponds to the domain value 0, and xScale(d.count) gives the horizontal position of the right side of the bar. To get the width of the bar, we need to subtract xScale(0) from xScale(d.count), because the width is just the distance between the left side of the bar and the right side of the bar. This will give an appropriately scaled bar width based on the count of each datum and the maximum count. We set the x attribute of the bar to xScale(0) to enforce the left margin ❸.

Reload the page and start typing into the text area. The first time you enter a character, a single bar will appear, at the maximum width. Try typing *abccc* into the text area; you'll see that as you add more c's, the first two bars (for a and b) get smaller.

Now let's create a scale for the height of the bars, to make full use of the vertical space of the svg element. The bars will start out tall but get shorter to accommodate more bars as new characters are added to the text field. Make the changes shown in Listing 14-33.

```
--snip--
function update(data) {
  let xScale = d3.scaleLinear()
    .domain([0, d3.max(data, d => d.count)])
    .range([margin.left, width - margin.right]);

❶ let yScale = d3.scaleBand()
    .domain(data.map(d => d.char))
    .range([margin.top, height - margin.bottom])
    .padding(0.5);

  svg
    .selectAll("rect")
    .data(data)
    .join("rect")
    .attr("width", (d, i) => xScale(d.count) - xScale(0))
❷ .attr("height", yScale.bandwidth())
    .attr("x", xScale(0))
❸ .attr("y", (d, i) => yScale(d.char));
}
--snip--
```

Listing 14-33: Scaling the bar heights

To create a scale for the heights of the bars, we use the d3.scaleBand helper ❶. This lets us create a set of evenly spaced bands. The domain here is slightly different, because instead of an array giving the minimum and maximum values, it contains the full set of values. For example, if the content of the text area were the word *hello*, the domain of the y scale would be ["e", "h", "l", "o"] (remember that we sort the data alphabetically). This would map to four evenly spaced bars.

The range here is from margin.top to height - margin.bottom, which gives the range of y values the bars will exist in (the first bar will be at the top and the last at the bottom). The padding value defines how much space there is between bars based on the space available: 0 means that they are as tall as possible and will be touching, while 0.5 means that the bars will take up half of the space available.

Scales created using scaleBand also have a bandwidth method that returns the scaled size of the bands, which we can use to set the height of the bars ❷. (The method is called bandwidth on the assumption that the bars are oriented vertically, whereas ours are oriented horizontally.) To get the y attribute of the bar, we pass d.char to the yScale function ❸, because the domain of this scale is all the characters present in the data.

Reload the page and type some text into the text area. The first character you enter will cause a single tall black bar to appear, but for every unique character you type a new bar will be added, and the heights of the existing bars will decrease to make space. Figure 14-12 shows how the visualization should look.

Figure 14-12: Our bar graph scaled in both dimensions

Try typing in different text to get a feel for how the bars update as the data changes. Next we'll add axes with labels, which will update along with the scaling to show the actual range of data. This will make it much easier to understand the graph.

Adding Labeled Axes

The D3 axis helpers allow you to draw axes along the sides of your diagrams. An axis in D3 includes a horizontal or vertical line, with small tick marks drawn perpendicular to this line and the value for each tick, as shown in Figure 14-13. The axis allows you to see the values in the data domain.

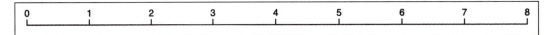

Figure 14-13: An axis for the numbers 0 to 8

Axes are closely linked to scales, and indeed you need a scale to create an axis. For example, the axis in Figure 14-13 is 540 pixels wide and contains the numbers from 0 to 8. This axis was created using a scale with a domain of [0, 8] and a range of [0, 540].

To draw an axis, you first have to define a g element that will contain the axis elements. You then create an axis generator object using one of the D3 axis helpers, and finally use the generator object to draw the axis elements into the g element.

Our diagram is going to have two axes: a top axis for showing the count values, and a left axis for showing the character values. First, we'll add the g elements, as shown in Listing 14-34.

```
--snip--
let margin = { top: 20, right: 10, bottom: 20, left: 50 };

// Top axis container
❶ let topContainer = svg
    .append("g")
    .attr("id", "top")
    .attr("transform", ❷ `translate(0, ${margin.top})`);

// Left axis container
❸ let leftContainer = svg
    .append("g")
    .attr("id", "left")
    .attr("transform", ❹ `translate(${margin.left}, 0)`);

function update(data) {
--snip--
```

Listing 14-34: Adding g elements for containing the top and left axes

We create the top axis container ❶ by appending a g element to the svg element and giving it an id of "top". Because we defined the range for xScale to be [margin.left, width - margin.right], that will also define the visual range of the axis. xScale doesn't have any knowledge of vertical positioning, however, which is why we have to translate it down by margin.top ❷. We store the element selection in a variable called topContainer so we have a reference to it for later when drawing the axis into the container. The left axis container is created similarly ❸, but this time we have to translate it to the right by margin.left ❹, since yScale has no knowledge of horizontal positioning.

Now that we have the containers, we can draw the axes. Make the changes shown in Listing 14-35 to the update function.

```
--snip--
  let yScale = d3.scaleBand()
    .domain(data.map(d => d.char))
    .range([margin.top, height - margin.bottom])
    .padding(0.5);

  let topAxis = d3.axisTop(xScale);

  let leftAxis = d3.axisLeft(yScale);

  topContainer
    .call(topAxis);

  leftContainer
    .call(leftAxis);

  svg
    .selectAll("rect")
    .data(data)
    .join("rect")
--snip--
```

Listing 14-35: Drawing the axes

Here we call d3.axisTop, passing xScale, and d3.axisLeft, passing yScale. This gives us two axis generators, topAxis and leftAxis. Axis generators take a selection of an element and draw an axis into that element. Instead of passing a selection to the axis generators, however, we instead pass the generators themselves to a D3 method called call. This method, when chained to a selection (such as topContainer or leftContainer, in this case), calls the provided function on the current selection. Thus, writing topContainer .call(topAxis); is equivalent to writing topAxis(topContainer);, with either statement drawing the top axis of the bar graph. It's considered more idiomatic to use call, and this makes it easier to chain other methods to the statement.

Reload the page and type some text in the text area. You'll see the axes, as shown in Figure 14-14.

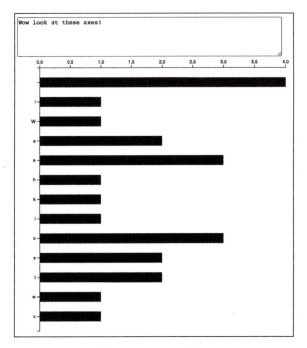

Figure 14-14: Our bar chart, now with axes

If you inspect the axes in the web inspector, you'll see that they're made up of g, path, text, and line elements. A line element is like a path, but it just defines the start and end points with the x1, x2, y1, and y2 attributes. These attributes default to 0 in the SVG specification, which often works just fine for the purposes of drawing these axes, so you'll notice in the inspector that many of the line attributes aren't set explicitly.

There are two things that are a bit off about the top axis right now. First, as you can see in Figure 14-14, the labels include numbers with decimal points, like 2.5, but we care only about whole numbers (you can't have half a character). So, we need to find a way to render only whole numbers, also known as integers. Second, if you enter a string of 15 of the same character (for example, *aaaaaaaaaaaaaaa*), then the labels will show only even numbers from 0 to 14, and there won't be a label for 15, as shown in Figure 14-15. You'll continue to see this problem as the maximum count increases, especially beyond 30, where the ticks switch to multiples of 5.

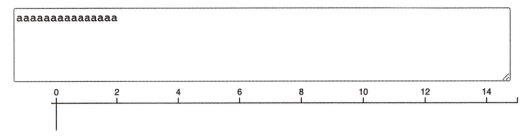

Figure 14-15: The top axis when the maximum count is 15

What we'd prefer here is for the domain to extend to 16, to give a nicer-looking axis. Luckily, this second problem is easy to fix. D3 scales have a nice method that extends their domain to the next "round" number, which in this case means the next number for which a tick would be drawn. Listing 14-36 shows how to incorporate this method.

```
--snip--
  let xScale = d3.scaleLinear()
    .domain([0, d3.max(data, d => d.count)])
    .range([margin.left, width - margin.right])
    .nice();
--snip--
```

Listing 14-36: Making our x scale "nice"

When you reload the page and again type in 15 of the same character, you'll see that the axis now extends to 16. Rendering only integers requires a little more effort. The basic approach here is to get the tick values, filter them to only integers, and then set those tick values on the axis. Additionally, we want to change the number rendering to exclude the decimal point, so we render 1 and not 1.0. These changes are shown in Listing 14-37.

```
--snip--
  let yScale = d3.scaleBand()
    .domain(data.map(d => d.char))
    .range([margin.top, height - margin.bottom])
    .padding(0.5);

❶ let topAxisTicks = xScale.ticks()
    .filter(tick => Number.isInteger(tick));

  let topAxis = d3.axisTop(xScale)
❷  .tickValues(topAxisTicks)
❸  .tickFormat(d3.format("d"));

  let leftAxis = d3.axisLeft(yScale);
--snip--
```

Listing 14-37: Rendering integer ticks on the top axis

First we have to get the ticks, which are available using the ticks method on the xScale generator ❶. We then filter the ticks to integer values using Number.isInteger. This will convert an array like [0, 0.5, 1, 1.5, 2, 2.5, 3, 3.5, 4] to [0, 1, 2, 3, 4]. Next, we set the filtered tick values on the top axis using the tickValues method ❷. Finally, we use the tickFormat method to set a rendering format for the numbers ❸. This method takes a formatting function that will be used to format each tick value. In this case, d3.format("d") returns a function that formats numbers without the decimal point.

Reload the page and enter some text again; you should see whole numbers rendered without the decimal point.

Styling with CSS and Regular Expressions

Next we're going to improve the appearance of our graph with some CSS styles. In order to better differentiate the types of characters, we'll give different colors to the bars depending on whether they're lowercase letters, uppercase letters, numbers, or any other character. To do this, we'll need a function that can distinguish between these types of characters. The function will use *regular expressions*, which are a way of specifying patterns in strings of text and then determining if other strings match those patterns.

NOTE *JavaScript's regular expression capabilities are very powerful, but we'll be considering only the features we need for this project. To learn more, check out the website* https:// www.regular-expressions.info, *or search MDN for "regular expressions."*

JavaScript has a regular expression literal syntax that is delimited by forward slashes. For example, /hi/ is a regular expression literal that matches any string containing the sequence of characters *hi*. The *hi* can occur anywhere in the string. For example, the regular expression /hi/ would match the words *hither*, *Chicken*, and *sushi*. You can more narrowly define a regular expression's pattern by adding special characters. For example, a caret (^) at the start of an expression indicates the character sequence should occur at the start of a string, so /^hi/ matches any string that starts with *hi*. Similarly, a dollar sign ($) at the end of an expression indicates the character sequence should occur at the end of a string, so /hi$/ matches any string that ends with *hi*.

You can use the test method on a regular expression to see if a particular string matches it. Here are some examples in the JavaScript console:

```
/^hi/.test("hi there");
true
/^hi/.test("Chicken");
false
```

The string "hi there" passes the test, because *hi* appears at the beginning of the string, whereas "Chicken" fails.

You can use ^ and $ together to create a regular expression where the full string must match. For example, /^hi$/ will match only the string "hi" and nothing else, as you can see here:

```
/^hi$/.test("hi");
true
/^hi$/.test("him");
false
```

To match a range of characters instead of a single character, use square brackets and a hyphen to describe the range. For example, /[a-z]/ matches any lowercase character from *a* to *z*. The regular expression /^[A-Z][a-z]$/ matches a string containing an uppercase letter followed by a lowercase letter, and no other characters. Try it out in your console:

```
/^[A-Z][a-z]$/.test("Hi");
true
/^[A-Z][a-z]$/.test("iH");
false
/^[A-Z][a-z]$/.test("Hip");
false
```

For this project, we need three regular expressions: /^[a-z]$/ (matching a single lowercase letter), /^[A-Z]$/ (matching a single uppercase letter), and /^[0-9]$/ (matching a single digit). If a character doesn't match any of those expressions, we'll know it's some other kind of character, like a space or a punctuation mark. See Listing 14-38 for the new getClass function, which uses those regular expressions to choose a CSS class name for a given character's bar. Add this function to *script.js* immediately before the update function.

```
--snip--
// Left axis container
let leftContainer = svg
  .append("g")
  .attr("id", "left")
  .attr("transform", `translate(${margin.left}, 0)`);

function getClass(char) {
  if (/^[a-z]$/.test(char)) {
    return "lower";
  } else if (/^[A-Z]$/.test(char)) {
    return "upper";
  } else if (/^[0-9]$/.test(char)) {
    return "number";
  } else {
    return "other";
  }
}

function update(data) {
--snip--
```

Listing 14-38: The getClass *function*

This function tests a character against the provided regular expressions and returns the appropriate class name: "lower", "upper", "number", or "other". Next, we'll update the rendering code to use this function to set a class name on each rect element, as shown in Listing 14-39.

```
--snip--
  svg
    .selectAll("rect")
    .data(data)
    .join("rect")
    .attr("width", (d, i) => xScale(d.count) - xScale(0))
    .attr("height", yScale.bandwidth())
    .attr("x", xScale(0))
```

```
    .attr("y", (d, i) => yScale(d.char))
    .attr("class", (d, i) => getClass(d.char));
}
--snip--
```

Listing 14-39: Applying the class name based on the character

Now every rect element will have a class name based on the character from that element's datum. The last step is to write the CSS that will give each class name a different fill color. Add the CSS code in Listing 14-40 to *style.css*.

```
.lower {
  fill: purple;
}

.upper {
  fill: orangered;
}

.number {
  fill: green;
}

.other {
  fill: #555;
}
```

Listing 14-40: Defining styles for the different classes

Now when you reload the page and type in some different characters, you should see something like Figure 14-16.

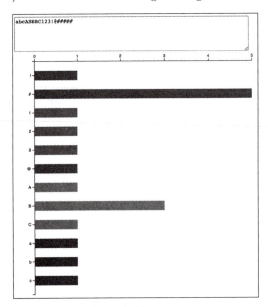

Figure 14-16: Color-coded bars

The bars should be assigned different colors based on the kind of character entered.

Cleaning the Data

Often it's necessary to clean a dataset by fixing any mistakes or irregularities it contains before visualizing it. For example, one problem with the current approach to our bar graph is that different whitespace characters show up as different bars, each with an invisible label (because the text of the label is just whitespace). These whitespace characters include spaces, newlines, tabs, and various other kinds of spaces that you can type with different key combinations (for example, a non-breaking space, which you can enter with OPTION-spacebar on macOS or CTRL-SHIFT-spacebar on Windows). To fix this, we'll convert all whitespace characters to the same "<space>" string before the character counting, so all whitespace will be visualized by a single bar with a readable label. Update your *script.js* file as shown in Listing 14-41. These updates come near the end of the file.

```
--snip--
function standardizeSpace(char) {
❶ if (char.trim() == "") {
    return "<space>";
  } else {
    return char;
  }
}

d3.select("textarea").on("input", e => {
  let frequencies = {};

  e.target.value.split("").forEach(char => {
❷   let standardized = standardizeSpace(char);
    let currentCount = frequencies[standardized] || 0;
    frequencies[standardized] = currentCount + 1;
  });
--snip--
```

Listing 14-41: Standardizing whitespace characters

We first declare a `standardizeSpace` function that takes a character and calls the `trim` method on it ❶. The `trim` method removes whitespace at the start or end of a string, so if it returns an empty string, we know the character is whitespace. In this case, we return the string "<space>". Otherwise, we return the character unchanged. We then have to modify the text processing code to call our function and standardize the whitespace characters ❷ before using them as keys in the `frequencies` object.

Now when you enter various kinds of whitespace characters in the text area, you should see a single bar labeled <space> instead of multiple bars with empty labels.

Animating the Changes

Our final task is to add animations to the axes and bars. This will make it easier to see when new elements are added and when the counts for existing elements change. To animate the axes, all we need to do is add a call to transition to the topContainer and leftContainer selections inside the update function, as shown in Listing 14-42.

```
--snip--
let leftAxis = d3.axisLeft(yScale);

topContainer
  .transition()
  .call(topAxis);

leftContainer
  .transition()
  .call(leftAxis);
--snip--
```

Listing 14-42: Adding animations to the axes

Now when the domains for the axes update to accommodate new data, the existing ticks will animate to their updated positions, and new ticks will fade in.

We have two options for adding transitions to the bars: we could keep the existing join code and just add a single call to transition, or we could use the advanced join technique described earlier, which would let us customize the transitions depending on whether the elements are entering, updating, or exiting. As you might guess, we're going to go with the advanced version! You can find the updated update code in Listing 14-43.

```
--snip--
  leftContainer
    .transition()
    .call(leftAxis);

  svg
    .selectAll("rect")
❶ .data(data, d => d.char)
    .join(
❷ enter => enter
        .append("rect")
        .attr("x", xScale(0))
        .attr("y", (d, i) => yScale(d.char))
        .attr("class", d => getClass(d.char))
        .transition()
        .attr("width", d => xScale(d.count) - xScale(0))
        .attr("height", yScale.bandwidth()),
❸ update => update
        .transition()
        .attr("width", d => xScale(d.count) - xScale(0))
```

```
        .attr("height", yScale.bandwidth())
        .attr("y", (d, i) => yScale(d.char)),
❹ exit => exit
        .transition()
        .attr("width", 0)
        .attr("height", 0)
        .remove()
    );
}
--snip--
```

Listing 14-43: Animating the bars

The first thing we have to do is set a key function ❶ to tell D3 that the datum's char property should be used as its identifier. Next, we switch to the advanced join technique, similar to Listing 14-25. The enter function ❷ first adds the rect element and sets its x, y, and class attributes before the call to transition, meaning that these attributes won't be animated. The width and height attributes come after the call to transition, so these attributes *will* be animated. This way, new elements will grow in place from the left axis.

The update function ❸ animates the width and height again, but also animates the y attribute. This means that existing elements will slide up or down to their new position when new elements are added.

Finally, the exit function ❹ animates the width and height to 0 before the element is removed, causing elements to shrink away to nothing at their previous position.

Reload the page and try adding and removing characters in the text area. Enjoy watching how the elements animate in, out, or update.

Summary

In this chapter you learned the basics of SVG, and how to use D3 to create, update, and remove SVG elements based on real-time changes in a dataset. By now, you should have a pretty good understanding of how to build a data-based application in D3. In the next chapter, we'll put this knowledge to work by building an application that reads data from an API and renders it into an interactive diagram.

15

VISUALIZING DATA FROM THE GITHUB SEARCH API

In this final project, you'll build an application that reads data from a public API and uses D3 to build an interactive bar chart based on that data. We'll be reading data from the GitHub Search API. This API allows you to search for data on GitHub, a service that hosts Git repositories (Git is a popular version control system for keeping track of software project source code). The API uses the HTTPS protocol and returns JSON-formatted data based on a search query you encode into a URL.

If you haven't used GitHub before, go to *https://github.com* to see what it looks like. At the top of the page, you'll see a search box that you can use to search for public, *open source* repositories (that is, repositories whose source code is available to anyone to read and use). Instead of using that search box manually, the GitHub Search API lets us perform searches programmatically—for example, with JavaScript. The API can search for various items on GitHub, such as repositories, users, and issues. We'll be using the repository search feature to find top JavaScript repositories. Then we'll draw a D3 bar chart ranking the repositories by popularity. The viewer will be able to learn more about each repository by hovering over its bar. We'll also add some interactivity by allowing the viewer to hide or show repositories based on their software license.

This project will give you experience working with real-world data from a JSON API. A huge amount of programming boils down to making requests to third-party APIs and then doing some work with the returned data, as you'll practice here. You'll also put everything you learned about D3 in Chapter 14 to work, building up a more interesting, interactive chart, and you'll learn some techniques for creating richer visualizations.

Setting Up

To get started, create a new directory called *github*, and add empty *style.css* and *script.js* files. Then make an *index.html* file and add the code in Listing 15-1.

```
<!DOCTYPE html>
<html>
  <head>
    <title>GitHub</title>
    <link rel="stylesheet" href="style.css">
  </head>
  <body>
    <script src="https://unpkg.com/d3@7.4.4/dist/d3.js"></script>
    <script src="script.js"></script>
  </body>
</html>
```

Listing 15-1: An index.html *file for our GitHub Search API visualization*

This is the same basic HTML file we used in Chapter 14. It gives us access to D3 through a script element linking to a copy of the library on *https://unpkg.com*.

Fetching Data

Now let's try getting some data from the GitHub Search API. To do this, we need to format our request for data as part of a URL. Visiting that URL retrieves the data. The whole URL, including the search query we'll be using, looks like this (note that it's been broken onto two lines here to fit the page):

```
https://api.github.com/search/repositories?q=language%3Ajavascript%20stars%3A
%3E10000&per_page=20&sort=stars
```

Rather than type out the URL manually, however, we'll build it up using JavaScript, which will make it easier to understand and modify.

The URL has two parts: a base URL, which gives us access to the API, and a query string, where we specify what data we want. These two parts are separated by a question mark (?). The query string contains pairs of keys and values that are used to send information to the API about the query we're making. Each key and value is joined by an equal sign (=), and each key-value pair is separated by an ampersand (&). In this URL, the keys are q (search query), per_page (number of results per page), and sort (how to sort the results). The keys and values in query strings are allowed to contain only a limited set of characters: a–z, A–Z, 0–9, hyphen (-), period (.), underscore (_), tilde (~), and a limited set of other special characters. All other characters must be represented using the *URL encoding* system, which is where all the percent (%) characters in the URL come from. For example, a colon (:) is encoded as %3A and a space is encoded as %20.

To simplify things, we'll write a function that takes an object with the unencoded query string parameters and converts it to a properly formatted and encoded URL. Add the code in Listing 15-2 to *script.js*.

```
function getUrl() {
❶ let baseUrl = "https://api.github.com/search/repositories";

❷ let params = {
    q: "language:javascript stars:>10000",
    per_page: 20,
    sort: "stars"
  };

❸ let queryString = Object.entries(params).map(pair => {
    return `${pair[0]}=${encodeURIComponent(pair[1])}`;
  }).join("&");

❹ return `${baseUrl}?${queryString}`;
}

let url = getUrl();

console.log(url);
```

Listing 15-2: Creating the URL

The code to create the URL lives in the getUrl function. This function first sets the base URL (the part of the URL before the query string) ❶. Then, to build the query string, we start by creating a params object ❷, with the search query q using GitHub's search query format. Specifically, we're searching for repositories whose language is JavaScript that have over 10,000 stars (users on GitHub can "star" repositories to save them for later, so the number of stars is a rough measure of popularity). You can try out this query in the search box on *https://github.com* if you want.

Next, we map over the key-value pairs in params, creating a string for each pair with the format *"key=value"* ❸. The keys don't need to be

URL-encoded—unquoted object keys don't contain any special characters, so they're already valid in URLs—but we encode the values using the built-in function encodeURIComponent, which replaces any disallowed characters with their percent-encoded versions. We then join the strings together, separating them with the & character, and build and return the final URL by combining the base URL, the ? character, and the query string ❹. We end the script by calling our getUrl function and logging the result to the console.

When you load the page and open the console, you should see the URL shown earlier printed there. If you copy that URL and paste it into your browser's address bar, you should see a bunch of JSON data. If not, make sure the URL matches the URL on the previous page, and check your code if it doesn't. If the URL looks correct and you're not getting data, or you're getting an error message, it's possible that GitHub has changed the way its API works. See the upcoming box "Authenticated vs. Unauthenticated APIs" for guidance on what to do in this case.

To bring the JSON data into your application you can use D3's json helper method, which fetches JSON from a given URL. Update the end of *script.js* as shown in Listing 15-3.

```
--snip--
let url = getUrl();

d3.json(url).then(data => {
  console.log(data);
});
```

Listing 15-3: Fetching JSON data

Fetching a bunch of data from an API may take a little time, so the d3.json method returns a Promise, a type of object that represents something that will be available in the future. The then method takes a function that will be called when the data is ready. D3 converts the JSON response string into a JavaScript object, so data will be an object. Here, we just log it to the console.

AUTHENTICATED VS. UNAUTHENTICATED APIS

The GitHub Search API is an HTTP API, meaning it exchanges data using HTTP over the HTTPS protocol. This kind of API can be either authenticated or unauthenticated. An *authenticated* API requires you to somehow prove your identity to the API owner, for example, by providing a secret key with your request, whereas *unauthenticated* APIs have no such requirements.

Unfortunately, with browser-based JavaScript applications like the one we're writing here, there's no easy way to use an authenticated API without exposing some secret information. For that reason, when you need to work

---

with an authenticated API, it's most common to break the application into two pieces: *backend* code running on a server that communicates securely with the authenticated API, and *frontend* code running in the browser that communicates with the backend. This way, the browser code and the API don't need to interact directly.

It's perfectly possible to write backend code in JavaScript using a framework called Node.js, but that's outside of the scope of this book. Instead, we'll keep all the application code in the browser, and stick to unauthenticated APIs like the GitHub Search API we're using here. On the off chance that GitHub is no longer supporting this unauthenticated API at the time you read this book, however, this arrangement will no longer work, and you'll have problems running Listings 15-2 and 15-3. In case that happens, I've provided a snapshot of the GitHub Search API data we'll be using for this project, which you can access through the URL *https://skilldrick-jscc.s3.us-west-2.amazonaws.com/gh-js-repos.json*. To use this snapshot of the data, replace the content of your *script.js* file with the following code:

```
let backupUrl =
  "https://skilldrick-jscc.s3.us-west-2.amazonaws.com/gh-js-repos.json";

d3.json(backupUrl).then(data => {
  console.log(data);
});
```

You'll now be able to continue with the rest of the project code as written, starting from Listing 15-4.

When you reload the page, after waiting a few seconds you should see the data in the console. Take a moment to inspect it. You should see three top-level properties: `incomplete_results`, `items`, and `total_count`. The `incomplete_results` property will be `true` if the query took too long and the API was able to return only partial results; otherwise, it will be `false`. The `total_count` property gives the total number of results for this search query (this is the total number of results the search found, of which only the first 20 are returned). The `items` array contains the results of the current call; it should contain 20 items. Each item is an object with some information about a particular repository, including its name, description, and various other details. Several of the fields are themselves GitHub API URLs that can be called to get additional information about the repository. For example, `languages_url` is an API URL that tells you what programming languages are used in the repository, broken down by the number of lines of code per language.

In this project, we'll be using several fields from each item: `full_name`, `stargazers_count`, `html_url`, and `license`. The `full_name` field holds the name of the repository owner and the name of the repository joined with a forward slash: for example, `"facebook/react"`. The `stargazers_count` field gives the number of times the repository has been starred by users. The `html_url` field holds the repository's URL on GitHub. Finally, license has data about which software license the repository uses.

Open source code owners use software licenses to tell other users what they can and can't do with their code. For example, some licenses are very restrictive, stating that the code can't be used in an application whose code isn't itself open source. Others are much more permissive, allowing you to do whatever you want with the code.

The Basic Visualization

Now that we have the data, we'll create a basic bar chart showing how many stars each repository in the dataset has received. To do this, we'll create the required SVG elements, draw the axes, and draw the bars themselves. Later we'll improve on this basic chart, making it more informative, stylish, and interactive.

Creating the Elements

To create our chart, we first have to create the svg element that will hold it and the two g elements for the axes. In this case, the axes will be on the bottom and left sides. Add the code in Listing 15-4 to the start of *script.js*, before the getUrl function.

```
const width = 600;
const height = 400;

let svg = d3
  .select("body")
❶ .append("svg")
  .attr("width", width)
  .attr("height", height);

❷ let margin = { top: 20, right: 10, bottom: 20, left: 50 };

// Bottom axis container
let bottomContainer = svg
❸ .append("g")
  .attr("id", "bottom")
  .attr("transform", `translate(0, ${height - margin.bottom})`);

// Left axis container
let leftContainer = svg
❹ .append("g")
  .attr("id", "left")
  .attr("transform", `translate(${margin.left}, 0)`);

function getUrl() {
--snip--
```

Listing 15-4: Setting up the elements

Much like we did for the character frequency chart in Chapter 14, we append an svg element to the page ❶ and set its width and height. We then create a margin object ❷ and append the g elements for containing the bottom ❸ and left ❹ axes, which we position based on the margins.

Drawing the Axes

With the elements created, we can make a start on the update function, which will draw the visualization. First, we'll create the scales based on the data and draw the axes. Make the changes to *script.js* shown in Listing 15-5.

```
--snip--
// Left axis container
let leftContainer = svg
  .append("g")
  .attr("id", "left")
  .attr("transform", `translate(${margin.left}, 0)`);

function update(items) {
❶ let xScale = d3.scaleBand()
    .domain(items.map(d => d.full_name))
    .range([margin.left, width - margin.right])
    .padding(0.3);

  let yScale = d3.scaleLinear()
❷ .domain([0, d3.max(items, d => d.stargazers_count)])
    .range([height - margin.bottom, margin.top])
    .nice();

❸ let bottomAxis = d3.axisBottom(xScale);
  let leftAxis = d3.axisLeft(yScale);

❹ bottomContainer.call(bottomAxis);
  leftContainer.call(leftAxis);
}

function getUrl() {
--snip--

d3.json(url).then(data => {
❺ update(data.items);
});
```

Listing 15-5: Drawing the axes

The update function takes the items array from the API response. Our bar chart will have a vertical bar for each repository, so we create the horizontal xScale using the scaleBand helper to evenly space the bars ❶. The domain is the full_name from each repository. Each repository's full name is unique, so this will result in 20 bands. The vertical yScale is used to visualize the number of stars that each repository has, so its domain goes from zero to the max stargazers_count ❷. We use nice here to round the top of the scale to the next tick value. After creating the scales, we create the axis generators ❸ and then use those generators to draw the axes to the containers ❹, as we did for the character frequencies project.

The last thing to do here is call our update function from inside the d3.json callback, passing the items array ❺. We're able to go straight from fetching the data to calling update because the GitHub Search API conveniently returns the data in the format we need for rendering. There's no need to do any processing of the data like we did in the character frequencies example, where the source data was just a string and we needed a sorted array of objects describing each character and its count.

When you reload *index.html* you should now see the axes, as shown in Figure 15-1. We'll fix the bottom axis labels shortly; they're a mess right now because D3 is trying to render the full name of each repository. Also, your left axis scale may go higher than the 200,000 shown in the figure, depending on how many stars the most popular JavaScript project has when you run this code. At the time of this writing, facebook/react had the most stars of any JavaScript project on GitHub, at around 196,000.

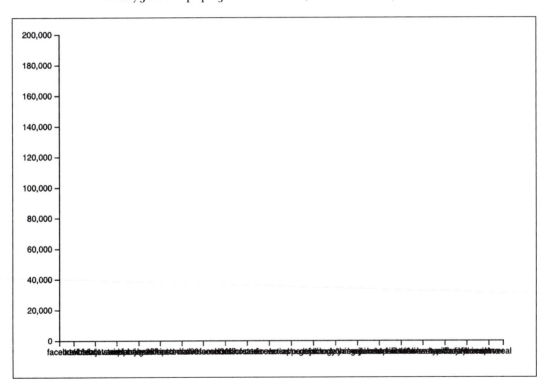

Figure 15-1: The axes

Given that we're working with such large numbers here (and getting larger every day), we can increase readability by using SI prefixes like *k* for 1,000. This is easy to do in D3 with the right number format. While we make that change, we'll also remove the ticks from the bottom axis. See Listing 15-6 for these changes.

```
--snip--
  let yScale = d3.scaleLinear()
    .domain([0, d3.max(items, d => d.stargazers_count)])
    .range([height - margin.bottom, margin.top])
    .nice();

  let bottomAxis = d3
    .axisBottom(xScale)
❶ .tickValues([]);

  let leftAxis = d3
    .axisLeft(yScale)
❷ .tickFormat(d3.format("~s"));

  bottomContainer.call(bottomAxis);
  leftContainer.call(leftAxis);
--snip--
```

Listing 15-6: Cleaning up the scales

For the bottom axis, we're updating the tick values to be an empty list ❶, which effectively removes the ticks. For the left axis, we're adding a tick format using the format specifier "~s" ❷, which will, for example, render the number 200,000 as 200k and 1,000,000 as 1M. Figure 15-2 shows how the updated axes should now look.

Figure 15-2: The axes after some cleanup

The numbers in the left axis are now easier to read at a glance, and the bottom axis is no longer a jumble of text.

Drawing the Bars

Now that the axes are drawn, we need to draw the bars themselves. Add the code in Listing 15-7 to the end of the update function.

```
--snip--
  bottomContainer.call(bottomAxis);
  leftContainer.call(leftAxis);

  svg
    .selectAll("rect")
    .data(items, ❶ d => d.full_name)
    .join("rect")
    .attr("x", d => xScale(d.full_name))
❷ .attr("y", d => yScale(d.stargazers_count))
    .attr("width", xScale.bandwidth())
❸ .attr("height", d => yScale(0) - yScale(d.stargazers_count));
}

function getUrl() {
--snip--
```

Listing 15-7: Drawing the bars

As in the character frequencies project, we're drawing a bunch of rect elements. The key function ❶ extracts the full_name property, which we're using here as the unique identifier for each repository. For now, we're using the simple join technique, without separate handling for entering, updating, and exiting elements (that will come later).

The x attribute is set based on looking up the full_name in xScale, and the width is based on the bandwidth method on xScale. The y and height attributes are a bit trickier this time and require some explanation. If you look back at the definition of yScale in Listing 15-5, you'll see that the domain is [0, d3.max(items, d => d.stargazers_count)] and the range is [height-margin .bottom, margin.top]. With the values we've set, that range expands to [380, 20]. The range goes from high to low, meaning that high values in the domain map to lower values in the range, and vice versa. This is because y values in computer graphics count down from the top of the screen, but in our graph we want y values to count up from the bottom of the graph. The other thing that makes this tricky is that SVG rectangles are drawn from the top-left corner, which will likely be different for each bar, so we need to set a variable height that makes all the bars hit the bottom axis.

Because of all this, we set the y attribute of the bar to yScale(d.stargazers _count) ❷, which gives the vertical position of the top of the bar. To calculate the height of the bar, we use yScale(0) - yScale(d.stargazers_count) ❸. Calling yScale(0) gives the vertical position of the bottom of the bar (all the bars should have their base at 0 in the domain), so subtracting the position of the top of the bar from the position of the bottom of the bar gives the height of the bar. We need to end up with a positive height, so we have to subtract the smaller number from the larger number. The top of the bar is a smaller number in the display range, even though it's a larger number in the domain. Figure 15-3 shows how the bars should look, though keep in mind that your bar heights may be different based on how the data evolves.

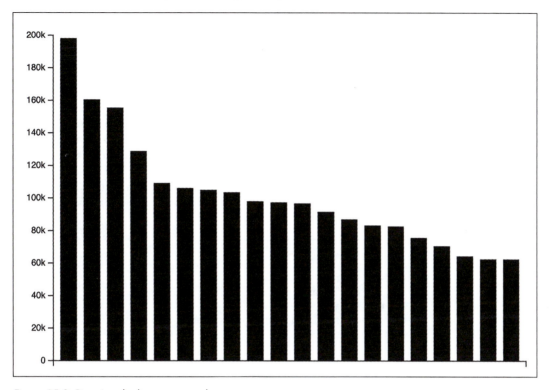

Figure 15-3: Drawing the bars as rect elements

As you look at the bars, remember that each bar is drawn from its top-left corner, and that the heights are calculated such that the bottoms of all the bars align.

TRY IT YOURSELF

15-1. Try modifying the width of the bars by changing the padding on the xScale object.

15-2. For more of a challenge, try modifying the domain of the data along the left axis so the minimum value is based on the minimum number of stars rather than starting at zero. Hint: this makes calculating the bar heights a little more complex, as you can't subtract from yScale(0) now. To get the appropriate height, you'll need to replace yScale(0) with yScale.range()[0]. yScale.range() gives you the two-element array of the minimum and maximum range values after applying the nice rounding.

Improving the Visualization

We now have a basic visualization up and running, but it isn't terribly informative. In this section, we'll implement some improvements to make the visualization more meaningful. We'll create a way to see more information about each repository. We'll also color-code the bars to show each repository's license type, and make sure the axes are properly labeled.

Showing Repository Info

The current graph doesn't give any way of identifying which repository each bar represents. There are various ways to solve this (for example, vertically or diagonally oriented tick labels, or some kind of *tooltip*, a text field that pops up when a bar is hovered), but for this project we'll add a permanent sidebar that shows more information about a bar when you hover over it. First, we'll add the HTML for the sidebar to *index.html*, as shown in Listing 15-8.

```
--snip--
  <body>
    <div id="sidebar">
      <div id="info" class="box">
        <p class="repo">
          <span class="label">Repository</span>
        ❶ <span class="value"><a target="_blank"></a></span>
        </p>
        <p class="license">
          <span class="label">License</span>
          <span class="value"></span>
        </p>
        <p class="stars">
          <span class="label">Stars</span>
          <span class="value"></span>
        </p>
      </div>
    </div>

    <script src="https://unpkg.com/d3@7.4.4/dist/d3.js"></script>
    <script src="script.js"></script>
  </body>
--snip--
```

Listing 15-8: Adding the sidebar HTML to index.html

Here we set up a div called info with the elements that we'll need to display the repository information. It's nested inside another div called sidebar. This outer div may seem superfluous now, but later we'll add another div element to the sidebar, so we'll need the parent div element to contain the two sidebar div elements.

The info div will show the repository name, its license type, and its number of stars. We use span elements to wrap parts of the text. A span is a container element like a div, but unlike div elements, which create a new block, span is an inline element, so it can enclose part of a line of text without making a new line. Later, we'll update the content of the value spans when you hover over a bar to show the relevant information about that bar.

One of the span elements contains an a element ❶, which creates a hyperlink to another page or website. The URL of the link is specified with an href attribute, which we'll set dynamically later. The target="_blank" attribute instructs the browser to open the link in a new tab or window.

The sidebar looks a bit ugly at this stage, so let's add some CSS. Add the code in Listing 15-9 to *style.css*.

```
body {
❶ display: flex;
  align-items: flex-start;
  font-family: Arial, Helvetica, sans-serif;
}

.box {
  padding: 0px 15px 0px 15px;
  border: 1px solid #888;
  margin-bottom: 15px;
}

#info .label {
  font-weight: bold;
  display: block;
}

#info a {
  text-decoration: none;
}

#info a:hover {
  text-decoration: underline;
}
```

Listing 15-9: Styling the sidebar

For this project we're using a CSS technique called *flexbox* ❶, which is a relatively recent addition to the CSS specification. Flexbox makes it much easier to define layouts, especially those that will work flexibly across a variety of screen and viewport sizes. Flexbox layouts have two main components: the *flex container* and the *flex items*. The flex container is a parent element that defines how its child flex items (the direct children of the container) are sized and how they flow. In our case, the flex container is the body element, and the flex items are the svg element and the #sidebar element. By default, the items are arranged left to right (meaning that the #sidebar element will appear on the left of the screen, followed by the svg element to its right). The declaration align-items: flex-start; means that the items will be aligned to the top of the parent container.

NOTE *If you want to learn more about flexbox, check out* https://css-tricks.com/snippets/css/a-guide-to-flexbox/.

TRY IT YOURSELF

15-3. Chrome makes it very easy to experiment with flexbox changes. If you open up the element inspector, you'll see a small `flex` icon next to the body element. Click that and the browser will add highlighting to show the flex container and flex items. In the Styles pane, you can click the icon next to `display: flex;` to open a dialog that will let you interactively modify the flex container properties.

Currently the svg element is being appended to the body element, meaning that it comes after the sidebar, but for layout reasons we want it to come before. To do that, we'll need to switch from the append method to the insert method when we create the svg element, since the latter allows us to specify an element to insert before. The *script.js* change for this is shown in Listing 15-10.

```
--snip--
let svg = d3
  .select("body")
  .insert("svg", "#sidebar")
  .attr("width", width)
  .attr("height", height);
--snip--
```

Listing 15-10: Inserting the svg element before the sidebar

Now the sidebar will appear to the right of the graph, as the svg element now appears before the sidebar in the flex container.

Before we write the code for displaying the details about a repository in the sidebar, we need a function for getting the name of the repository's license. Accessing the other pieces of information will be straightforward, but not all repositories have a license, so our function has to handle the case where no license data is available. Listing 15-11 shows the new getLicense function, which you can insert into *script.js* just before the update function.

```
--snip--
// Left axis container
let leftContainer = svg
  .append("g")
  .attr("id", "left")
  .attr("transform", `translate(${margin.left}, 0)`);
```

```
  function getLicense(d) {
❶ let license = d.license?.name;

❷ if (!license) {
    return "No License";
  } else {
    return license;
  }
}

function update(items) {
--snip--
```

Listing 15-11: The getLicense function

If a repository has a license, the license name will be available as
`d.license.name`, but if it doesn't have a license, `d.license` will be undefined.
We test for this situation using the `?.` operator, called the *optional chaining
operator* ❶. Like the regular `.` operator, `?.` attempts to take the object specified to the left of the operator and access the method or property specified
to the right of the operator. Unlike the regular `.` operator, however, `?.` will
return undefined if the object to the left of the operator is `null` or `undefined`.
Thus, if `d.license` is undefined (meaning the repository doesn't have a license),
our license variable will be set to undefined, but if `d.license` is an object (meaning the repository has a license), then license will be set to `d.license.name`.
If license ends up undefined ❷, our getLicense function returns the string
`"No License"`. Otherwise, the value of license is returned.

Now we can add the code that will update the sidebar when the bars are
hovered over. We'll do this by adding a mouseover event handler to the rect
elements. Update *script.js* with the code in Listing 15-12. This code goes at
the end of the update function.

```
--snip--
    .attr("width", xScale.bandwidth())
    .attr("height", d => yScale(0) - yScale(d.stargazers_count))
    .on("mouseover", (e, d) => {
      let info = d3.select("#info");
      info.select(".repo .value a").text(d.full_name).attr("href", d.html_url); ❶
      info.select(".license .value").text(getLicense(d));
      info.select(".stars .value").text(d.stargazers_count);
    });
}

function getUrl() {
--snip--
```

Listing 15-12: Updating the sidebar on hover

D3 event handlers are called with two arguments: the event object (e)
and the datum bound to the element that the event was triggered on (d).
The first thing we do in the handler is select the #info element, because

all the elements we want to modify are children of that element. We then update the a element inside the `.value` element inside the `.repo` element ❶ (refer back to Listing 15-8 or look at *index.html* to remind yourself of the HTML structure). We're setting both the text content of this element and the `href` attribute. This has the effect of making a link to the repository, with the full name of the repository as the link text. We similarly set the text of the `.value .license` element to whatever getLicense returns for this datum and the text of the `.stars .value` element to the number of stars.

Reload the page and try hovering over some of the bars. You should see something like Figure 15-4.

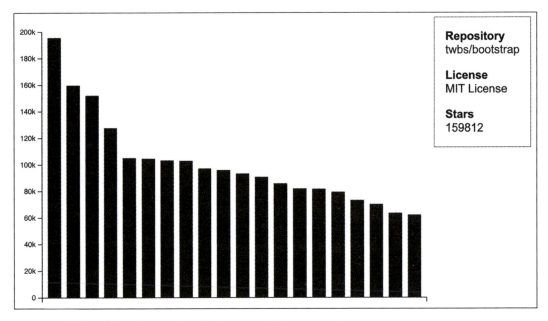

Figure 15-4: The sidebar showing details about one of the repositories

For each bar you hover over, the details for that repository should show up in the new sidebar. If you click the repository name, your browser should open up a new tab and take you to the repository's GitHub page.

Color-Coding the Bars

In order to convey some additional information visually, we're going to color-code the bars based on the license types. D3 lets you create scales whose inputs (the domain) are values and whose outputs (the range) are colors. You'll see how to do that in Listing 15-13.

```
--snip--
function update(items) {
❶ let licenses = new Set(items.map(d => getLicense(d)));

❷ let colorScale = d3.scaleOrdinal()
    .domain(licenses)
```

```
    .range(d3.schemeCategory10);

  let xScale = d3.scaleBand()
--snip--
```

Listing 15-13: Creating a color scale for the licenses

First, we need to collect all the unique license names. To do this, we map over the items, calling our getLicense function for each one ❶. This gives an array of the license names. In the same line, we pass the resulting array to the Set constructor. In programming terms, a *set* is a collection of unique items, so the Set constructor can take an array of items and filter out any duplicates. In JavaScript, sets maintain their order, like arrays.

The d3.scaleOrdinal helper ❷ creates a scale with discrete inputs and discrete outputs. Here, the inputs are the unique license names and the outputs are color names. For the scale's range, we're using d3.schemeCategory10, which is an array of 10 hex color strings. You can check it out in the console:

```
d3.schemeCategory10;
▶ (10) ['#1f77b4', '#ff7f0e', '#2ca02c', '#d62728', '#9467bd', '#8c564b',
 '#e377c2', '#7f7f7f', '#bcbd22', '#17becf']
```

Each license in the set will map to one of these colors, index-wise. If there are more than 10 licenses, the colors will wrap around to the beginning again (the eleventh and twelfth licenses will use the same colors as the first and second ones).

Next we have to set the color of the bar based on its license and the color scale. Listing 15-14 shows how to make that change near the end of the update function.

```
--snip--
  svg
    .selectAll("rect")
    .data(items, d => d.full_name)
    .join("rect")
    .attr("x", d => xScale(d.full_name))
    .attr("y", d => yScale(d.stargazers_count))
    .attr("fill", d => colorScale(getLicense(d)))
    .attr("width", xScale.bandwidth())
    .attr("height", d => yScale(0) - yScale(d.stargazers_count))
--snip--
```

Listing 15-14: Setting the fill color of the rect

We have to call our getLicense function on d to get the license name (because it could be "No License"), before passing the license name to the colorScale. This gives us the color value for setting the fill attribute of the rect.

With color-coding like this, you really need a key so users know what each color means. We'll create that key as another box in the sidebar, beneath the repository info box. It will include squares of color alongside the corresponding license names. First, we'll need some more HTML. Update *index.html* with the changes in Listing 15-15.

```
--snip--
      <p class="stars">
        <span class="label">Stars</span>
        <span class="value"></span>
      </p>
    </div>

    <div id="key" class="box">
      <h1>Key</h1>
    </div>
  </div>
--snip--
```

Listing 15-15: Adding the div and heading for the license key

Here we're creating another div called key inside the sidebar div and giving it a heading. We'll create the other elements for the key using JavaScript.

Next comes the CSS for styling these new elements and the children we'll be adding with JavaScript. Add the code in Listing 15-16 to the end of *style.css*.

```
--snip--
#info a:hover {
  text-decoration: underline;
}

#key h1 {
  font-size: 1.5em;
}

#key .color {
  display: inline-block;
  width: 10px;
  height: 10px;
  margin: 0px 10px 0px 10px;
}
```

Listing 15-16: Styling the key

The font size for the h1 element here is set to 1.5em, which means 1.5 times the font size of the parent element. This ensures that this heading will be 1.5 times bigger than the rest of the text. The #key .color ruleset is used to style the squares of color that will appear as part of the key. These will be div elements, but display: inline-block means that they'll act like a cross between an inline element (like a span), in that they won't force a new line, and a block element (like a div), in that they'll be able to have fixed dimensions and margins. (Inline elements are unable to have a width and height because they're sized based on their content, and in this case the squares have no content.)

Now we can add the JavaScript that will generate the key. This will entail a new data join at the end of the update function, to join the licenses to the elements used to render them. Update *script.js* with the changes in Listing 15-17.

```
--snip--
    .on("mouseover", (e, d) => {
      let info = d3.select("#info");
      info.select(".repo .value a").text(d.full_name).attr("href", d.html_url);
      info.select(".license .value").text(getLicense(d));
      info.select(".stars .value").text(d.stargazers_count);
  });

  d3.select("#key")
    .selectAll("p")
    .data(licenses)
    .join(
      enter => {
      ❶ let p = enter.append("p");

      ❷ p.append("div")
          .attr("class", "color")
        ❸ .style("background-color", d => colorScale(d));

      ❹ p.append("span")
          .text(d => d)

        return p;
      }
    );
}

function getUrl() {
--snip--
```

Listing 15-17: Generating the key

Here we're using the #key element as the container for our new join, and we're joining in a bunch of p elements to bind to each license datum. We're using the advanced join technique, but just with an enter function; we don't need custom behavior for updating or exiting items. (We can't use the regular join technique here because then the element appends would happen every time update is called.) First we create the p element for each new datum ❶, then we append a div element where we'll display the square of color to the p element ❷. Adding the color class to the div means that it will have the styling from Listing 15-16. To give it the right color, we use the style method ❸, which sets an inline CSS style on the element. We set the color to the appropriate value for the datum using colorScale. Finally, we add a span element to the p element for holding the actual name of the license ❹.

Reload the page and you should see something like Figure 15-5.

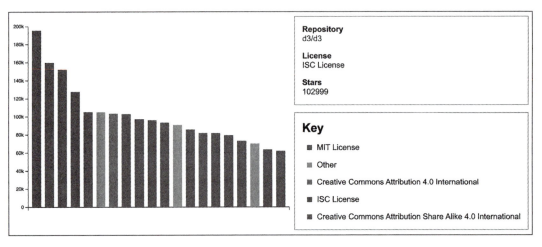

Figure 15-5: Color-coded bars with a key

Our visualization now has a full key showing the license that each color maps to, making the colors much more meaningful.

Labeling the Left Axis

It's implied that our graph's left axis shows the number of stars each repository has, but that isn't explicitly stated in the chart. To fix this, we'll add a text element to label the left axis. The code for this is in Listing 15-18. Add this code right before the getLicense function.

```
--snip--
// Left axis container
let leftContainer = svg
  .append("g")
  .attr("id", "left")
  .attr("transform", `translate(${margin.left}, 0)`);

let chartHeight = (height - margin.bottom) - margin.top;
let midPoint = margin.top + chartHeight / 2;

svg
  .append("text")
  .text("Stars")
  .style("font-size", "14px")
❶ .attr("text-anchor", "middle")
❷ .attr("transform", `translate(12, ${midPoint}) rotate(270)`);

function getLicense(d) {
--snip--
```

Listing 15-18: Adding a left axis label

First, we need to calculate where to draw the label. Its vertical position should be in the middle of the chart. We calculate the height of the chart based on the total height and the two margins, then calculate the midpoint based on adding the top margin and half the height of the chart.

Next, we append a text element with the word *Stars* to the svg element. We set the font earlier in *style.css* by applying a font-family to the body element. Setting the text-anchor attribute to middle ❶ causes the text to be centered around its calculated position. We also specify two transformations ❷: a translate followed by a rotate. The translate moves the center of the label to the correct position, and the rotate turns it 90 degrees counterclockwise (or 270 degrees clockwise).

Adding Interactivity

Our visualization is already somewhat interactive in the sense that hovering over a bar shows details about that repository in the sidebar. It would be fun to add another interactive element that allows the user to filter the data. For example, now that we have a key listing the different license types, we could use it to selectively show or hide repositories with those licenses. We'll implement this interactive feature now, while also adding animation to smooth out the changes to the graph.

Filtering the Data by License

To let the user filter the data by license type, we're going to add a checkbox to each of the items in the key. We'll then use those checkboxes to determine which repositories to (temporarily) exclude from the graph. This will require keeping track of the licenses we want to hide and removing any repositories that use those licenses before rendering.

First we'll add the checkboxes. Change *script.js* as shown in Listing 15-19 to do this.

```
--snip--
    d3.select("#key")
      .selectAll("p")
      .data(licenses)
      .join(
        enter => {
        let p = enter.append("p");

        p.append("input")
         .attr("type", "checkbox")
         .attr("checked", true)
         .attr("title", "Include in chart");

        p.append("div")
         .attr("class", "color")
         .style("background-color", d => colorScale(d));
--snip--
```

Listing 15-19: Adding checkboxes

In HTML, a checkbox is an input element with a type attribute value of checkbox. In the code, we add one of these at the start of each p element in the key. The checked attribute determines whether the checkbox is checked or not; we set them to be checked by default, so all the repositories will be shown when the visualization first loads. The title attribute gives a tooltip with helper text if you hover over the element.

Next, we need to create a mechanism for keeping track of which licenses should be hidden. The code for this is in Listing 15-20.

```
--snip--
function getLicense(d) {
  let license = d.license?.name;

  if (!license) {
    return "No License";
  } else {
    return license;
  }
}

❶ let hiddenLicenses = new Set();

function update(items) {
  let licenses = new Set(items.map(d => getLicense(d)));

--snip--

      p.append("span")
        .text(d => d)

      return p;
    }
  );

❷ d3.selectAll("#key input").on("change", (e, d) => {
    if (e.target.checked) {
    ❸ hiddenLicenses.delete(d);
    } else {
    ❹ hiddenLicenses.add(d);
    }

    console.log(hiddenLicenses);
  ❺ update(items);
  });
}

function getUrl() {
--snip--
```

Listing 15-20: Keeping track of the hidden licenses

First, we create a new empty Set called hiddenLicenses, just before the update function ❶. We're using Set here to make it easier to add or remove licenses—with an array it's trickier to remove a specific element. Then, after the code that renders the key, we create a change event handler for the checkboxes ❷. Whenever a checkbox changes from checked to unchecked or vice versa, this handler will run. In the handler, e is the change event and d is the bound datum (even though the license is bound to the p element, the children, like this checkbox, also inherit the datum). We use e.target.checked to determine whether, after the change, the checkbox is checked or not. If it is, then we know the datum should be removed from the hiddenLicenses set, using the delete method on the set ❸. Conversely, if the checkbox is now unchecked we add that datum to hiddenLicenses, using the add method on the set ❹.

Finally, with the hiddenLicenses set modified, we log the set to the console and call the update function again ❺, with the same items it was called with originally. When you reload the page, you won't see any new behavior because we're not actually updating the graph yet, but if you open the console you'll see how the hiddenLicenses set changes as you check and uncheck the various checkboxes. The hiddenLicenses set should always correspond to the unchecked licenses in the key.

Now we need to determine which repositories to show when there are hidden licenses. To do that, we'll create a new array called filtered at the top of the update method. It will be a version of the items array with the repositories with hidden licenses removed. The code for this change is in Listing 15-21.

```
--snip--
let hiddenLicenses = new Set();

function update(items) {
  // Items with the hidden licenses removed
  let filtered = items.filter(d => !hiddenLicenses.has(getLicense(d)));

  let licenses = new Set(items.map(d => getLicense(d)));
--snip--
```

Listing 15-21: Determining the repositories with hidden licenses

To filter the list of items, for each item we check to see if its license name is in the hiddenLicenses set, using the set's has method. If the name isn't included the set, then it will be in the filtered list. Otherwise, it's filtered out.

Finally, we need to switch to using the filtered array rather than the items array for rendering. The new graph will be rendering only the filtered data, so we need to change the scales and the bar drawing code to work with filtered. On the other hand, we shouldn't filter the licenses set because it's needed to maintain a consistent color scheme and to render the key, regardless of whether certain licenses are currently hidden in the bar chart. Listing 15-22 shows all the places in the update function that need to be changed to use filtered instead of items.

```
--snip--
  let xScale = d3.scaleBand()
❶ .domain(filtered.map(d => d.full_name))
    .range([margin.left, width - margin.right])
    .padding(0.3);

  let yScale = d3.scaleLinear()
❷ .domain([0, d3.max(filtered, d => d.stargazers_count)])
    .range([height - margin.bottom, margin.top])
    .nice();

--snip--

  svg
    .selectAll("rect")
❸ .data(filtered, d => d.full_name)
    .join("rect")
    .attr("x", d => xScale(d.full_name))
    .attr("y", d => yScale(d.stargazers_count))
--snip--
```

Listing 15-22: Replacing items *with* filtered *for rendering the bar chart*

We update the code for creating the bottom ❶ and left axis ❷ scales, as well as the code for drawing the bars ❸, changing items to filtered in each case. Refresh the page and deselect some of the licenses in the key. You should now see the corresponding bars disappear from the bar chart. The changes are rendered because, as you saw in Listing 15-20, we're calling update from the change event handler for the checkboxes.

Animating the Changes

For the icing on the cake, let's add some animations. These will make it easier to see changes to the bars as licenses are shown or hidden, and also just make the visualization look cooler. We're going to animate two parts of the graph: the left axis and the bars. To do this, make the changes shown in Listing 15-23.

```
--snip--
  let leftAxis = d3
    .axisLeft(yScale)
    .tickFormat(d3.format("~s"));

  bottomContainer.call(bottomAxis);

  leftContainer
❶ .transition()
    .call(leftAxis);

  svg
    .selectAll("rect")
    .data(filtered, d => d.full_name)
```

```
  .join(
    enter => enter
      .append("rect")
      .attr("x", d => xScale(d.full_name))
      .attr("y", d => yScale(d.stargazers_count))
      .attr("fill", d => colorScale(getLicense(d)))
      .attr("width", xScale.bandwidth())
      .attr("height", d => yScale(0) - yScale(d.stargazers_count))
    ❷ .style("opacity", 0)
      .transition()
    ❸ .style("opacity", 1),
    update => update
      .transition()
    ❹ .attr("x", d => xScale(d.full_name))
      .attr("y", d => yScale(d.stargazers_count))
      .attr("width", xScale.bandwidth())
      .attr("height", d => yScale(0) - yScale(d.stargazers_count)),
    exit => exit
      .transition()
    ❺ .style("opacity", 0)
    ❻ .remove()
  )
  .on("mouseover", (e, d) => {
    let info = d3.select("#info");
    info.select(".repo .value a").text(d.full_name).attr("href", d.html_url);
    info.select(".license .value").text(getLicense(d));
    info.select(".stars .value").text(d.stargazers_count);
  });
--snip--
```

Listing 15-23: Adding animations

Animating the left axis is straightforward: we just call `transition` on the axis's container before the axis is drawn to it ❶, and the left axis will transition anytime the scale changes (which will happen only if the biggest bar is hidden or unhidden, which changes the upper bound of the domain).

To animate the bars, we follow the standard practice of switching to the advanced join technique and adding transitions for entering, updating, and exiting elements. Entering elements start out with all their attributes set and an opacity of 0 (meaning that they are 100 percent transparent) ❷. We then call `transition` and animate up to 100 percent opaque ❸, which has the effect of fading in entering elements. Updating elements remain the same color and opacity, but their position and dimensions can change, so we animate all of these ❹. This has the effect of stretching and sliding these updated elements to their new size and position. Exiting elements do the opposite of entering elements and fade out, which we achieve by transitioning their opacity back to 0 ❺. Remember that we also have to call `remove` on any exiting elements after the transition is complete ❻.

Reload the page and try hiding and unhiding various licenses. The first license in the key should always correspond to the repository with the most stars (because the repositories are ordered that way and we extract the license names from the repositories in order), so if you want to see the left axis resize, you'll need to turn off that license. You should see the repositories with that license fade out and the other repositories expand to fill the space and the recomputed scale. Figure 15-6(a) shows the chart with all the licenses shown, and Figure 15-6(b) shows the chart with the MIT license (at the time of writing, the most popular license in the dataset) hidden.

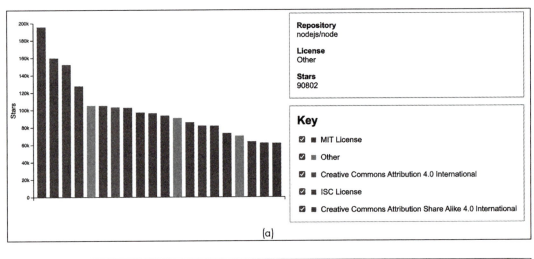

(a)

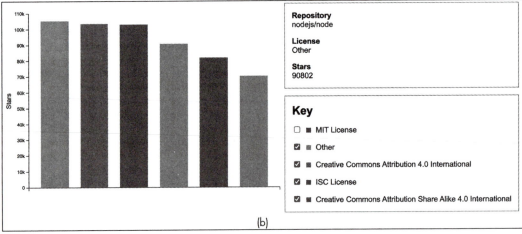

(b)

Figure 15-6: The final chart showing all licenses (a) and with the top license hidden (b)

Try showing and hiding different licenses to get a feel for how the animations work. Is there anything you would change about them? How else might you make the visualization more interesting?

15-4. Add an input element that lets you change the page of search results, so you can see the 20 repositories on the next page, or any other page. Hint: you'll need to listen for change events on the input element and use the new value to set the page parameter in the request to the GitHub Search API.

15-5. Add a button element called "Load More" that loads the next page of search results into the chart, combining them with the existing data (so you'd have 40 bars after one click, and 60 after two clicks).

15-6. Instead of color-coding based on the license, try using a different dimension, such as d.owner.login (which gives the name of the account that owns the repository).

The Complete Code

If you'd like to see what the full *script.js* file should look like, you can find the complete code in Listing 15-24.

```
const width = 600;
const height = 400;

let svg = d3
  .select("body")
  .insert("svg", "#sidebar")
  .attr("width", width)
  .attr("height", height);

let margin = { top: 20, right: 10, bottom: 20, left: 50 };

// Bottom axis container
let bottomContainer = svg
  .append("g")
  .attr("id", "bottom")
  .attr("transform", `translate(0, ${height - margin.bottom})`);

// Left axis container
let leftContainer = svg
  .append("g")
  .attr("id", "left")
  .attr("transform", `translate(${margin.left}, 0)`);

let chartHeight = (height - margin.bottom) - margin.top;
let midPoint = margin.top + chartHeight / 2;

svg
  .append("text")
```

```
    .text("Stars")
    .style("font-size", "14px")
    .attr("text-anchor", "middle")
    .attr("transform", `translate(12, ${midPoint}) rotate(270)`);

function getLicense(d) {
  let license = d.license?.name;

  if (!license) {
    return "No License";
  } else {
    return license;
  }
}

let hiddenLicenses = new Set();

function update(items) {
  // Items with the hidden licenses removed
  let filtered = items.filter(d => !hiddenLicenses.has(getLicense(d)));

  let licenses = new Set(items.map(d => getLicense(d)));
  let colorScale = d3.scaleOrdinal()
    .domain(licenses)
    .range(d3.schemeCategory10);

  let xScale = d3.scaleBand()
    .domain(filtered.map(d => d.full_name))
    .range([margin.left, width - margin.right])
    .padding(0.3);

  let yScale = d3.scaleLinear()
    .domain([0, d3.max(filtered, d => d.stargazers_count)])
    .range([height - margin.bottom, margin.top])
    .nice();

  let bottomAxis = d3
    .axisBottom(xScale)
    .tickValues([]);

  let leftAxis = d3
    .axisLeft(yScale)
    .tickFormat(d3.format("~s"));

  bottomContainer.call(bottomAxis);

  leftContainer
    .transition()
    .call(leftAxis);

  svg
    .selectAll("rect")
    .data(filtered, d => d.full_name)
    .join(
```

```
      enter => enter
        .append("rect")
        .attr("x", d => xScale(d.full_name))
        .attr("y", d => yScale(d.stargazers_count))
        .attr("fill", d => colorScale(getLicense(d)))
        .attr("width", xScale.bandwidth())
        .attr("height", d => yScale(0) - yScale(d.stargazers_count))
        .style("opacity", 0)
        .transition()
        .style("opacity", 1),
      update => update
        .transition()
        .attr("x", d => xScale(d.full_name))
        .attr("y", d => yScale(d.stargazers_count))
        .attr("width", xScale.bandwidth())
        .attr("height", d => yScale(0) - yScale(d.stargazers_count)),
      exit => exit
        .transition()
        .style("opacity", 0)
        .remove()
    )
    .on("mouseover", (e, d) => {
      let info = d3.select("#info");
      info.select(".repo .value a").text(d.full_name).attr("href", d.html_url);
      info.select(".license .value").text(getLicense(d));
      info.select(".stars .value").text(d.stargazers_count);
    });

d3.select("#key")
  .selectAll("p")
  .data(licenses)
  .join(
    enter => {
      let p = enter.append("p");

      p.append("input")
        .attr("type", "checkbox")
        .attr("checked", true)
        .attr("title", "Include in chart");

      p.append("div")
        .attr("class", "color")
        .style("background-color", d => colorScale(d));

      p.append("span")
        .text(d => d);

      return p;
    }
  );

d3.selectAll("#key input").on("change", (e, d) => {
  if (e.target.checked) {
    hiddenLicenses.delete(d);
```

```
    } else {
      hiddenLicenses.add(d);
    }

    console.log(hiddenLicenses);
    update(items);
  });
}

function getUrl() {
  let baseUrl = "https://api.github.com/search/repositories";

  let params = {
    q: "language:javascript stars:>10000",
    per_page: 20,
    sort: "stars"
  };

  let queryString = Object.entries(params).map(pair => {
    return `${pair[0]}=${encodeURIComponent(pair[1])}`;
  }).join("&");

  return `${baseUrl}?${queryString}`;
}

let url = getUrl();
let backupUrl = "https://skilldrick-jscc.s3.us-west-2.amazonaws.com/gh-js-repos.json";

// Replace url with backupUrl in following line if needed
d3.json(url).then(data => {
  update(data.items);
});
```

Listing 15-24: The full script.js *file for this project*

Summary

In this final project, you created a pretty complex interactive chart using live data fetched from the GitHub Search API. You now have the tools you need to create your own custom charts using D3. We've touched on only a small part of what this library offers, however; it has support for many different kinds of visualizations, like trees, cartographic maps, and other more esoteric layouts. Each of these visualization types has the same basis in SVG, data binding, joins, scales, and transitions, so what you've learned here will set you up well if you decide to explore data visualization with JavaScript further. The D3 website, *https://d3js.org*, is an excellent starting point for further research.

AFTERWORD

You've learned the core of the JavaScript language, you've worked through the book's three projects, and you're wondering what to do now. The good news (or the bad news, depending on your outlook) is that the learning never stops. There are many different directions in which you can take your programming career. Here are some suggestions about possible next steps and tools and resources to explore.

Projects

You should have a fairly good understanding of how to set up a new JavaScript project at this point, so why not try building something new? One option would be to make your own game, using the techniques you learned in this book. Some relatively simple arcade games in a similar vein to *Pong* include *Snake*, *Space Invaders*, *Tetris*, and *Breakout*. Or you could try something completely different and make a word game, like *Wordle* or *Hangman*.

You could also try to build on what you learned in the book's other projects by making your own musical creation or data visualization. On the music side, you might want to experiment with making a drum machine, or perhaps an endless music generator. You could also use your knowledge to add sound effects to one of your games. On the data visualization side, there are countless other APIs you can try out for fetching data from other services. As discussed in Chapter 15, many APIs require some sort of authentication, which isn't feasible for browser-based applications; with Node.js, however, you can experiment with building your own backend applications as well.

Of course, you shouldn't feel limited to the sorts of projects you worked through in this book. If there's something that interests you, try to build it! If you're not sure where to start, use Google to get some ideas. JavaScript is one of the most popular languages in the world, so chances are somebody has written up instructions on doing whatever it is you want to do.

Node.js

This book only explains how to write JavaScript for running in web browsers, but with Node.js you can also run JavaScript on backend web servers. Check out *https://nodejs.dev/en/learn/* for a great guide to getting started with Node.js. Once you have a backend for your app, you can start to do more interesting things, such as storing data on the user's behalf, accessing third-party authenticated HTTP APIs with a secret key, and much more.

Tools

There are many tools of various kinds that will help you as you continue your programming journey. This section introduces a few of them, but it's in no way comprehensive.

Git

Git is a popular version control system that allows you to keep track of changes to your code and go back to earlier versions. When I first started programming, I would often find myself making changes to my code and breaking something, then not understanding how I had broken it and not being able to get back to the previous state. To avoid that, I started making backups of my code so I could go back to an earlier version. Git is a much better way to achieve the same goal. With Git, you make *commits* that store the state of your code at a particular point in time. Each commit builds on previous ones, while keeping track of what's changed.

There are a lot of online resources for learning Git. Many of them can be found at *https://git-scm.com/doc*.

GitHub

Once you have Git installed on your computer, using GitHub (the service from which we drew our data in Chapter 15) is a great next step. GitHub provides a way to upload and share your local Git repositories so they can be accessed anywhere.

GitHub also gives you access to millions of open source repositories that you can *fork* (make your own copy of) and modify to your heart's content. For example, to see all my public repositories, go to *https://github.com/skilldrick*.

CodePen

To share your projects with others, you'll need a way to make them accessible via the web. You could set up your own web hosting, but a much easier option is using CodePen (*https://codepen.io*). This is also the tool used for hosting the companion resources for this book, available at *https://codepen.io/collection/ZMjYLO*.

With CodePen, you can create and share projects built using HTML, CSS, and JavaScript. The code is all viewable on the page in separate panels. For example, Figure A-1 shows a sample Pen I put together that adds an extra exclamation mark every time you click the text. Check out the Pen online at *https://codepen.io/skilldrick/pen/abKaQpo*.

Figure A-1: A sample Pen on CodePen

In the HTML panel, only the contents of the body element are needed. CodePen supplies the rest of the HTML structure automatically. You can also easily include external JavaScript libraries through the Settings dialog.

Glitch

Like CodePen, Glitch is a service that hosts your code for you and lets you share it with the world. What sets Glitch apart is its ability to run frontend *and* backend code. Instead of just providing panels for HTML, CSS, and JavaScript, Glitch allows you to define a full directory structure with all the files you need. You can even add a SQLite database to store data. Go to *https://glitch.com* to learn more, or check out *https://glitch.new* to choose from a list of starter apps.

Web Development

Although this book's focus is on JavaScript, along the way you also learned some general web development skills. If this has whetted your appetite, you may want to spend some more time learning about other aspects of web development.

HTML and CSS

HTML is the language that the vast majority of web pages are written in, so it's valuable to have a deeper understanding of its intricacies. To learn more, check out the MDN docs at *https://developer.mozilla.org/HTML*. CSS is used for styling web pages, so if you want your pages to look nice, it's essential to understand how it works. Learn more on MDN at *https://developer .mozilla.org/CSS*.

JavaScript Frameworks and Libraries

Web development today is very complex, with web apps regularly containing thousands of lines of HTML, CSS, and JavaScript. To greatly reduce the amount of code needed to write a fully functional modern web app, many developers use JavaScript frameworks and libraries. Two of the most popular at the time of this writing are React and Vue.js. Knowledge of such tools isn't necessary, but it can dramatically simplify the process of building complex websites and frontend applications. You can try out React and Vue.js in CodePen, or check out their websites:

- React: *https://reactjs.org*
- Vue.js: *https://vuejs.org*
- React on CodePen: *https://codepen.io/topic/react/templates*
- Vue.js on CodePen: *https://codepen.io/topic/vue/templates*

Testing

One essential tool for programmers is an automated testing framework. Automated tests are designed to run against your code regularly, to confirm it does what you expect it to do. A common problem when writing code is adding a new feature without realizing that the change breaks some other aspect of your program. By writing good tests and running them regularly, you can identify the moment something breaks, and fix it. You can also work on large refactors of your code with confidence, knowing that as long as the tests pass, it's unlikely that you've broken anything.

There are a huge number of testing libraries and frameworks for JavaScript. One of the most popular at the time of this writing is Jest: check it out at *https://jestjs.io*.

More JavaScript!

If you want to deepen your JavaScript knowledge, there are many resources available to you. Here are a few recommendations of where to get started:

- MDN JavaScript Portal: *https://developer.mozilla.org/JavaScript*
- *Eloquent JavaScript*, 3rd edition, by Marijn Haverbeke (No Starch Press, 2018)
- *JavaScript: The Definitive Guide*, 7th edition, by David Flanagan (O'Reilly Media, 2020)

Other Languages

You might decide at this point that you want to broaden your programming knowledge rather than dig deeper into JavaScript. Go for it! Every language you learn gives you valuable insights into programming in general, so this is actually a great way to get better at JavaScript.

TypeScript

One of the problems that people have with JavaScript is its weak, dynamic typing, which allows values to be implicitly coerced to different data types depending on the surrounding code. For example, the + operator will convert a number operand to a string if the other operand is a string, while the - operator will convert a string operand to a number if the other operand is a number.

The TypeScript language is an attempt to add static typing to JavaScript. *Static typing* means that a variable of a certain type can only contain values of that type, and conversions between types must be explicit. TypeScript is syntactically a superset of JavaScript, which means that a valid JavaScript program is also a valid TypeScript program. TypeScript code can be converted to JavaScript using the TypeScript compiler.

Using static types makes it impossible to write code with certain bugs. For example, in JavaScript you might take a value from a text box, assume that it's a number, and add it to another number. Unfortunately, any value from a text box is treated as a string, so the other number will be implicitly converted to a string as well, and you'll end up with the two strings concatenated. TypeScript doesn't allow this. It knows that the value from the text box is a string, and it forces you to decide whether you want to convert both operands to strings for concatenation or convert both operands to numbers for addition.

The downside of TypeScript is that it can sometimes be more difficult to write code that otherwise seems like it should work. This is sometimes known as *fighting the compiler.*

If you'd like to learn more, here are some books and other resources that can help you get started with TypeScript:

- The TypeScript Handbook: *https://www.typescriptlang.org/docs/handbook/intro.html*
- *Effective TypeScript* by Dan Vanderkam (O'Reilly Media, 2019)
- *Learning TypeScript* by Josh Goldberg (O'Reilly Media, 2022)

Python

Python is a scripting language, like JavaScript, but it has a different philosophy. The language takes a "batteries included" approach, meaning that its standard library comes fully featured with a wide array of functionality (JavaScript's standard library, by comparison, is very limited). Like JavaScript, Python is dynamically typed, so the same variable can hold values of different data types. But whereas JavaScript is weakly typed, Python is *strongly typed,* meaning that there are no implicit coercions. Syntactically, Python looks very different, using indentation (which is required, not optional) rather than braces to define nested blocks of code.

Python is a popular language of choice for web servers, as well as for scientific and numeric programming. If you're looking to broaden your skills, it's a good choice. The following book (in the same series as *JavaScript Crash Course*) is a great introduction to the language, and its projects highlight some of the areas in which Python shines:

- *Python Crash Course,* 3rd edition, by Eric Matthes (No Starch Press, 2023)

Rust

One of the languages I'm most excited about today is Rust. Like TypeScript, it's a statically typed language, but it has a much more powerful type system than most languages in use today. Rust aims to replace the older languages C and C++ for developing high-performance code.

C and C++ are both languages without *garbage collection,* the process that tells the computer which values and objects are no longer used, in order to free up the computer's memory. Instead, C/C++ programmers must manually free data that is no longer in use—a process that's error prone and can often lead to bugs. These languages are commonly used in performance-critical environments, and they don't use garbage collection because it can reduce the performance of software. Rust avoids this problem with a compile-time *borrow checker*, which keeps track of which objects are in use at any given time, and by which parts of the program.

Rust is also used heavily as a source language for compiling to Web-Assembly, which is an exciting new technology for running extremely efficient and performant code in the browser. Here are some resources for learning more:

- *The Rust Programming Language*, 2nd edition, by Steve Klabnik and Carol Nichols (No Starch Press, 2023)
- Rust and WebAssembly: *https://rustwasm.github.io/docs/book/*

INDEX

arrays *(continued)*
    methods *(continued)*
        finding index of element in array, 45
        removing element from array, 43–44
        turning array into string, 45–46
    nesting
        exploring nested objects in console, 54–55
        with literals, 52–53
        printing nested objects with JSON.stringify, 55–56
        with variables, 53–54
    taking callback functions, 85–87
arr.includes(*elem*) method, 46
arrow functions, 82–83
arr.reverse() method, 46
arr.slice(*start, end*) method, 46–47
arr.sort() method, 46
arr.splice(*index, count*) method, 47
artificial intelligence (AI), 181
assignment operator (=), 13
attack, ADSR, 211–212, 234
attributes, 116–118
attr method, 269
audio context, 207–208
authenticated APIs, 302–303
axes
    drawing, 305–307
    labeling, 288–291
    labeling left, 318–319

B

backend code, 303
backslash (\), 23
backticks (`), 24
ball, Pong, 161–162, 195–197
bandpass filter, 226
bandwidth method, 287
bar graphs, 279–297, 304–319
    animating changes, 296–297
    calculating character frequencies, 280–282
    cleaning data, 295
    color-coding bars, 314–318
    creating elements, 304–305

    drawing, 282–291
        axes, 305–307
        bars, 308–309
        labeled axes, 288–291
        scaling bars, 284–288
    labeling left axis, 318–319
    setting up, 279–280
    showing repository info, 310–314
    styling with CSS and regular expressions, 292–295
baseline, 257
base URL, 301
bass lines, 240–242
beats per minute (BPM), 217
bezierCurveTo method, 147
bindings, 12–16
    constants, 14–15
    naming conventions, 15–16
    variables, 13–14
block body syntax, 82–83
body
    of control structure, 59
    function, 74
body element, 113
Booleans, 26–30
    comparison operators, 29–30
    as conditions, 60–61
    logical operators, 27–28
    using subexpressions in, 171
bouncing
    near paddle ends, 174–175
    overview, 165–166
BPM (beats per minute), 217
braces, 63
bubbling events, 130

C

callbacks
    array methods taking, 85–87
    custom functions taking, 88–89
    defined, 78
    event handlers and, 129
calling functions, 74–78
    parameter types, 77
    return values, 75–76
    side effects, 77–78
calling methods, 21
call method, 289

camelCase, 15

C and C++, 334

Canvas API, 144, 256

canvas elements, 141–154

    animating, 152–153

    creating, 142

    drawing Pong game on, 160–161

    interacting with, 147–151

    making static drawings, 142–147

        drawing other shapes using paths, 145–147

        drawing outlined rectangles, 144–145

caret (^), 292

Cascading Style Sheets. *See* CSS

case sensitivity, 15

CDN (content delivery network), 210

chained `if...else` statement, 61–63

chaining methods, 130, 269

`change` event handler, 151

characters

    frequencies of, 280–282

    from strings, 21–22

`checkCollision` function, 165–166

child elements, 114

chords, 242–244

Chrome

    accessing JavaScript console, 4

    calling functions in, 75–76

    exploring nested objects in, 54–55

    indentation in, 40

    Web Audio API, 206

`circle` element, 260–261

    advanced joins, 276–279

    data binding, 270–271

    data joins, 271–273

`class` attribute, 122

classes, 93–108

    creating instances and, 94–97

    inheritance, 97–101

    prototype-based inheritance, 101–108

        comparing constructors and classes, 104–105

        exploring `Object.prototype`, 105–106

        overriding method, 107–108

        using constructors and prototypes, 102–104

        walking the prototype chain, 106–107

class selectors, 123

cleaning data, 295

`clearInterval` function, 83

`clearRect` method, 151

`click` handler, 148

clock, JavaScript, 220–221

closures, 90

CodePen, 331

coercion, 30–35, 77

    equality with, 31–32

    truthiness, 32–35

collision detection

    bouncing, 165–166

    defined, 163–164

    in object-oriented Pong, 195–197

    for paddles, 170–173

color

    color-coding bars, 314–318

    RGBA color, 150

    RGB color, 261

    sound of oscillator as, 213

combining arrays, 44–45

combining objects, 51–52

comments, 165

comparison operators, 29–30

complete code

    GitHub Search API, 325–328

    Pong, 185–188

    song writing, 247–252

composition, 199

compound data types, 37–56

    arrays, 38–47

        arrays of arrays, 39–41

        creation and indexing, 38–39

        methods, 41–47

    nesting objects and arrays, 52–56

        exploring nested objects in the console, 54–55

        with literals, 52–53

        printing nested objects with `JSON.stringify`, 55–56

        with variables, 53–54

H

I

J

transitions, 275–276, 296–297
translation, 258–259
transport, Tone.js. *See* Tone.js transport
trim method, 22
triple equals (===) operator, 29
true constants, 15–16
true value, 32–33
trumpet notes, 233
truthiness, coercion, 32–35
tune playing, 244–246
TypeScript language, 333–334

U

ul element, 131
unauthenticated APIs, 302–303
undefined behavior, 117
undefined value, 26
unshift method, 43
update, element, 277
update function, 153, 164
URL encoding system, 301
URLs, 300–301

V

valid identifiers, 48
values, object
    accessing, 48
    setting, 49
variables
    naming conventions, 15–16
    nesting with, 53–54
    overview, 13–14
var keyword, 13
vector graphics, 256
visualizing data
    D3 library, 255–297
        advanced joins, 276–279
        bar graphs, 279–297
        data binding, 270–271
        data joins, 271–273

real-time updates, 273–275
    selections, 269–270
    setup, 268
    SVG graphics format, 256–268
    transitions and key functions,
        275–276
GitHub Search API, 299–328
    adding interactivity, 319–324
    basic visualization, 304–309
    complete code, 325–328
    fetching data, 300–304
    improving visualization,
        310–319
    setting up, 300
VS Code (Visual Studio Code)
    if statement in, 58–59
    indentation in, 40
    overview, 5–6
Vue.js, 332

W

W3C (World Wide Web
        Consortium), 206
walking the prototype chain, 106–107
Web Audio API, 206–209
    generating tone with, 207–209
    setting up, 206–207
web development, 332
while loop, 63–64
white noise, 224
whitespace, 22, 295
World Wide Web Consortium
        (W3C), 206

X

XML (Extensible Markup
        Language), 256

Z

zero-based indexing, 21, 38, 218

JavaScript Crash Course is set in New Baskerville, Futura, Dogma, and TheSansMono Condensed.